進士五十八の日本庭園

Theory of
Japanese Gardens

Isoya SHINJI

ボタニカルガーデン アートビオトープ『水庭』 設計：石上純也
Botanical Farm Garden Art Biotop "Water Garden", designed by Junya ISHIGAMI+associates

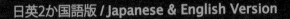
日英2か国語版 / Japanese & English Version

進士五十八の日本庭園

技心一如で自然に順う

Theory of Japanese Gardens

The Spirit and Techniques of Design in Accordance with Nature

Isoya SHINJI

市ケ谷出版社 / Ichigaya Publishing Co. Ltd, Japan

まえがき　　読者のみなさんへ － 「庭2つの心：平和＋自然」

　私の造園研究の核心は、「平和と自然」である。世界の現在は、「人類の知よ」いずこ？を痛感するほど貧困だからである。

　各国の歴史と共にある庭園の本質は、エデンの園、パラダイス、極楽浄土、桃源境にある。平安、安寧、美しく平和な環境空間の実現である。また、日本庭園の特質は、日本人の自然観に順い自然を熟知し自然と共生する環境デザインで、21世紀地球社会の要請とも重なる。2つの庭をみてほしい。

　1つは、ハンガリー動乱下、自ら西側に亡命した哲学者彫刻家 Wagner Nándor（1922-1997）作の「哲学の庭」。キリスト、仏陀など宗教の祖のすべてが同じ球一点を見ている。宗派はちがうが誰もが「平和」を目指している。ナンドールは「違いよりも共通性を分かり合うことで、平和を具現したい」という。800 年前、越の国（福井県）に曹洞宗大本山永平寺を開山した道元禅師は「他の宗教を誹るものは正しい宗教でない」と語ってもいる。

　だから私も、単なる異国趣味で JAPANESE GARDENS を読むことなく、日本庭園の基底を流れる DNA：「平和志向と自然共生の知恵」を、誰にでも理解できる本を世界に提供したいと思った。

Preface　　The Heart of Two Gardens: Peace + Nature

At the core of all my landscape architecture research, is the theme "Peace and Nature". In light of the world's present unrest, I feel increasingly and acutely aware of the degrading and impoverished state of the world and wonder, "Where did humanity's wisdom vanish to?" and hence my research theme.

The essence of garden designs of the various countries of the world, influenced by their histories, can be found in that country's version of heaven or paradise: Eden, Arabic Jannah Paradise, the Buddhist Amitabha's Pure Land, China's Táoyuán jìng (Shangri-La), etc. These gardens are the representation of an ideal, serene, tranquil and beautifully peaceful environment. At the foundation of the essence and characteristics of Japanese garden design is the Japanese people's perception of nature, one compliant with nature's principles of coexistence - fundamentally environmental design - which I see beautifully overlapping with the needs of our 21st century society. Case in point, I present to you these two gardens.

The first is the Garden of Philosophy in Nakano Ward, Tokyo, conceived by philosopher and sculptor Nándor Wagner (1922-1997) who had been forced to flee to Sweden from his native Hungary in the turmoil of the Hungarian revolution, and eventually landed in Japan. As part of his sculpture which forms the heart of the garden, he depicts Christ, Buddha, Abraham, Echnaton, and Lao Tse standing in a circle looking at the same sphere in the center of the circle. His message being that regardless of the differences in their religions, they all were seeking "peace." Nándor declared that "Rather than looking for differences in culture and religion, I want to find similarities. It is only through those things we share that we can become closer."

Similarly, 800 years before, Japanese Buddhist priest, writer, poet, philosopher and founder of the Eihei-ji Temple (the main temple of the Sōtō school of Zen Buddhism) Dōgen Zenji, had said something very similar, "The one who denigrates another's religion does not belong to the right religion."

「哲学の庭」 ワグナー・ナンドール（日本名:和久奈 南都留）1994年完成作品。ハンガリーと日本の外交関係開設140年・国交回復50年記念として、ワグナーちよ夫人からの寄贈で東京都中野区哲学堂公園内に2009年建立された（構想：進士五十八、設計：加園貢＋中野区公園課。進士「哲学の庭」からのメッセージ『東京人』、2016）庭は 3つの輪で、第1の輪は方形で地を、円形で天を表す。台上5体はすべて中央の球を注視。球は真善美・平和を象徴。祈りにひれ伏すアブラハム、左にエクナートン、キリスト、仏陀、老子へ、宗教の祖が続く。2の輪は聖フランシスコ、達磨、ガンジー。3の輪は聖徳太子、エスティニアヌス、バビロン王ハムラビ。

Photo: Part of the Nándor Wagner (1922–1997) sculpture collection donated by his wife Chiyo, to commemorate the 140th anniversary of the establishment of diplomatic relations between Hungary and Japan, which forms the heart of the Garden of Philosophy in Nakano Ward, Tokyo (design concept - Isoya Shinji, design drawings - Mitsugu Kazono and Nakano Ward parks dept.).

There are three concentric rings of people in this sculpture arrangement - representing religion, philosophy, and law - symbolizing the idea that in order for the different people of the world to become closer, we need to return to a common philosophy and values. The first ring has the five patriarchs of the world's major religions standing in a circle, all transfixed on a common sphere, as described in the text of the book. The second ring features Bodhidharma, Saint Francis, and Gandhi and the third Prince Shotoku, Justinian I, and Hammurabi.

自然の庭 石上純也設計の2018年作品、ボタニカルガーデンアートビオトープ「水庭」。栃木県那須町所在、二期クラブ創業20周年記念として2007年オープンしたアート・ビオトープ・レジデンスの隣接地。その土地の記憶を再構成した自然再生の先端的作品。森林→水田→放牧地→水庭が、建築家石上により318本の樹々、水系により連結する160個の池のビオトープに結実した（施工：櫻井淳・静岡グリーンサービス）。

ecology+landscape+biodiversity+biotope+artを統合化、地球時代の日本庭園を示唆している。「建築の未来の道筋を再定義できる影響力」が評価され、デンマークの「オベル賞(2019)」を受賞。(画像提供:株式会社nikissimo)
本文p.107生き物術参照。

2つめの庭は、現代日本の建築家の石上純也（1974-　）の作品「ボタニカルガーデン　アートビオトープ『水庭』」。かねて著者は「日本庭園は美しいビオトープ」と主張してきたが、石上作品はエコロジーのみならず美しい自然の再生にチャレンジしており、正に地球環境の世紀における「日本庭園の未来像」を象徴している。自然共生的自然観の日本文化は深刻な地球環境問題への対処にも有効だろう。

旧来の英語直訳本は背景の日本を知らないひとには理解できない。本書は日本文化を熟知しない英語圏の読者にもわかるように、大局からの合理的説明、ビジュアルや英語

ネイティブスピーカーの翻訳による解説を工夫。日英2カ国語版「日本庭園の心と技の全てが分かる完全版」を完成させたと自負している。

本書を通読されれば直ちに分るだろうが、数ある世界の庭園のなかで、地場の自然材料を活用する造園が特徴の「日本庭園」は、立地、規模、用途、意匠ほかあらゆる面で景観多様性に富んでいる。「庭園多様性」は、多様な生き方を求めている世界の環境市民にとってJAPANESE GARDENS最大の魅力となるだろう。

ぜひ本書で Garden-diversity をエンジョイしてほしい。

進士 五十八

In this book, I do not want to emphasize the unique exoticism of Japanese gardens but rather uncover the primary foundation or DNA of Japanese garden design founded in the wisdom of coexistence with nature and orientation towards peace and relay that to the world in an easily understood manner.

The second garden is the Botanical Farm Garden Art Biotop "Water Garden", designed by architect Junya Ishigami (1974 -) which is located in the Nasu-kougen highlands in Tochigi Prefecture. This garden features 318 trees which were saved and relocated from a nearby land development and then situated carefully between 160 small pondlets made with traditional rice field construction techniques to allow for beautiful flowing water, with moss carpets established throughout, creating a "new nature." It combines the various elements in a new configuration emphasizing aspects of nature that could not be made by man, and the elements of manmade art that cannot be found in nature. It plays with light, reflections and combinations of natural elements in a density not found in nature, while serving an ecological conservation mandate.

I have always declared that Japanese gardens are in essence beautiful biotopes but Ishigami's creation is not only a successful attempt at creating a beautiful natural environment art form but represents the future of Japanese garden design in the century of world environmental awareness. I believe that the culture and tradition of Japan which strives to respectfully

coexist with nature, offers solutions to the world for how we can address the serious environmental problems we face in our world today.

Books on this topic in the past were hard for non-Japanese speakers to understand, suffering from the bane of direct translation and requiring too much detailed knowledge of history and cultural implications. This book endeavors to simplify the explanations, concepts and background information and explain it in more naturalized English while combining all this with an abundance of pictures and visual aids.

As I hope you will understand thoroughly after reading this book, Japanese gardens differ from other garden design styles of the world in their flexibility and adaptability, embracing the use of locally available materials, making masterful use of naturally occurring topographical features and the surrounding natural scenery, complying with the needs and limitations presented in each locale and above all showcasing diversity. I believe this serves as a template for how society can more sustainably live, embracing diversity in unison with nature, further enlarging the appeal Japanese gardens have to the citizens of the world.

May everyone enjoy the "garden diversity" presented in this book.

Isoya SHINJI

Photo: The Botanical Farm Garden Art Biotop "Water Garden", a 2018 creation by architect Junya Ishigami (1974 -) located in the Nasu-Kougen highlands of Tochigi Prefecture. This creation draws on and reflects the historical land-use faces of this property which was originally wooded, then cleared for rice fields and then became meadowlands, taking elements from each era and recombining them into a manmade natural biotope art form water garden. 318 trees were relocated from a nearby land development and situated carefully between 160 small pondlets made with traditional rice field construction techniques to allow for beautiful flowing water and then moss carpets established throughout creating a "new nature." This garden is touted to have, "The influential power to redefine the path of the future of architecture" and has been awarded numerous prestigious prizes including Denmark's 2019 Obel Award for Architecture. (Photo credit: nikissimo Inc.)

Designed by © junya ISHIGAMI+associates, construction by Jun Sakurai, Shizuoka Green Service Co.

進士五十八の日本庭園
技心一如で自然に順う

第6章 現代に生きつづける日本庭園

Theory of Japanese Gardens
The Spirit and Techniques of Design in Accordance with Nature

by Isoya SHINJI

明治神宮の森
The Forest of the Meiji Jingu Shrine (Tokyo)

Introduction

The Forest of the Meiji Jingu Shrine

*The Japanese Perspective
on Nature and a Century of
Modern Landscape Architecture in Japan*

世界の庭園の中で日本庭園ほど、神や先祖とつながっている精神性を重視している庭園はない。太陽、雷、風、山、川、岩などの自然神と、天皇、学者などの人格神などが祭神だが、すべての神社は濃い緑（樹林）で荘厳される。

前頁序章の扉写真は、東京都心の明治神宮。

写真上は、日本最大の古墳で、ギゼーの第一ピラミッドの3倍半の長さがある、世界遺産、仁徳天皇陵（御陵：ごりょう）。これらに見られる日本人の自然観を日本庭園も共有している。

Many overseas tourists visit the forest of Meiji Jingu Shrine while they are in Tokyo. On the approach to the main shrine buildings, one can overhear snatches of conversation in languages from around the world. The deep forest, a rare place of peace and tranquility in the hustle and bustle of the capital, seems to suggest to people from all cultures, a spiritual character that is distinctive to Japan.

Keiji Uehara, who possessed a doctorate in forestry (mentor to the author - Isoya Shinji), was an active participant in the early days of modern landscape architecture in Japan. He believed three genres within landscape architecture were uniquely Japanese - shrine forests, imperial mausoleums, and Japanese gardens - and helped implement all three in the project to develop a forest around Meiji Jingu Shrine.

Garden styles have generally been referred to by the

外国人の多くが、東京に滞在中「神宮の森」を訪れる。参道では、世界中の言葉が聞こえてくる。喧噪の東京都心で唯一、緑濃い森は静寂かつ深遠であり、異文化の人たちにも何故か、日本らしい精神性を感じられる場所であるようだ。

　著者（進士五十八）の恩師上原敬二林学博士は、日本の近代造園草創のひとである。上原は世界のランドスケープ界を俯瞰したうえで、日本独自の造園領域は、①神社林、②陵墓、③日本庭園の３つであると考え、神宮の林苑計画にもその3要素を感じていたようである。

　およそ世界の庭園様式は「国名」で呼ばれてきた。イタリア式、フランス式、イギリス風景式のように。作庭や造園のテーマは、その国の民族や宗教、人々の自然観や環境観の反映だからである。また、造園の形や材料は、その土地の自然条件や地場材料に規定されざるを得なかったからである。

names of countries because the design themes of gardens and landscapes found in a particular country reflect that country's unique perspective on nature or the environment, as well as the general character of the religion or people of that country. Furthermore, the forms and materials used in the creation of gardens, by necessity, are largely determined by the surrounding natural environment and locally available materials.

Emperor Meiji, who died on July 30, 1912, was widely venerated by the people of Japan, traveled often on official visits throughout Japan and interacted extensively with the citizenry. Two days after his death, on August 1, a group that included Eichi Shibusawa of the Tokyo Chamber of Commerce and Yoshirō Sakatani, the mayor of Tokyo, suggested creating the Inner and Outer Precincts of Meiji Jingu Shrine in memory and honor of this beloved Emperor. There was an outpouring of support for the idea. It was determined that the Inner Precinct of the Shrine would be funded by the national government and the Outer Precinct through public donations.

A commission of experts was formed, which guided a

Among all the gardens of the world, none have an emphasis on spirituality, connection to god and one's ancestors, in the way Japanese gardens do. The Japanese expression of spirituality or reverence is almost always innately conducted via a setting with awe-inspiring attributes of natural elements as opposed to human constructs of awe such as a pyramid or palace. Whether reverence for greatly respected human figures such as an emperor, famous scholars or others given god status, in the form of a memorial park or the imperial palace grounds, or reverence for the power and sanctity of elements of nature in Shintoism or even Buddhism, the conduit is invariably established by emulation of the deep green richness of the natural world.

The photo on the cover page is of Meiji Jingu Shrine and **the photo to the left** is of Japan's most ancient gravesite, the mausoleum of Emperor Nintoku, which is a World Heritage Site. Looking at these design attributes of these sacred sites as well those of Japanese gardens, we recognize how the use of emulation of nature garners reverence.

ところで、明治天皇は日本国中を行幸され、国民みんなに崇敬された天皇であったが、明治45（1912）年7月30日に崩御された。その翌々日の大正元年8月1日、東京商業会議所の渋沢栄一、東京市長阪谷芳郎らが発意した神宮内外苑構想は、国民から圧倒的に支持され、内苑は国の予算で、外苑は国民の寄付によって造園されることになった。

　ナショナルプロジェクトの造営事業は、一流の専門家からなる調査委員会指導の下、その弟子達の実行体制で進められた。

　社殿や記念館などの建築は、東京帝国大学教授の伊東忠太、関野貞の両工学博士が、樹木の選定や林苑造成は、東京帝国大学教授の川瀬善太郎、本多静六の両林学博士。内苑の芝生園地や外苑の並木・緑地デザインは、園芸系の宮内省技師の福羽逸人、農学博士で東京帝国大学教授の原熙が指導した。こうして1920年11月神宮鎮座祭が挙行された。

team in executing this national project. Professors Chūta Itō and Tadashi Sekino of Tokyo Imperial University (now the University of Tokyo), who possessed doctorates of engineering, were in charge of the architectural design of the main shrine and the Meiji Kinen-kan (Constitution Memorial Hall); Professors Zentarō Kawase and Seiroku Honda of Tokyo Imperial University, who possessed doctorates in forestry, were in charge of the selection of trees and the planning of the shrine forest; and Hayato Fukuba, a technical expert in horticulture for the Imperial Household Ministry, and Professor Hiroshi Hara of Tokyo Imperial University, who possessed a doctorate in agriculture, were in charge of the design of the lawn area in the Inner Precinct, the trees lining the avenue and the green area in the Outer Precinct. The ceremony consecrating the shrine was held in November 1920.

　　The Inner and Outer Precincts are a direct expression of the current of thought that prevailed in the Meiji and Taisho periods, namely the tendency to assimilate Western learning while retaining a Japanese spirit. The Inner Precinct is Japanese; its stately main shrine and majestic

内外苑の造園構成は、近代日本人の西洋文明の受容態度であった「和魂洋才」の考え方が直截表出している。内苑は「和」、荘重な本殿、森厳な社叢など日本古来の伝統である鎮守の森と境内計画を踏襲したもの。外苑は「西洋」的で、聖徳記念絵画館（明治天皇の業績顕彰ミュージアム）を主景観とするvistaとsymmetry designによる西洋式造園計画を踏まえたものであった。

　内苑の森づくりは林学博士の本多静六、本郷高徳らが、その弟子上原敬二による全国80余の神社林の実測調査など科学的知見により作成した『植栽直後0、50、100、150年後のシミュレーション』（自然の時間的経過による林相の遷移予想図）にもとづき man madeの「永遠の森」が目指された。

　また神宮外苑は、原博士、その弟子折下吉延技師により設計された近代的スポーツ・レクレーション施設配置の洋式大規模公園緑地で、当初はイチョウ並木のある乗馬道で内苑と外苑をつないでいた。

forest are based on the precincts and layouts of shrines and temples traditional to Japan. The Outer Precinct is modeled on Western-style landscape architecture projects based on principles of vista and symmetry.

To create the forest of the Inner Precinct, Seiroku Honda and Takanori Hongō, who both possessed doctorates in forestry, used scientific findings including detailed surveys of over 80 shrine forests around the country undertaken by their mentee, Keiji Uehara, to prepare a four-stage simulation of the development of the forest at 50-year intervals. The aim was to create a human-made "eternal forest" which would arrive at a diversified, mature forest state at an accelerated pace and sustain itself perpetually while capturing the revered mystique of the natural forests of Japan.

The Outer Precinct, designed by, among others, Hiroshi Hara and his mentee, technical expert Yoshinobu Orishimo, is a large-scale Western-style park, visually organized around the Meiji Memorial Picture Gallery (a museum of paintings portraying the achievements of Emperor Meiji) and featuring modern sports and recreation facilities. The Inner and Outer Precincts were originally connected by a ginkgo-tree-lined equestrian path.

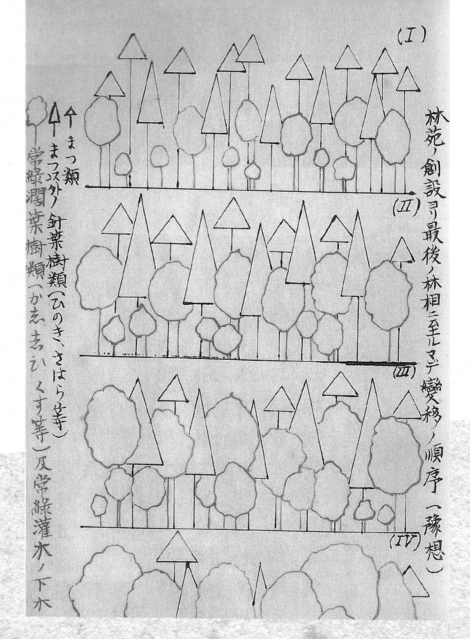

林苑ノ創設ヨリ最後ノ林相ニ至ルマデ變移ノ順序（豫想）

まつ類
↑まつスギノ↑

常緑濶葉樹類（かし、しひ、くす等）及常緑灌木ノ下水

まつ類以外ノ針葉樹類（ひのき、さはら等）

『明治神宮御境内 林苑計画』（本郷高徳、1921年）
（Ⅰ）植栽時、（Ⅱ）50年後、（Ⅲ）100年後、（Ⅳ）150年後の林相変化を予測した。
章末の写真を見ると、シミュレーションが正しく、風景が生長したことを実感できる。いろいろな樹種、また、いろいろな樹齢、樹高を混ぜて植栽し、自然の時間にゆだねると、人工的に植林しても自然林に育っていく。神宮の森は、その壮大な実験でもあった。（写真提供：明治神宮）

An illustration of the different 50-year stages in Hongō Takanori's development manual for the Meiji Shrine forest. The project planners anticipated that broadleaf evergreens like chinquapin, oak, and camphor would gradually replace pines and other conifers.
Photo credit: Meiji Jingu Shrine

林苑造成の主役は、責任者本多静六（1866-1952）。東京帝国大学教授で日本初の西洋風公園・日比谷公園の設計者でもある。林苑整備の技師は、本多の弟子ドクトル本郷高徳（1877-1949）、現場主任は、後に日本初の造園技術者養成機関（東京高等造園学校：現在の東京農業大学造園科学科）の初代校長となる上原敬二（1889-1981）の林学系造園家３名で、林苑造成上のポイントは三つ。

　　一つは、神社林はスギ林でなければいけないという当時の世間的常識に捉われず、あくまでも科学的に、この土地にふさわしい常緑照葉樹を主とする森林を目標と考えること。二つは、神社林の理想は、人手をかけずに自然の力で持続できる"永遠の森"であるべきだとしたこと。そのためには、多様性に富んだ樹種構成とし、樹高も多層性に配慮して植樹すること。三つ目、植栽後は林内の枯木や落葉落枝を、林内から一切持ち出すことを禁止し、腐葉土と発芽条件を充すものとすること。

The three landscape architects specializing in forestry who were responsible for the creation of the forest were led by Seiroku Honda (1866-1952), the designer of Hibiya Park, Japan's first Western-style park; Honda's mentee, Takanori Hongō (1877-1949), the technical expert for the development of the forest; and Keiji Uehara (1889-1981), the site foreman who later became the first director of Japan's first school for landscape engineering (which eventually became the Department of Landscaping Architecture Science in the Faculty of Regional Environment Science at the Tokyo University of Agriculture).

The planners established three conditions for developing the forest. First, they rejected the idea, widely accepted at the time, that the woods of a shrine must be Japanese cedar, but instead believed that, from a scientific standpoint, the aim ought to be to develop a forest of mainly evergreen broadleaf trees appropriate for the location. Second, they believed that ideally, the forest ought to be a self-sustaining "eternal forest." It was vital that it mature naturally without human intervention. For that to happen, the trees had to be of diverse species and planted so that they were diverse in height. Third, they insisted that after

This introduction text was based on a previously published article in nippon.com titled *The Forest of Meiji Jingu Shrine: A National Project Accomplished by Forestry Science and Landscape Architecture Professionals* (June 10, 2020). Nippon.com is a public interest foundation seeking to contextualize Japan for readers throughout the world, publishing in seven different languages, employing professional translators and native speaker writers. They help connect Japan's top communicators, allowing them to share their insights with the world for consideration and discussion of ideas that affect the world as a whole.

次頁：日本人の大自然や庭園を愛する心は、古代から現代までずっと続いている。ちょうど100年前、尊敬された明治天皇を祀る神社を、人々は計画。森のない敷地に、神社林を造成し、明治神宮境内の一角には、参拝後の余韻にひたり、神の恩恵を感じられる広場もデザインした。

それまでの日本の造園では職人的経験の上に名園を生み出してきたが、明治神宮林苑事業が「日本における近代造園学の発祥」といわれるのは、科学的な調査と造林学知識を基本とした本格的プロジェクトであったからである。

以上のような、①日本の気候風土における天然林—神が宿る森林を「常緑照葉樹林」とし、②究極の林相への遷移プロセスを実地的・科学的に予測、③シミュレーション・モデルを作成、その理論にもとづいて整備，育林、管理してきたことが正しかったことは、著者らがすすめた『明治神宮鎮座百年記念境内第二次総合調査』（2013）によって実証されたところである。

本書は、主として近代以前の日本庭園を対象としてJAPANESE GARDENS の自然・歴史・文化・政治・経済的背景と、その下での造園の手法・技法などの技術的な特色と、その基調をなす日本人の自然観や風景観、庭園観について日本の建築家や環境デザイナーはもとより世界各国の読者にもわかり易く解説するものである。著者はそのことが、未来の世界と日本のランドスケープの発展に不可欠だと信ずるからである。

※本書序章の明治神宮に関する内容は、著者のニッポンドットコム掲載記事「明治神宮の森；林学者や造園家によるナショナルプロジェクト」を基本に、若干加筆したものである。
掲載日：2020年6月10日
出典：nippon.com
公益財団法人ニッポンドットコムは、国連公用語（英語・フランス語・スペイン語・中国語・アラビア語・ロシア語）、および日本語の7言語で日本の今を発信。日本を熟知するネイティブスタッフと日本人エディターが、海外にもわかりやすく伝えている。

trees had been planted, fallen branches and leaves be left on the forest floor to decay, further enriching the soil and promoting natural germination of the forest's seed production.

Until then, the design and construction of well-known gardens in Japan had largely been the work of experienced traditional gardener craftspersons. The project to create the forest and precincts of Meiji Shrine is considered the origin of the modern study of landscape architecture in Japan because it was the first project undertaken in earnest on the basis of scientific surveys and knowledge in forestry.

At its basis, as previously described, the principle design philosophy was: (1) the idea that a natural forest in Japan's climate - a forest in which traditionally *kami* (i.e. gods) were thought to reside - was a forest comprised mainly of evergreen broadleaf trees; (2) the forest would be designed based on practical and scientific prediction of the succession process by which the forest would achieve stable diversity and maturity in the shortest possible period; and (3) the

　この本がいまも広く市民や観光客に親しまれている
国内外各都市の公開 JAPANESE GARDENSの背後にある、日
本人の自然共生的態度を踏まえた正しい見方、味わい方
を理解する助けになればと願っている。

creation of a simulation model, and the adoption of a program, based on that model, for the ongoing improvement, nurturing and management of the forest.

The successful results of that program was verified by "The Second Comprehensive Survey of the Meiji Jingu Shrine Forest on the Centennial of Its Consecration (2013)," in which the author took part.

This book considers mainly the premodern gardens of Japan and is intended to provide, not just Japanese architects and designers, but readers throughout the world, with a clear explanation of their technical characteristics and the Japanese perspective on nature, landscape, and gardens, which is based on their natural, historical, cultural, political, and economic context.

It is hoped that this publication will help readers understand the proper way to look at and appreciate the public Japanese gardens in cities throughout the world which both local residents and tourists have come to feel deep affection for.

Since ancient times, Japanese have had a love for the beauty of unspoiled nature and Japanese gardens. 100 years ago, in an expression of reverence for the passing of the much respected Emperor Meiji, a project was planned. The goal was to create an awe-inspiring, natural looking shrine forest, on a site where no trees existed, around the imperial palace. In one corner of this park, a huge open lawn space was included in the design. This open space provided a balancing contrast to the solemnity of the memorial forest.

神宮の森　造成時100年前
A giant wooden *torii* towers over the newly planted forest during the construction of Meiji Shrine.

神宮の森　100年後の現在
A century later, the same *torii* is now shrouded by trees.

写真提供：明治神宮　Photo credit: Meiji Jingu Shrine

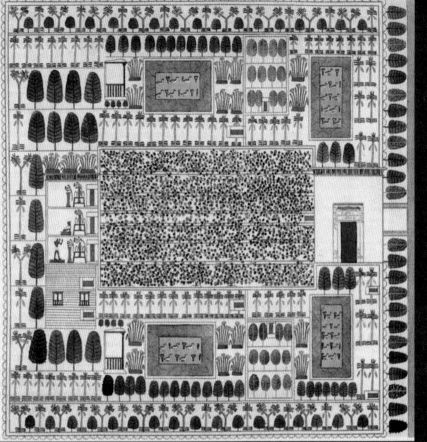

第一章　庭園とは何か　人が生きられる理想境

古代エジプトの庭園図。囲まれて安全な敷地内には、果実がなり、植物が美しく
配され、gardenの定義の原点が見える。

Ancient Egyptian garden design plan which includes fruiting trees and
beautiful plants all within an enclosure, allowing us to see and understand
the origins of gardens.

Chapter 1

The Garden

The Ideal Human Living Environment

前頁扉絵：**古代エジプトの庭園図** それぞれの民族が自然風土にふさわしいガーデンスタイルを形成してきた。その土地に生育する植物や理想とする景観の違いから、各国庭園様式はそれぞれ個性的で、一見して異なって見える。しかし表面上は違っていても、基底にある名園の条件や空間構造の本質は共通する。エジプトの図では、周囲を高い塀で囲んで敵から身を守り、敷地内には池や緑陰、果実がなり、植物が美しく配されてgardenの定義そのものだ。邸宅と門の軸線にシンメトリカルにレイアウトされた格式高い美の世界がエジプト庭園の特徴。以後、西洋ではルイ14世のヴェルサイユ宮苑までこの構成原理が活用される。

庭園の歴史は人類の歴史とともにある。古代は国王や皇帝の愉しみと権威のために、完全に囲まれた閉じられたGardenであった。中世には、領主や貴族、修道院のために、外部の山や湖への眺望をとり入れたLandscape Gardenが、そして近世・近代になると、広く市民の安全や健康、豊かな生活のために、地域社会に開かれたOpen Spaceを扱う Landscape Architectureへと発展する。

このように、時代と共に造園の主体と方法は変化してきたが、自然環境との調和を基本として、人間生活を美しく豊かなものにする「環境デザイン」としての空間・景観構成の手法・技法は、古来からの知恵が現代まで継承されている。デザイナーが庭園史を学ぶ必要性はここにある。

庭園デザインのモデルは、キリスト教の世界では「エデンの園」、イスラム教の世界では「パラダイス」、古代ギリシャでは「アルカディア」、古代中国で

The love of gardens, and their creation, use and enjoyment, are as old as human history. In ancient times, enclosed "gardens" were created for the pleasure of kings and emperors and were symbols of their status and authority. In the middle ages, "landscape gardens" that incorporated views of mountains and lakes, were devised for lords, aristocrats and monasteries. In the modern era, works of "landscape architecture", with spaces accessible to the local community, are intended to promote the health of the general populace and to enrich the quality of their lives.

Many of the ideas behind the design of gardens have changed over time, but the basic techniques of spatial and scenic composition - known in our present age as "environmental design" - are based on design devices that have endured from ancient times until today. These design techniques aim to arrange landscape elements in harmony with the natural environment, to help make human life richer and more beautiful. By studying the history of gardens we can enhance our understanding and appreciation for these techniques.

は「桃源郷」、そして日本では「極楽浄土」である。端的に言えば、全て人間の理想境を目標とした環境デザインということになる。

　英語の「ガーデン（garden）」は、「ガン（gan, gun）：守る、囲われる」と「エデン（eden, oden）：悦び、愉しみ」の合成語で、塀や濠で囲まれた空間に緑陰や果実、飲水があり、生物としての「人間が生きられる環境」、すなわち「安全で快適」な環境となる。中世ヨーロッパでは「愛の園」があった。現代都市計画の目標「アメニティ（amenity）」にも通じる。「アメニティ」の語源は「アモーレ（amare）：愛」に遡る。

　庭園は、自然風土に規定される。例えば、砂漠地帯では、唯一『オアシス』だけが生きられる場所で、水は、地下から泉が湧き出てくる。一方、雨がたくさん降る日本では、川さえ滝のようだといわれる。西洋庭園の噴水と日本庭園の滝のデザインとの違いが生まれる。

Garden design was born out of historical garden archetypes; Christianity's Garden of Eden, the Paradise of Islam, Arcadia of ancient Greece, Peach Blossom Spring (Táohuā Yuán) of China, and the paradisaical Pure Land of East Asian Buddhism (Gokuraku Jōdo in Japanese). These archetypes are ancient examples of environmental design that essentially embody perceptions of the ideal human world.

The English word "garden" comes from the Hebrew word "*gan*", which means to protect or defend, and "*oden*" or "*eden*" which means "pleasure" or "delight": together these can be translated as "the enclosure of land for pleasure and delight". The ideal garden is a space that includes water and food and which is safe, secure and imbued with love, in a spiritual sense.

In medieval Europe there was a concept of a "Garden of Love", which was related to the word "amenity". Amenity has etymological roots in *amore*, which means "love". Different styles of gardens evolved in various regions of the world according to their climates and landscapes. For example, in the desert regions of the

Chapter one cover:
Ancient Egyptian garden design
Each culture of the world developed garden styles appropriate to their respective environments. As each country has different vegetation that will thrive in that climate, the garden designs of each country look quite different at first glance. However, garden designs of the world, though different superficially, share common principles in their fundamental design. In this ancient Egyptian garden design, you will notice the hedge enclosure making it safe from threats, with water, shade, fruit and beautifully arranged plants inside which fulfills the basic universal definition of a garden. The symmetrical layout in this Egyptian garden that accentuates the residence, giving it importance, was typical of Egyptian gardens but is also found in other gardens such as the garden of Versailles developed for Louis XIV.

漢字の「庭園」は近世日本人の造語。これが逆に中国でも普及した語だ。もともと「庭（テイ）」は建物で囲まれ、磚（セン）、黒レンガの舗装のようなdryarea（ドライエリア）であり、「園（エン）」は日本では「その」の意味で植栽地（中国では園林ーエンリン、樹華園）の意味。日本の空間文化上の特色が「庭屋一如（ていおくいちにょ）」といわれ、自然＋人工、outdoor＋indoorの一体感や連続感の重要性を示唆している。

　造園学とは、そういった空間や環境の基本と実際がテーマの科学技術であり芸術であるのである。

Middle East, oases were the only places where life could exist. In an oasis, water wells up from below ground, and thus fountains are a common feature of gardens in countries with dry or desert climates. In Japan, where rain is plentiful and water often runs off and cascades from higher ground, waterfalls are a common garden feature, mimicking the characteristics of the natural environment. Differing cultures, climates and landscapes result in distinctive differences in garden design.

The unique word for the Japanese garden in Japanese is 庭園 (*teien*). Unlike most kanji character words, which originated in China and were adopted by the Japanese, this word originated in Japan and has been adopted by the Chinese. The word consists of two separate kanji characters, 庭 (*tei*) which originally meant the stone-paved, dry area around a building, and 園 (*en*) which means an area planted with trees. This is a reflection of Japanese architecture's distinctive characteristic of 庭屋一如 (*teioku ichinyo*) which is the combination of garden and architecture, with emphasis on the importance of the inclusion of, and the harmony between, both man-made and natural elements in garden design.

Landscape architecture is both a science and an art that consciously accounts for the characteristics of a particular space and its surrounding environment.

第二章　日本庭園の特質

Design with Nature

Animism

自然共生の造園思想

日本人は老大木に神を感じ、そのしるしとして注連縄を廻らす
（東京・明治神宮の拝殿前のクスノキの大木）

The Japanese believe large old trees and other natural spectacles
are residence to gods and mark such sites with sacred Shinto rice
straw rope. Meiji Jingu Shrine, Tokyo

Chapter 2

Characteristics of
the Japanese Garden

*Animistic Beliefs and
Designing with Nature*

Left: Amatsu-iwakura - Throne of Gods rock formation (Tsurugatayama, Kurashiki City, Okayama Pref). These rocks are arranged in such a way that they look like they are part of the earth and their imposing, towering nature makes them look divine. This is a very basic and important design pattern in Japanese gardens.

右頁写真：御神木（神籬／ひもろぎ）（福井県小浜市の式内社・若狭姫神社）
著者（身長171㎝）と比べると樹高は100ft超、樹木径5ft超がわかる。草本類は緑でしかないが、樹木（巨木・老木）は大地に根を張り年輪を重ねて樹霊が宿ると信じられた。

Opposite page: Himorogi sacred tree (Shikidaisha, Wakasahime Shrine, Obama City, Fukui Pref). Compared to the height of the author (5'7") this tree at over 100 feet height and 5 feet in diameter, has an imposing presence. Unlike grasses or smaller plants, this tree has a massive root system grounding it deep into the earth. Such old growth trees are considered sacred places where tree spirit gods reside.

Japan, with an Asian monsoon climate, has warm temperatures and plentiful rains, abundant vegetation, and rich soils and rock materials. The Japanese archipelago stretches from a subtropical zone in the south to a subarctic zone in the north, and from the ocean level to tall peaks in the 3,000-meter range; 70% of the land is forested. It is a country with over 2,000 years of history, rural regions, each with their own local character, and variegated natural landscapes of great beauty. As a result of living in such a land, the Japanese developed animistic beliefs that *kami* (gods) resided in nature and thus their rich natural environment was the realm of a myriad of spirits. Landscapes and forces of nature were held in awe. The Japanese have coexisted with nature from ancient times and after the introduction of Buddhism, embraced the idea of respect for all life which is expressed, for example, in the phrase, *sōmoku kokudo shitsū busshō*, which means that even those objects without feelings such as grass, trees and land have the capacity to attain Buddhahood.

Natural elements are essential components of gardens and living environments. Trees in particular,

古来、日本人は、自然を畏れ自然を敬って生きてきた。アジアモンスーン気候で、高温多雨、豊かな植生や土壌、石材に恵まれた日本の国土は、南の亜熱帯から温帯、北の亜寒帯へ、また、海抜3000mの高山はじめ、国土の70%の森林でおおわれている。2000余年の歴史や郷土色豊かな田園地帯と自然性豊かで美しく変化に富んだ風景の国である。そんな国土で育まれた日本人は、山川海、巨岩大木の大自然にあまねく神を感じ、「八百万神（やおよろずのかみ）」とうやまった。自然の全てに霊魂が宿ると考え、畏敬の念を抱くアニミズム的感性は、古代日本人から現代日本人にまで、自然共生の生き方の　DNAを伝えている。加えて、仏教の「草木国土悉有仏性（そうもくこくどしつうぶっしょう）」の考え方が入り、生命尊重の思想をもち続けてきた。

providing protection from wind and snow, and shade from the sun, are appreciated for their important functional and aesthetic roles and are even thought to possess spiritual significance, connecting *kami* and humans.

In ancient times, when humans were far more subject to the forces of nature, it was common to believe that the *kami* could descend to the human realm through especially big trees. The *kami* were believed to reside in these large trees as well as impressive boulders and headwaters or sources of water. Such rocks, and trees were decorated with straw rope called *shimenawa* to mark them as sacred areas known as *himorogi*. Sacred rocks were referred to specifically as *iwakura* and the area around them in which *kami* resided, *iwasaka*. Headwaters and sources of water, being of great importance for life, were revered and referred to as *mizugaki*.

The projection of human emotions and characteristics into elements of nature such as trees, rocks, and water continues to be a characteristic of Japanese culture even in the present day, and is at the heart of the unique beauty of Japanese gardens.

In cities and gardens around the world, water is a fundamental compositional element. In landscapes, water is often the expressive element that people most

日本庭園の「用と景」：戦国時代の日本越前の国の大名、朝倉氏の城下町一乗谷の「下の城戸」と「諏訪館庭園」。

Functional and aesthetic designs of Japanese gardens: Ichijōdani Asakura Family Historic Ruins (Suwayakata-ato Garden, Fukui Pref) built during the Warring States Period of Japan (late 15th - late 16th century) by the Asakura *daimyō* of the Echizen region.

下の城戸は城下の入り口を守る要塞（**上**）であり、諏訪館（**下**）は朝倉義景の愛する女性のための庭園の滝石組。用(機能性)と景(美観性)のバランスが庭園美の根本である典型例（一乗谷朝倉氏庭園 諏訪館跡庭園、福井県）。

Top: Rock wall made to guard the castle entrance.
Bottom: Waterfall rock placement formation made in honor of the woman Daimyō Asakura loved. The balance of these features in the garden exhibits a fundamental design pattern creating beauty in Japanese gardens.

庭園や生活環境を構成する重要な要素が自然材であり、特に樹木は、防風や日射コントロールなど、物理的、機能的、さらに美観的にも、また神と人間をつなぐなど精神的にも重要な存在である。

古代人は自然よりもはるかに弱い存在であったため、特別に目立つ大きな樹木に神が降り、巨石に神が宿ると考え注連縄（しめなわ）をめぐらせ「神籬（ひもろぎ）」、「磐座・磐境（いわくら・いわさか）」と呼んだ。また、清らかな水にも神が宿るとし、水源や池沼には水神を祀り、「水垣（瑞垣）（みずがき）」と呼んだ。こうして日本人の、木・石・水などへの強い感情移入は、現代人にも通じ「日本庭園の美」の根源となってい

admire and that leaves the deepest impression; waterscapes of every conceivable form are highly valued scenic elements. Typically, in garden design, where there is an abundance of water, designs often include the use of large ponds; like the Grand Canal in Versailles which covers several square kilometers. In areas where there is a shortage of water, designs trend towards the use of elements like dynamic fountains rather than large ponds to make the presence of water felt.

Designing in harmony with nature is the essence of Japanese gardens. The best Japanese gardens begin with respect and awareness of the location or site selection. Gardens of diverse forms and designs are created and influenced by variables such as the flow of air, quality of daylight, topography and views, availability of water - such as a spring or a stream from a mountain - whereas the size and

る。もちろん世界中、古今東西を問わず「水のない庭園風景」はない。水が豊富なベルサイユ宮苑の場合は数キロの長さのグランカナルを造成し、少ない場合は運動的な噴水で迫力を表現している。

　Design with Nature が、日本庭園の本質だ。最良の日本庭園は、立地や敷地選定に始まる。通風や日照はもとより、背山臨水の地形と眺望、湧水や山からの流水など清らかな水利、施主の社会的立場や庭園のふさわしい規模や格式などによって、実に多様な形式や意匠が作出された。

　日本人は、庭園を「山水」とか「林泉」と呼んだように、敷地の中で土を掘って池を造り、土を盛って山水風景を再現した。庭園風景の表現法は「自然学習性」による。先人は大自然の構成を写生したのである。このとき、園景の骨格づくりには「自然石」（庭石という）を多用した。石の形や質を生かした「石組」や「飛び石」、「石灯籠」

level of formality are often determined by the intention and resources available to the client.

　The Japanese traditionally called gardens "mountain streams" (*sansui*) or "forest springs" (*rinsen*). As those terms suggest, gardens are created by either excavating ponds or by creating raised mounds to imitate landscapes of mountains and streams. The basic principle of garden landscape design is to learn from nature. Gardens imitate the way nature is organized. Large numbers of boulders are used to construct the framework of the garden landscape. Designers employ "rock groupings" and stepping stones that utilize the shape or qualities of rocks and garden lanterns that utilize the characteristics of sculpted materials to create gardens in which utility and scenery are in harmony. The fundamental goal of garden design is to integrate functionality and the scenic beauty of nature. Attentiveness to both is essential for a successful design.

　In Japan, the creation of space has yet another goal; harmony between both technical skills and *kokoro*, literally translated as "heart". Japanese place a high value on making skillful and appropriate use of materials, not just in gardens, but in all aspects of culture, including, for example, Japanese cuisine (*washoku*), which accordingly

Next page: French garden design features geometrical design features with absolutely straight canals, perfectly circular ponds and symmetry whereas Japanese garden design uses primarily organic curves and shapes, mimicking nature. The landscape of Japan, which other than man-made civil engineering works, is full of diversity and unpredictability with no straight lines and is the source of inspiration for Japanese garden design.

日本庭園は、自然曲線本位

フランス式庭園では、直線のカナールや正円の噴水池など、明快な幾何学的なデザインが支配しているが、日本庭園では、自然曲線がほとんど。

変化に富んだ日本の国土風景では、人工的な土木建築以外に直線をみることはなく、それが日本庭園へも大きな影響を与えた。

上：フランス庭園、ベルサイユ宮苑のグランカナールの直線
下：日本庭園、毛越寺庭園の自然護岸の曲線

Geometrically straight lines of the Grand Canal, the Palace of Versailles (**top**); Curved organic lines in the Mōtsu-ji Temple garden (**bottom**)

など石造美術品の特徴を上手に活用して作庭した。日本では、建築や土木では「用強美」、造園では「用と景」が基本とされ、「用」は実用性・機能性、「景」は景観性・美観性への気配りが環境デザインの基本とされる。

さらに、日本の空間創作においては「技」と「こころ」の一体的調和が追求されてきた。これは世界無形文化遺産の「和食」など日本文化に共通する特徴で、木や草花、石や砂など、その土地、その季節にふさわしい生き生きした材料を効果的に活用するのが、日本の庭師の腕である。

その結果、水利が無理なら「枯山水」を工夫し、真水が得られなければ、海水を生かした「汐入りの庭（しおいりのにわ）」を生み出したのだ。

また、山から滝、流れ、池へと、多様な大自然を狭い敷地にミニァチュール化するため、角張った山石、丸みのある沢石、貝殻の付着する海石へ。また杉など濃い常緑樹から風にそよぐ落葉樹の柳へと、石や植栽も適材適所で配置した。変化ある土地利用であったので生物多様性に富むビオトープ Biotope ともなっている。日本庭園は、地球的課題でもある Bio-diversity にも有効なのである。

has been declared by UNESCO to be an Intangible Cultural Heritage. The Japanese garden designer displays their skill by using rocks, sand, trees, and flowering plants in such a way.

Japanese gardens are intriguing for their local character; available stones and trees are different from place to place and thus each garden has a very specific regionally appropriate "flavor". If there is no water available on the site, a *kare sansui* garden (raked gravel, dry stream bed) might be created. If no fresh water is available but seawater is, a garden into which saltwater is introduced might be an alternative.

For Japanese gardens to miniaturize the beauty and biodiversity of nature - a waterfall cascading down a mountain or a stream flowing down to a pond, etc. - on a limited site, appropriate elements, ranging from rugged mountain rocks to rounded river stones to verdant evergreens and swaying willows, are exquisitely employed in appropriate places, producing a biotope rich in organic variety at an appropriate scale.

復元整備された、日本最古の庭園・平城京左京三条二坊六坪の発掘遺跡
（奈良市）
Part of the archaeologically excavated and restored Imperial Villa
Garden of Nara, the ancient capital, Japan's oldest known garden.

第三章　日本庭園の変遷

神仏境域から諸国名所に遊ぶ回遊式庭園へ

Chapter 3

Changes in the Japanese Garden

*From the Realms of Kami and Buddha in
Sacred Gardens to Kaiyū-Style Gardens with
Thematic References to Famous Scenic Views*

上：仏教の極楽浄土の世界を地上に再現した宇治平等院鳳凰堂池庭（京都）**下**：同、平等院。近年、想像的復原された浄土庭園の平橋と反橋

Top and bottom: Garden re-creation of heaven on earth, also known as Gokurakujōdo or the Pure Land, in the Byōdō-in Garden in Uji City, Kyoto Pref. Byōdō-in is the most famous Jōdo-style garden in Japan. The flat and arched bridges were restored according to educated guesses as to what the originals looked like (**bottom**).

「庭園」の種類や形は、施主（クライアント）とその庭の利用目的によって、時代背景や資金力・技術力により変遷してきた。「日本式庭園（ジャパニーズ・ガーデン）」も天皇家、貴族、社寺、武家、大名、また茶人、農家や町人へと時代と施主を変え、形式、細部構成を変化させてきた。イタリア式はルネサンス期の Villa を、フランス式は17、18世紀の絶対王政を象徴する様式を指すが、日本では、古代から現代まで連綿として「日本式庭園」と呼ばれる特徴的な形がつくられつづけてきた点は他国とちがってめずらしい。

なお、日本の造園は、おおよそ①神のにわ（yard）②仏の庭園、③人のにわ（武士・農家）、④自然の庭園へと変遷。現代日本のランドスケープ作品・空間・環境の多彩なデザインに特色をもたらした。

（1）古代の庭園

鎮守の杜や神体山への祈り、先祖を敬う古墳（天皇御陵ほか）等、日本的造園がはじまる。稲作のための溜池や用水路が整備されるなか、大きな池泉には島がつくられ海景への憧れをも表現した。古代「島（しま）」は「にわ」の同義語であった。

1. Gardens of the Ancient Period

Garden design has changed over time, adapting to the clients for whom they are created, their uses, different time periods, prevailing conditions, financial resources and technical skills available in the period in which they are created.

Japanese gardens have been made for many different parties - the imperial family, aristocrats, temples and shrines, the samurai class, *daimyō* warlords, tea masters, farmers, and townspeople - and subsequently have undergone changes in style and compositional details. However, a distinctive form called "the Japanese garden" has continuously existed from the ancient period to the present day in a contiguous and fluid manner, whereas garden design styles in other cultures are less contiguous. Italian-style gardens generally feature a villa reminiscent of the Renaissance period, and French-style gardens generally feature the linear, symmetrical and formal style born out of the absolute monarchy governance of the seventeenth and eighteenth centuries.

Japanese garden design began with guardian shrines

538年に日本に仏教が伝来し、朝廷は仏教による国家鎮護を目指す。仏教の基本思想は、草木国土悉有仏性で、古代日本人のアニミズムの延長線上に重なり、日本文化の基層を形づくる。

　京都の蒸し暑さをやわらげ、やさしさを象徴する池泉の水平展開、また中国伝来の貴族の遊び「曲水宴（きょくすいのえん）」をテーマとしたり、前栽（せんざい）、坪庭、遣水（やりみず）による寝殿造庭園が造られた。

　池泉舟遊式、池泉周遊式。古代の平安貴族たちは、広大な敷地に池を設け、舟を浮かべたり、池畔をめぐり景色を楽しむ庭園形式を営む。京都北の嵯峨院離宮（大沢池）や市中の寝殿造が作られる。平安後期、仏教で末法の時代といわれ世が乱れると、貴族たちは地上に極楽浄土を再現して救済されようとし、藤原頼通の宇治・平等院鳳凰堂が建てられる。この形式が「浄土式庭園」であり、平等院のほかに平泉の毛越寺、磐城の白水阿弥陀堂が現存する。

平泉、毛越寺浄土庭園。水平に広がるゆるやかな曲線の汀線（**上**）と、垂直で強さを表現する立石組（**下**）。水平と垂直の両面のバランスが絶妙。

to recognize sacred mountains and to honor the graves of ancestors. Ponds and irrigation canals were developed for the purposes of rice cultivation, but islands were sometimes created in these large ponds to imitate seascapes. For the people of the ancient period, a *shima* (island) was synonymous with a *niwa* (garden).

These early gardens were often designed with horizontally extended bodies of water to mitigate the heat of the capital and to enable aristocrats to engage in a pastime called *kyokusui-no-en* ("meandering stream parties") that originated in China. Gardens of the Heiankyō (the ancient period) were typically based on seascape themes and characterized by gently curved lines. Gardens of the *chisen shūyū / funa asobi* ("Leisure Pond Boating Garden") style or *chisen shūyū* ("pond-strolling garden") style, were designed on spacious sites with large ponds so the aristocrats of the ancient period could float in boats or stroll around. Examples include the Ōsawa Pond of the Saga-in Detached Palace in a northern suburb of Kyoto, or the *shinden*-style gardens within Kyoto. In the late Heian period, in anticipation of the end times forecast in Buddhism, aristocrats recreated the paradisaical Pure Land to which Amida would come to lead them in Jōdo-style gardens such as the Garden of Hōō-dō of Byōdō-in in Uji.

Horizontal and vertical lines: In the Pure Land re-creation Jōdo garden of Mōtsu-ji Temple (Hiraizumi Town, Iwate Pref) examples of both can be seen. **Top**: Gentle, sweeping horizontal lines of the pond and shoreline create a tranquil mood. **Bottom**: The austere vertical lines of the *tateishi* sea cliff emulation vertical rock grouping formation in winter communicate a sense of strength.

夢窓疎石作庭、瑞泉寺の池と座禅窟（鎌倉市）。洞も池も、鎌倉地方の軟らかい石の山を彫りだしてつくったもので、いわゆる「引き算」の庭づくり手法。夢窓疎石(1275-1351)は、禅僧の中で、作庭を禅修行の作務（さむ）として、名園を数多く作り出した石立僧（いしだてそう）で、造園家。

In Japanese garden design, rocks are usually brought in and placed and ponds formed or dug out but in this instance, an existing soft rock formation was sculpted to make a cave and pond feature. The designer for this feature at the Zuisen-ji Temple in Kamakura City and also the temple's founder, Musō Soseki (1275-1351), or as he was known professionally by his "gardener name" Musō Kokushi, was one of the rock arrangement monks who performed their Zen practice through Japanese garden design and were responsible for the design of many famous Japanese gardens and rock arrangements within them.

（2）中世の庭園

　日本の鎌倉・室町期の主役は、平安期までの貴族（公家）から武家に移り、彼らは自力本願の仏教：禅宗に帰依。禅僧の道元は宋（中国）の伽藍配置（七堂伽藍）をそのまま日本に移して永平寺を建立。厳しい自然環境のもとで、自らの衣食住を担保する作務、只管打坐（しかんたざ）の修行をすすめた。京都の禅寺の塔頭（たっちゅう）では禅修行のほか、書画、茶花など教養を身につけ、居室としての書斎（書院）を整える。

　日本建築の特色は、「庭屋一如（ていおくいちにょ）」で、禅寺の書院のみならず民家と庭、茶室と露地の関係として一般化して、現代住宅にまで継承されている。日本の木造家屋は、縁（えん）を介して園庭と一体化しており、室内から眺められる庭園形式を「座観式・定視式・鑑賞式」という。書院や座敷から、縁側の向こうの囲まれた庭を眺める。座敷に座ったまま注視するので、凝視に耐える景観構成が求められ、中国の山水画など手本とした立体絵画的構成の庭園形式が生まれた。

2. Medieval Period

In the Kamakura and Muromachi periods, the aristocrats (kuge), who were dominant in the Heian period, gave way to the samurai class. Members of this class embraced Zen, a sect of Buddhism that emphasized salvation through one's own efforts. Zen monks introduced the monastery traditions of the Song dynasty in China to Japan which is how Dōgen, the Zen monk who founded Eihei-ji Temple. was introduced to them. Aspects of Zen culture were introduced, including activities such as calligraphy and flower arrangement. The inclusion of study space (shoin), as well as environmental design techniques such as daylighting and ventilation became widespread in the shoin building designs within these gardens.

　　　The integration of gardens with buildings, so called tei-oku-ichinyo, has been a distinctive characteristic of Japanese architecture. Although this relationship began with the shoin study halls of Zen temples, it eventually spread to common houses and their gardens and to tea houses and their tea gardens (roji) and it continues to characterize contemporary houses today. This transition between interior and exterior space, achieved by the elevated, covered veranda space (en), is one of the most well-known design aspects of Japanese wooden architecture and is a classic example of how nature and man-made architecture can be harmoniously joined.

In contrast, gardens of the *zakan, teishi* or *kanshō* "contemplation" style were enclosed and appreciated from within a reception room beyond the veranda. Since the garden was appreciated by an observer sitting at a certain point within the reception room, a pictorial composition that could withstand intense viewing was required. A garden form with a pictorial composition inspired by the Song-dynasty "mountain stream" (Chinese: *shan shui*) paintings was often a theme for these gardens. The basic character of this style is relatively easy to convey in photographs and books and was exported overseas since the modern period which led to worldwide admiration of the gardens of Japan.

"Zen gardens" are another commonly referred to garden style, however, strictly speaking, Zen temples are typically located in natural environments in the mountains and thus have no need for gardens. It is the author's speculation that these gardens were created to make amends for temples located inside the city with the gardens emulating the wild landscapes that normally surround temples in the mountains. Where water was in short supply, *kare sansui* ("dry mountain stream") gardens were introduced.

There are three fundamental styles of *kare sansui* gardens:

写景的枯山水の典型、大徳寺大仙院庭園（132頁）。左手高山の滝が右へ、渓流、堰、大河、やがて大海（南庭）に。向かう中ほどは、古図に基づき中根金作氏らが復原した、亭橋。右は宝船。
写真提供：大徳寺大仙院

Realistic representation style in this *kare sansui* garden of the sub-temple Daisen-in at Daitoku-ji Temple (see page 132). There is a dry waterfall in the unseen left of the picture forming a mountain stream with rapids which then turns into a large river and finally terminates in a large dry pond representative of the ocean in the south garden outside of the right perspective of this picture. The stone on the viewer's right mid-ground is an archetypal "treasure boat" shaped boulder. Photo credit: Daisen-in, Daitokuji Temple

Opposite page top left: The garden of Myōshin-ji Temple Taizō-in Villa, Kyoto City. This *kare sansui* garden was designed by the painter and calligrapher Kano Motonobu (1476 - 1559) exhibiting an artist's sense and is an example of an **impressionistic representation** style of *kare sansui*. He was a member of the Kanō School of Painting which dominated the painting world from the end of the Muromachi period (1336–1573) to the end of the Edo period (1603–1868).

Opposite page top right: A typical example of symbolic representation in the Ryōan-ji Temple in Kyoto

Opposite page bottom: Diagram of the Urasenke school of tea ceremony's roji compound, including the Konnchi-an and Yūin teahouses originally built by the grandson of Sen no Rikyū, Sōtan in 1646 and 1653 respectively. A unique and famous pattern of stepping stones attributed to Sōtan, which paves the path between the *tsukubai* purification basin and Yūin, looks like scattered beans and is appropriately named *mamemaki* or thrown beans.

近代以降、日本の美しい庭園として海外に評価紹介された多くがこれ。立体絵画は写真映りがよく、普及しやすく①**写景的枯山水**として京都大徳寺大仙院、②**写意的枯山水**として妙心寺退蔵院、③**象徴的枯山水**として東海庵、龍安寺石庭に3分類することもできる。一般に「禅の庭」といわれるが、本来山中の自然環境（＝禅境）であるべき禅宗寺院が市中につくられたので、仮山水はその代償的環境であったのかもしれない。当初、枯山水は水利困難なときの便法だったが、背景に広く園林が存在する境内の一角の庭（てい・ドライエリア）には最適な象徴的空間として枯山水や茶庭が禅文化のひとつとして普及、中世日本人の精神史の反映とされる。

国際商業港で雑踏のまち、堺の商人たちは、市中の山居を理想とし茶室への道すがらを常緑樹で構成、地味な山里を演出。「一期一会（いちごいちえ）」の精神的気分を醸成した。「侘茶（わびちゃ）」といわれる千利休（せんのりきゅう）

- **Realistic Representation** - strives to make a realistic representation of an actual natural landscape by mimicking an actual landscape using stones, stone groupings, trimmed trees or raked sand or gravel. eg. Daisen-in of Daitoku-ji Temple of Kyoto
- **Impressionistic Representation** - strives to create imagery through impressionistic representation of a scenic composition, leaving the viewer with a residual, impressionistic image of a scenic composition by use of shapes or combinations of rocks, trees and sand or gravel raking patterns. eg. Taizō-in of Myōshin-ji Temple in Kyoto
- **Symbolic Representation** - symbolic representation of a concept, often beyond a scenic composition, for example, the universe, by using symbolism in landscape elements to leave an impression on the viewer. eg. Tōkai-an of Myōshin-ji Temple and the rock garden of Ryōan-ji Temple in Kyoto

There is also a style of garden within Zen culture called the *chaniwa* or *roji* ("tea garden") style. Congruent with the spiritual character of the Japanese in the medieval period, it gave meaning and order to the approach walkway of the teahouse. To evoke the feeling that the tea ceremony to come would be a unique, once-in-a-lifetime experience (*ichigo ichie*) for the visitor, plants, mainly evergreen trees, were simply arranged to suggest a location in the mountains. *Tobi-ishi* (stepping-stones) and *nobedan* (a paved path made by combining natural stones of

左：写意的枯山水の例、妙心寺退蔵院狩野元信の庭。
画家らしく景勝地を造園　　　　　　　　**右：象徴的**枯山水の典型、龍安寺石庭

（1522-1591）の茶道、その系譜を引く今日庵、不審庵露地な
ど、茶事（Tea ceremony）のための茶禅一味の姿勢が、より内
面的で深い精神性を日本庭園に付与したのはまちがいない。

different sizes and at times larger rectangular cut stones) were used to create the feeling of a journey down a mountain village path. The *roji* tea gardens of Konnichi-an and Fushin-an teahouses, and the Zen religion itself, undoubtedly endowed Japanese gardens with an enduring, profound, spiritual character.

右図：茶道裏千家流家元邸内の今日庵、又隠露地などの構成。今日庵(こんにちあん)(1646年創建)と、又隠(ゆういん)(1653年創建)は、ともに利休を祖父に持つ3代宗旦（そうたん）による。蹲踞(つくばい)から又隠の躙口(にじりぐち)にかけての飛石は宗旦の豆撒き飛び石と呼ばれ、豆を撒いたように数多くの飛び石が打たれ、無作為に見えながらも計算され尽くされた美。
（北尾春道著『露地・茶庭』（彰国社1956）より作図）

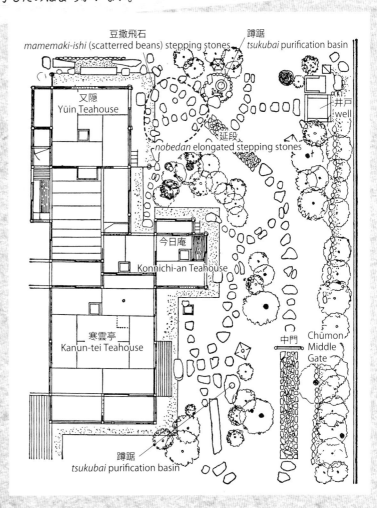

公家の桂の御所が大名の回遊式庭園へ発展

禅文化として茶華道が茶庭（露地）を完成。複数の御殿と茶庭を池泉の周囲に配し、古代以来の日本造園ディテールを総合化した八条宮家の月の名所・桂の里「桂の御所」（現桂離宮）が発展し、回遊式庭園となった。

Zen culture was the influence that developed the tea and flower arrangement culture of Japan in the Heian medieval period from which was born the uniquely Japanese tea ceremony, tea garden and teahouse and the *roji* approach path of the teahouse through the tea gardens. The garden design pattern of multiple tea gardens and houses distributed around a pond was the foundational concept for the Hachijonomiya royal family's construction of the Katsura Detached Palace and its garden as a place for moon viewing. From this was born the pattern for the circuitous strolling garden.

右：彦根城天守閣と玄宮園（滋賀県彦根市）。彦根城内楽々園には、地震のときの避難用の建物もある。

Right: Hikone Castle Tower and Rakuraku-en Genkyu-en Park (Hikone city, Shiga Pref): In Rakuraku Park, there is a building that was designed in 1814 to be earthquake proof to provide shelter after an earthquake.

（3）近世の庭園

徳川幕藩体制の下、江戸と国元には大名の権威を象徴する数ヘクタールないし10数ヘクタール以上の大面積の回遊式庭園が営まれた。大名ら封建領主の政治力は米の収穫高で象徴される農本主義経済の時代でもあり、庭園にも勧農精神の表象として水田、茶畑、梅林など「農」の風景をとり入れている。一方で儒教精神に準拠する園名（偕楽園）や亭榭（ていしゃ）名（涵徳亭）が多用される。大名の庭園は軍事、宴遊、社交、殖産など多機能的であり、それまでの日本の全時代の形式や意匠を総合的に活用した大規模オープンスペースとなっている。

茶庭を大池泉の周囲に複数配置して、これをつなぎ合わせたものが桂離宮で、この形式が全国各地に一般化したのが江戸期大名庭園であり、後楽園、栗林園、兼六園など日本各地に現存し内外から訪問者を集めている。

3. The Feudal Period

Under the Tokugawa shogunate, gardens in the *kaiyū* ("circuitous strolling garden") style that exceeded tens of hectares in area and displayed the authority of *daimyō* (feudal lords) were created in both Edo and the respective domains of the *daimyō* warlords. The political power of feudal lords was measured by rice crops (i.e. - food production capacity); thus, agrarian landscapes such as paddy fields, tea fields, and Japanese apricot groves were incorporated into gardens. Meanwhile, gardens and teahouses were often given names that aligned with the Confucian spirit

回遊式は、広大な敷地を建築区（御殿や茶屋など）、築山区、泉水区、樹林区、農地区などにゾーニングし、各所に点景として国内外の名所、富士山や近江八景、中国の名勝、杭州西湖十景や寺塔景観を縮小して園景を構成している。それを利用者が移動しながら景観変化を味わう形式である。そのためには八方正面構成で、築山と池、樹林と芝生を対比的に配置、園路をアップダウンし明暗、曲折させシークエンス景観（移動景観）を演出する。回遊式は、大面積で多機能、多数者の利用を可能とし、美しくエコロジカルでもあるので、現代の都市公園にも援用できる近代性がある点に注目したい。

Above: The Satoyama landscape of Santome Shinden - Developed under the feudal lord of the Kawagoe domain of Yoshiyasu Yanagisawa (1658-1714) from the wild grasslands of the Musashino plateau. These strip-shaped plots of land, protected from the winds by a planted shelter belt, are productive sweet potato fields. Using composted fallen leaves from the shelter belt, the land grew rich and continues to be impressively productive today 300 years later and has become a world agricultural heritage site. (Edo Period Agriculture Techniques Club, Santome, Miyoshi-cho, Tokorozawa City, Saitama Pref)
Photo credit: Tokyo Shimbun

which preached an orderly relationship between lord and vassal. Daimyō gardens had many uses including military and social functions as well as industry-related uses. Their large open spaces synthesized styles and designs from different periods of Japan.

For example, multiple tea gardens were arranged around a large pond and linked together at the Katsura Detached Palace and the Shūgaku-in Detached Palace. This arrangement was adopted in the *daimyō* gardens of the Edo period which were designed all over the country, such as Kōraku-en, Ritsurin-en, and Kenroku-en gardens.

In a *kaiyū* style garden, a spacious site was divided or zoned into a number of areas; these were scenically organized according to themes such as the Eight Views of Ōmi or the views of the 53 Stations of the Tokaido, so that users moved within the garden and enjoyed changes in scenery. That being the case, the garden was composed to be viewed from all directions, and changes or sequences in scenery were staged with hillocks, ponds, groves, lawns, buildings, and garden areas, as well as with ups and downs, light and darkness, and curves in the garden path. This style was capable of serving many functions in a large area and accommodating many users simultaneously. This style created both ecologically balanced and beautiful spaces which have a modern character and thus is suitable for use in contemporary urban parks.

（4）近代の庭園

　やさしいアンジュレーション、芝生地に点在する背丈の低い刈込み物、目立たない腑せ石の護岸にナチュラルな流れ。それが文人政治家山縣有朋と庭師植治（うえじ）こと小川治兵衛の協働によって創作された近代日本の自然主義、田園自然風景式庭園であった。植治の代表作は、京都東山の南禅寺界隈に作庭された無鄰庵や対龍山荘、野村碧雲荘、住友有芳園などだが、それまでの鶴亀の庭のような定形を避け、人々に懐かしい田舎的原風景を表現した。

　フレデリック・ロー・オルムステッド（1822-1903）設計のニューヨークのセントラル・パークが追求したパストラル（田園美）は、ゆったりとしたカーブ園路と大芝生地に自然樹形の大木が疎林をなす形式で、新宿御苑や明治神宮内苑など日本近代の造園デザインに影響を与えた。

近代自然主義の作庭家、植治（うえじ）の作品、現在の国際文化会館の庭園(東京都港区鳥居坂、六本木)。
ガーデンパーティーにも利用される明るい芝生庭と自然主義のゆるやかな自然曲線園路（**上の左右**）。江戸技法の黒ボク石（熔岩）による涸流には紅葉が重なる（**下左**）。ゆるやかな土のアンデュレーションと自然風石段（**下右**）。すべて植治の技。

Above: One corner of **the Meiji Jingu Shrine Kyu-gyoen Inner Garden, Tokyo.** Here is found the Kakuun-tei teahouse created as a resting place for dowager Empress Shoken. In front of the teahouse, there is a lawn garden from which one can see the south pond and slope covered in 150 different varieties of Japanese water irises planted in a slope with water running down it from the Ikimasa well, which then collects in the pond. The entire garden is embraced by lush, thick forest which is reminiscent of the Musashino Plateau virgin forests. In the appraisal of Meiji era landscape architecture scholar Shyunkichi Kodera, the Kyu-gyoen Inner Garden exemplified the beauty of traditional Japanese rural town scenery.

4. The Modern Period

Gentle undulations, spacious lawns, low, pruned plants, inconspicuous and strategically arranged rocks, embankments and the natural flow of water are hallmarks of the naturalistic and rural landscape-style gardens created through a collaboration of a group of intelligentsia and the garden designer Ueji (also known as Ogawa Jihei) which marked a new era in garden design in modern Japan. Among Ueji's best known works are the Garden of Murin-an, Tairyū-sansō, Nomura Hekiun-sō, and Sumitomo Yūhō-en in the Nanzen-ji area of the Higashiyama district in Kyoto. He avoided conventional garden forms such as the so called *tsuru-kame* (Crane and Turtle) garden and instead recreated the primary landscapes of traditional countryside scenes that Japanese view with nostalgia.

The pastoral appearance achieved, for example, in New York's Central Park (designed by Frederick Law Olmsted), where large trees form scattered, isolated groves on lawns, interwoven with numerous curved paths, has been welcomed by residents of many metropolises. This same style was also implemented in the Shinjuku Gyoen National Garden as well as the Inner Precinct of Meiji Shrine.

Previous page: Creation of the famous modern period naturalistic garden designer Ueji (Ogawa Jihei), the garden of the International House of Japan in Roppongi, Tokyo. A man-made waterfall, fed by pumped well water, runs into a beautiful pond in a conceptual high grassland plateau forming the focal point of the garden. With an emulation of the Musashino Plateau forests in the background, a dry stream bed accented by carefully placed, black volcanic rocks looks especially beautiful in fall colors. This garden allows the drama of the four seasons to be felt and serves as a cheery venue for international cultural exchange events. (Roppongi, Toriizaka, Minato Ward, Tokyo)

左上：明治神宮旧御苑（東京都渋谷区神宮内苑の一角）昭憲皇太后行啓の御休息所としての隔雲亭、その芝庭から臨む南池。また清正井を水源とし武蔵野林の谷戸田に流れるように咲く花菖蒲の田園的庭苑の景観が見事。総面積21,000坪。

造園学者小寺駿吉は、旧御苑は東京の郷土地理的所産であり、明治期の歴史的遺産として極めて重要であると述べ、明治期、宮内省林苑技師の感性を高く評価している。

41

六本木ヒルズの「屋上田圃」（構想は著者・進士五十八）では、昆虫・野鳥のバイオダイバーシティが見られる。田植え、米の収穫、餅つきなど、年間を通じた農体験が、都心のランドスケープのみならず、人々のライフスタイルにも多様性を与えている。

写真：東京都心の超高層オフィス居住ビルの住民にも土と緑と生き物体験を提供する屋上庭園（森ビルの六本木ヒルズ、けやき坂コンプレックスの屋上庭園）（提供：森ビル）

（5）現代の造園

　現代日本は第二次世界大戦敗戦後、荒廃した国土緑化推進に始まり、列島改造ブームと高度経済成長（1960s）による海岸埋立など自然破壊に対する自然保護や公害反対運動の高まりを経て、現在ではエコロジー（ecology）とエコノミー（economy）の調和、さらにはSDGsの達成、美しい草花による安らぎや土とのふれあい等、アメニティ（amenity）や景観美の具現化に国民の支持が高まっている。

　そんな中、ジャパン・ランドスケープ（Japan Landscape）は、多様な展開を歩んでいる。近代造園が創出した明治神宮の森のような生物多様性に富んだ都市林の価値が見直され、東京新宿の京王ホテルでは東京の原風景の武蔵野や雑木林が、また六本木ヒルズの屋上には日本の原風景である水田風景が再生されている。

5. The Contemporary Period

After the Second World War, modern Japan started the National Land Afforestation Promotion Program in order to restore the landscape after the extensive damage from the war. In response to the rapid industrialization of the sixties and seventies, the "Plan for Remodeling the Japanese Archipelago" was developed to facilitate the dispersion of industry from concentrated urban centers to smaller centers throughout Japan by the development of improved and expanded transport networks and infrastructure. In response to the massive landfill projects and environmental pollution and destruction brought on by this period of high economic growth, came a surge in environmental conservation and pollution opposition movements. In more recent times, public support for policies that encourage harmonization between the economy and ecology is growing rapidly, as is support for the implementation of SDG's (Sustainable Development Goals), Amenity Design and scenic beauty development projects.

　　Ecology-based, urban forests are designed as a remedy to the choking urban environments of the mega-cities of today. For example, the woodland scenery once typical of the Musashino Plateau, and the rice paddies that constitute the primary landscapes of Japan, have been recreated in the modern landscapes of Tokyo.

　　In the midst of all these movements and reforms, Japanese landscape architecture has a role to play. As the world's major cities

世界都市間競争に対応する東京の都市再開発で高層高密化がすすみ、多彩な緑化技術が駆使されているが、緑量のみならずアメニティ質の向上を工夫している。また国際観光インバウンド（inbound）に対しては、ランドスケープのみならず、できるだけ日本らしさ・地方らしさ（locality）等、クール・ジャパンの風景づくりの工夫が重要である。そのとき自然材・地場材・地方技術を駆使する「日本庭園の手法・技法」は大いに有効であると強調しておきたい。

なお、インバウンドにも人気の芸術性豊かな枯山水には重森三玲作が多い（写真下）。日本庭園史図鑑の刊行を通じ立石組に力強さを発見した重森の古典への造詣の表出を感じるのであろう。

compete for preeminence, and as urban density intensifies, Tokyo's redevelopment plan must include more than just simply increasing the amount of greenery. It must also add meaningful amenities and improve the quality of life of residents, employing innovative and advanced landscape architectural techniques to make the most of unused space or difficult terrain, to maximize green space aesthetics and benefits.

As Japan works to rebrand its image as a tourist destination by highlighting the unique beauty and culture of Japan, through programs such as the Cool Japan Program and Inbound Tourism Goal Strategy, the attractiveness and global uniqueness of regionally flavored Japanese garden design techniques must not be forgotten or overlooked.

右：東福寺本坊枯山水（京都）、現代の代表的作庭家重森三玲作品

Right: The South Garden of Tofuku-ji Temple designed by the famous avant-garde Japanese garden designer Mirei Shigemori (1896-1975). A genius polymath, lover of *Ikebana* and extremely knowledgeable about Japanese culture and philosophy, but without traditional apprenticeship in garden design, he went on to design numerous gardens. Perhaps his most famous creation is this *kare sansui* garden and Hōrai-jima motif rock grouping; exaggerated and unconventional in how tall and long the rocks he chose were, a style previously unseen in temple gardens.

A: 田瀬理夫（たせみちお）設計の人工地盤上の森づくりと現代の造園アクロス福岡（福岡市）。 **B**: 急傾斜の山地を石積段を造成し、狭い農地でジャガイモ栽培して、いずれ遊ぶ子どものいる地域にしたいと願った。貧しい農漁村の人々の生きる努力が美しい風景を創る。重要文化的景観（愛媛県宇和島市遊子水荷浦）。 **C**: 東京都心のオフィスビルの壁面緑化、日本橋の江戸らしい土地柄か、日本の梅など花木を壁面に活用（東京都中央区日本橋）。 **D**: 宇治茶の郷、和束町（わづかちょう）の茶畑。重要文化的景観（京都府）。 **E**: 精神性を感じる、禅の修行道場福井県永平寺七堂伽藍（しちどうがらん）。800年前に中国杭州の杭州大工の手によって建築され、近年国の重要文化財に指定された。永平寺は七堂以外のコンクリート構造建築を今後「減築」（敷地の70％の建物を無くしていく方針）を決定し、七堂のみは修復しながら永続的に保存すると宣言している。（写真提供：曹洞宗大本山永平寺）。 **F**: 谷口吉生（たにぐちよしお）設計の「禅と日本文化」の著者である鈴木大拙（すずきだいせつ）記念館水鏡（みずかがみ）の庭（石川県金沢市）。

A: On reclaimed land, the forested modern park of ACROS Fukuoka. Designed by Michio Tase. (Fukuoka City, Fukuoka Pref) **B**: Stone wall terraced fields on steep slopes. This area has very limited flat land and the original inhabitants of this fishing/farming village were consequently poor and starving and created these very labor intensive fields to grow potatoes. The hardship and intense effort of these villagers makes this scenery beautiful. This is a Japanese government designated cultural asset. (Yusumizugaura, Uwajima City, Ehime Pref) **C**: The greenification of a Tokyo office building. Flowering trees typical of Japanese classical scenery are used to decorate this wall. (Nihonbashi, Chuo Ward, Tokyo) **D**: The tea groves where the famous Uji-cha tea of Kyoto is grown; a Japanese government designated cultural asset. (Wazuka-cho Town, Kyoto Pref) **E**: A place of spirituality. Shichido Garan (lit - seven-halls) Zen Buddhism compound within the Eihei-ji Temple grounds (main temple of Sōtō school of Zen Buddhism). It was built by a famous carpenter and his crew from Hangzhou, China 800 years ago. It recently became designated as a significant national cultural asset. While the original Shichido Garan hall was made of wood construction, 70% of the compound consists of modern reinforced concrete buildings. The temple made a declaration that they will remove these, while maintaining the wooden structures, with the goal of restoring and maintaining this historic and cultural asset into perpetuity. Photo: Eihei-ji temple **F**: The Water Mirror Garden at the D. T. Suzuki Museum. Dedicated to the life, writings, and ideas of Kanazawa-born Buddhist philosopher Daisetsu Teitaro Suzuki. Designer: Yoshio Taniguchi (Kanazawa City, Ishikawa Pref)

囲繞が独立世界を創る（慈照寺銀閣庭園の高垣、京都）

Enclosure creates a separate and comfortable space
(Garden of the Silver Pavilion, Jishō-ji Temple, Kyoto)

第四章 日本式庭園の空間・景観構成の手法

五原理 囲繞（いにょう）・縮景・借景・樹藝・然び

Arboriculture

Agingの美

Chapter 4

Techniques of Spatial and Scenic Composition in Japanese Gardens

Enclosure, Shukkei, Shakkei, Jugei and Sabi

第4章では、日本庭園は自然と人間の共生関係が基本だということを踏まえた上で、日本庭園の空間や景観構成の５つの基本原理−①囲繞、②縮景、③借景、④樹藝、⑤然び（さび）で庭園が成立していることを解説。この５点を理解すれば、日本庭園の特質がよくわかる。4章を科学的な視点から説明すると世界中すべての庭園構成に共通する普遍的原理、①空間、②景観、③眺望、④自然、⑤時間、の５つに対応する。

第4章から第6章までの読み方と理解のために

　いよいよ日本庭園のデザイン、つくり方を解説しよう。第4章では、空間や景観の構成手法、端的には広がる大地の中で、敷地を選定し目標となる庭園を構成し、外部との関連性をどのように「計画」するか（planning）を説明する。第5章では、材料や、形状寸法など、細部を構成し目標とする景観イメージや美しさをいかに実現するか、「設計」（designing）を説明する。ただし、実務的な多彩な知識や知恵、テクニックは庭園の目的、規模で千差万別なので、第6章個々の名園を実地に訪れ、体験的に学んでほしい。

　庭園というものは、いったいどのようにつくられているのか。わかりやすくいえば、①〜⑥となる。
　①人が安心して生きられるように、濠や塀垣で空間を「囲う」。

Let us now discuss the ways Japanese gardens are designed and created. In this chapter, spatial and scenic composition techniques are discussed including how the site is selected, how the garden is arranged, and how its relationship to the outside world is established.

Specific design principles and details, such as materials and dimensions of shapes and how they are organized to create harmonious beauty or a scenic image, are covered in Chapter 5. There are a wide range of skills and techniques used to achieve these arrangements depending on the objective and scale of the garden. The reader is encouraged to study those skills and techniques by visiting and experiencing the famous gardens described in Chapter 6 first hand.

How is a garden created? Simplified, there are six basic steps for the process.

① The space and its shape must be defined either by a waterway, a fence, or other means of enclosure, so that people can feel secure, enclosed and at ease.

②囲われた空間のなかに水を湛え、樹草を植えて「快適な空間」につくりかえる。

③閉じた空間のなかにいると人は不安になり、外界とつながりたくなるので、外を眺めたり「借景」するように工夫する。

④樹木は生長するので適切に手入れし、メンテナンスし、コントロールする。

⑤庭園は永い年月を重ねると、樹石は自然そっくりになり、周囲に馴じみ一体化する。

⑥庭園空間は安全安心で快適となり、時間的にも限られた人生の人間に「永遠の時間」（然び、エイジングの美）を感じさせてくれる。そのための土地自然と利用の適切なガーデン・マネージメントが必要である。

② The enclosed space needs to have water or the suggestion thereof, and greenery and flowers planted to create a pleasant atmosphere.

③ A connection to the outside world needs to be established by means of a view to the external world or with the use of "borrowed scenery." Being inside an enclosed space, while feeling secure, can make people uneasy unless a connection with the familiar, outside world is provided.

④ Plants must be maintained and controlled otherwise they will grow excessively, compromising the orderly atmosphere and proportion of the landscape.

⑤ Exposure to the elements over many years, allows trees and stones to come to resemble those in nature and the garden becomes integrated with its surroundings.

⑥ Ultimately the garden space needs to feel safe, secure and comfortable, evoking in humans, whose lives are of limited length compared to the time scale of nature, a sense of eternity while bringing awareness to the beauty of aging.

In this chapter, it is established that Japanese gardens are places where nature and humans can co-exist. From that relationship, the five basic principles of Japanese garden design can be explained: 1) enclosure, 2) *shukkei*, 3) *shakkei*, 4) arboriculture, 5) *sabi*.

With a firm understanding of these five fundamental techniques, the essential qualities of Japanese gardens can be better understood and appreciated.

In this chapter, garden design will be examined from a scientific perspective. All of the world's gardens have shared, fundamental elements:1) site; 2) landscape; 3) view; 4) nature; 5) time.

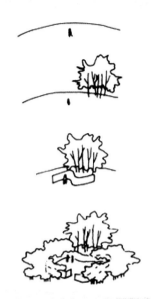

（Simonds, 1961）

（1）囲繞（いにょう）（囲い）— やすらぎの空間

　人間は、後ろには眼がない。自分の身を守るために
は背後がどっしり安定した壁で囲まれていることが必要
である。背後が大樹や林縁（フォレストエッジ）で囲ま
れた場所には最も長く滞留する。彼らの行動原理は外敵
から身を守る「生命保全第一」の構えである。

　「囲い」は住居空間を物理的に保護するばかりか、
心理的にも快適やくつろぎを感じさせる。ドイツ語で
は、生垣で囲まれた意味のBehaglichが「快適と感じ
る」であるし、山並みに囲まれた雰囲気の言葉
Gemütlich が「くつろいでいる」だからである。

　竹の豊富な日本では、多彩な竹垣が発達して、日本
庭園の独自性に大きく寄与している。

囲繞が独立世界を創る
囲うことで自分のための空間が
生まれる。それが落ちつきと安心
の安定空間をもたらす。
Gardenの基本構造が囲みだ。

**Enclosure Creates a
Separate and
Comfortable Space**

As you can see in the
diagram above, the space
does not feel comforting
or attractive with only the
addition of trees or a
barrier but rather needs
the hedge's complete
enclosure before gaining
these qualities. Enclosure
is the most basic principle
in garden design.

1. Enclosure: Secure Space

Lacking eyes in the back of our head, having a solid, secure
and stable environment behind us creates a feeling of safety
and security. Accordingly, we have a tendency to choose a
bench to relax on, or a place to linger, when there is a large
tree or a grove of trees behind us. This is a basic human
survival instinct.

　An enclosure not only provides physical space for
habitation with protection against animals or enemies, but
it can also be important psychologically, imbuing a sense of
comfort and relaxation. It is interesting to note that the
German word *behaglich*, which literally means "to be
surrounded by a hedge", means "to feel comfortable," and
the word *gemütlich*, which is an area surrounded by
mountains, means "to be relaxed."

　Also, the Hebrew etymological root of garden is *gan*
or *gun* meaning "to be protected." Moats, fences, walls,
hedges, and groves of trees have been created throughout
the world in all periods of history for the same reason.
Eventually, the pursuit of scenic beauty came to be as
important as the achievement of utility and safety in the
design of enclosures and culminated in elaborate forms such
as the bamboo hedges of Japan. (See Chapter 5, the
techniques of fences, for details.)

右：日本人の「こころのふるさと」の原型が盆地地形でもある。盆地に立地する飛鳥坐(あすかにいます)神社（奈良県）

Right: The archetypical nostalgic "hometown" for Japanese is most often pictured in a valley or basin where the hills or ridges create a sense of enclosure around it as is Asukaniimasu-jinja Shrine. (Nara Pref)

左：屋敷林（富山県、砺波平野）

Left: Typical enclosure formed by planted trees around a residence (Tonami Plain, Toyama Pref)

左：二段垣（大徳寺大仙院方丈）
写真提供：大徳寺大仙院

Left: Two-tiered hedge at the Hojo or Abbot's quarters of Daisen-in, Daitoku-ji Temple (Kyoto, Kyoto Pref)
Photo credit: Daisen-in, Daitoku-ji Temple

右：高さがちがう穂垣（京都、梅小路朱雀の庭）

Right: Varied height fence made of young bamboo (Sujyakuno-niwa Garden, Umekoji Park, Kyoto Pref)

個人では美しい花園をつくると
か、西洋庭園では、有力者は
経済力の誇示や政治的権威を
造形化するためにデザイン構成
を考えることが常だった。人々が
憧れる神仏世界にはじまり、富
士山のような名山、日本三景の
名所、和歌の枕詞となる景勝
地など、実在する自然景観を
「縮景」した。

（2）縮景 － 理想世界をつくる

　庭園の主題は「ミクロコスモス（小宇宙）」の実現
であった。人間は自然があって生きていける、いわば自
然によって生かされる存在である。しかしダイレクトの
自然のなかで、生きることは難しい。そこで、人にやさ
しく、快適に暮らせる環境構成として庭園を営むことに
した。それは人間の要求や都合に合わせて加工された
「二次自然」や「人為自然」で、いわば「家畜化した自
然」、「文化化された自然」、人間がコントロールした
「小自然」ともいえる。

　garden の語源が、gan、gun でガードされていること
からもわかるし、歴史的にみて世界中で濠、柵、塀、垣
や屋敷林がつくられたことでも十分理解されよう。それ
らは防衛など実用性のみならず美観性をも追求し、特に
日本の竹垣にみられる工芸品のような高質の造形に到達
した（詳細は第5章の垣根術を参照。）

Garden design evolved
from beautiful flower
gardens of individuals, or
in the case of politically or
economically powerful
members of society,
Western style, imposing,
symmetrical gardens, to
shukkei or reduced
scenery gardens which
emulate famous scenic
views of nature as design
philosophy shifted to
embrace natural wonders
or the "realm of the gods"
as its guiding theme.

2. Shukkei: Creating an Ideal World

In many ways, gardens represent a microcosmos. While we
are entirely dependent on the natural world for survival and
thus deeply connected to it, living in untamed nature is
intimidating. Gardens feel hospitable to us because nature is
molded into a pleasant   environmental composition where
human ideas are incorporated. Created in places that are
conveniently accessible, gardens allow us to comfortably
interact with nature without leaving the familiar environs of
civilization. Gardens feel peaceful to us because nature is
scaled down and domesticated. They are places where we
have bestowed order and nature is under our control.

　The only way the universe, the world, or large scale
scenic objects can be emulated in a small garden is by
utilizing reduction or miniaturization techniques. Thus,
shukkei ("reduced scenery") is a basic technique employed
in garden creation.

　The renowned gardens of the feudal period feature
many examples of reduced scenery that imitate places such
as Mt. Fuji and views which are traditionally identified as

さて、狭い庭のなかに宇宙や世界を表現するには縮小するしかない。ミニアチュールである。これを日本では「縮景」といい、日本庭園の本領であった。

近世の名園には、富士山や日本三景などの写景的「縮景」が多い。熊本市の水前寺成趣園の富士山、桂離宮の天の橋立、筑後、柳川藩立花家の松濤園の松島などリアルである。その特徴は、自然景観の本質をおさえた上で、巧みに省略、強調している点である。富士山でいえば、山頂の頂角をやや鋭くするとか裾野を水平に長く引き伸ばして雄大に見せるという技法である。

およそすべてのデザインや創造は、模倣から始まる。オリジナリティを強調する芸術の世界でも、なお「模倣」から始まるとされる。庭園でもまったく同じだが、著者は作庭において模倣が真の意味で創造だといえるのは、先人のつくった「名園」を模倣するのではなく、名園を成立させた「大自然」を学習し、模倣することでなければならないと考えていて、これを「日本庭園の自然学習性」と呼んでいる。

日本庭園は、大自然の模倣によってつくられた名園が多い。作庭家たちは自然のもつ「秩序性」、「多様性」、「依拠性」、「安定性」を、より具体的に造景技法の模範にしたのである。

the most famous in Japan. Some famous examples are: Mt. Fuji as recreated in the Jōju-en Garden of Suizen-ji Temple in Kumamoto; the Amanohashidate sandbar as recreated in the garden of the Katsura Detached Palace in Kyoto; and Matsushima island as recreated in the Shōtō Garden of the Tachibana Residence in Fukuoka.

縮景／秋吉台（**右**）からの自然学習性による常栄寺の雪舟庭園（**左**）

Example of *Shukkei* - The Akiyoshidai Plateau (**right**) and its emulated *shukkei* form in Sesshu Garden in the Joei-ji Temple grounds (**left**). (Yamaguchi Pref)

縮景／憧憬の美しい自然風景を、省略と強調して造形

Much admired examples of *shukkei* reduced scenery - beautiful natural vistas, reduced and exaggerated in garden designs

桂離宮の松琴亭(しょうきんてい)(**左**)前に
日本三景の一、丹後の天橋立(**右**)を縮景

Considered one of the three most scenic spots in Japan, Amanohashidate Sandbarnin northern Kyoto Prefecture (**right**) is the scenery which is emulated in front of the Shōkin-tei Teahouse in the Katsura Rikyū Detached Palace Garden (**left**).

水前寺成趣園(**左**)に富士山(**右**)を縮景

The *Shukkei* version of Mt. Fuji in Jōju-en Garden of Suizen-ji Temple in Kumamoto (**left**). The actual Mt. Fuji (**right**).

日本三景の一、奥州の松島(**右**)の縮景、立花家の
松涛園 (福岡県柳川市) (**左**)

Matsushima, a group of 260 tiny islands (*shima*) in Miyagi Prefecture covered in pines (*matsu*), considered one of the three most scenic spots in Japan (**right**), is emulated in the Tachibana family Shōtō-en Garden of Yanagawa City, Fukuoka Pref (**left**).

中国杭州西湖蘇堤の跨虹橋(ここうきょう・太鼓橋)(**右上**)の写し、縮景園(広島市)(**左上**)と琉球庭園の識名園(那覇市)(**左下**)

The Kokō-kyō Bridge and the Taikobashi bridge in Shukkei-en Garden in Hiroshima City (**upper left**), the Shikina-en Ryukyu Teien Garden in Naha City, Okinawa, (**bottom left**) and Yosui-en Garden in Wakayama City, Wakayama Pref (**bottom right**) are all emulations of the famous West Lake Causeways in Hangzhou, China (**top right**).

All of these examples use exaggeration and ingenious abbreviation of the shape and form observed in the actual scenery. In the case of the faux Mt. Fuji, the slope of the peak is accentuated and more vertical, and the lowland skirting the mountain is flatter and more extended than it actually is.

All creation begins with imitation. Imitation is a basic principle, even in the world of art, where originality is prized. The same is true in garden design. However, it is the author's supposition that imitation in garden design is creation only if one studies and imitates, not a famous garden created by a predecessor, but rather natural scenery like that which inspired the famous garden design originally. In this respect, the study of Japanese garden design is in fact the study of nature.

The imitation of nature has yielded many famous Japanese gardens. Garden designers have developed specific techniques inspired by the orderliness, diversity, and stability found in nature as well as our dependence on it.

養翠園（ようすいえん）の西湖堤（和歌山市）

53

All gardens of the world have beautiful views but Japanese gardens are unique in that they also incorporate the beauty of scenery outside the garden, making it part of the scenic composition in the garden. In order to capture borrowed scenery, one technique used, is to create sharp contrast between the distant object and scenery within the garden. One device employed for this, is a contrast created by the white sand of a *kare sansui* garden and the richness of the green mountain scenery beyond the confines of the garden. A famous example, that was not widely realized until Kinkichiro Honda pointed it out in his book Famous Gardens of Japan (Nihon Meien Zufu, 1964), is the *kare sansui* garden in Ryōan-ji Temple (**below**) which acts as the contrasting foreground to capture Mt. Otoko Yama in the background (home to Iwashimizu Hachimangu Shrine) to accomplish a *shakkei* composition.

（３）借景 – 外部世界とつながる / 外部の景を生けどる

　日本庭園では、「借景」手法が重要である。世界中の庭園には、必ず「眺望（view）」がある。庭園からは、園内も園外も必ず視野にはいる。しかし日本庭園の「借景」は、単に園外が眺望できるだけではない。園外の借景対象となる山や仏塔が、その庭園の景観構成の中核（主景）として取り込まれる場合のみ「借景庭園」という。したがって、何らかの事情で借景が見えなくなった場合には、名園としての評価も消滅する。

　これほど外部景観を重要視する「借景」では、次の3つの条件が必要で「風景の生けどり」とも呼ばれている。

①借景対象（山、湖、島、仏塔など建物、石灯籠など）
②見切り、区切り（借景対象をフレーミングする。築地塀、生垣、竹林などで額縁を形づくる）

3. Shakkei: Creating Connections to the Outside World; Capturing Outside Scenery

Shakkei ("borrowed scenery") is an important technique employed in Japanese gardens. Garden designs throughout the world, all create "views"either inside the garden or afford ones of the outside world. In Japanese gardens however, *shakkei* is not simply a matter of being able to view impressive scenery outside the garden from

借景とは認識されていなかった龍安寺の石庭だが、本多錦吉郎の『日本名園図譜』（1964年）によると石清水八幡宮の男山が背後に明確に示されている。

54

③庭園・園内景観（借景対象を引き立てるような白砂敷、芝生、苔、刈込みなど）

ところで借景手法は、本体の自然・仏塔等に手を加えることなく、人間の側に取り込む方法でもある。対象物には、さわりもせず完全に庭園の主景とすることができる。外部の相手を尊重しながら、自分の側の見切りや園内をコントロールすることで一体化する方法といえる。自他の柔らかな結合といった考え方は欧米とちがう日本的手法のすばらしさである。

within the garden. It is when the view of that scenery or object outside the garden, such as a mountain or pagoda, is intentionally incorporated in such a way that it becomes a focal point or centerpiece in the garden's scenic composition. Therefore, such a garden will lose its value if for some reason, that borrowed scenery becomes no longer visible.

Three physical components are necessary to create "borrowed scenery," which is also referred to as "live-captured scenery ":

① An object such as a mountain, lake, island, or a building such as a pagoda, etc. is visible from within the garden site.

② A separator; e.g. wall, hedge, bamboo grove exists to define the garden from the outside world.

③ A garden or a perspective from within a garden, that includes something like a bed of white gravel, a lawn, a bed of moss or a pruned plant, is positioned in such a way to create a setting that will frame the borrowed scenery.

Shakkei is a way of assimilating an object like a natural feature or a pagoda, capturing it within the garden's view without altering it. One can make this borrowed scenery the centerpiece of the garden; assimilating it while respecting it as is. The idea of establishing a loose, elastic union between large-scale scenery outside a garden with the controlled scenery within a garden, is a unique and exceptional Japanese technique.

借景の景観構造と借景の条件
／上段、左図の園外景のうち、遠景だけをフレーミングして、右図のように借景する。下段は借景にふさわしい地形と配置

The Structure and Conditions for Creating *Shakkei*

As seen in the upper left diagram, to create *shakkei* (borrowed scenery) it is necessary to frame the distant scenery focal point using garden elements. As shown, framing with the trees is not enough. The fence was also necessary to eliminate the clutter of the foreground of the distant focal point. The lower diagram shows how suitable topographical forms are necessary to accomplish *shakkei*.

借景／外景を生けどる。園外景観にフォーカスがある
Shakkei - Capturing Distant Scenery and Making it a Focal Point

右：京都、清水寺本坊の成就院庭園の借景／園内の石灯籠に呼応するように、湯屋谷の向こう側の山の斜面に石灯籠を立てることで、園の内外が結合し、対岸の風景を借景する(京都市)

Right: Another famous example of borrowed scenery can be found at Kiyomizu-dera Temple where a stone lantern in the garden emulates a large-scale stone lantern on the slopes of an adjacent mountain outside the garden. (Kyoto City, Kyoto

写真：公益財団法人京都市都市緑化協会

左：高松の栗林園：庭園正面の紫雲山の稜線（スカイライン）と園内の反橋（堰月橋-えんげつきょう）のカーブのパラリズム（平行手法）で内外景が一体化する。「隣借」。（香川県高松市）

下：庭内外の景観構成が互いに呼応し、広がりと奥行きを演出。NY椿山荘からハドソン川をはさみコロンビア大学を望む（伊藤邦衛作、1989年、ニューヨーク市）

Left: In Ritsurin-en Garden yet another variation of *shakkei* can be found where the arched shape of the Engetsu-kyo Moon Bridge emulates the skyline ridge of Mt. Shiun that can be seen behind the garden, uniting the scenery of both outside and inside the garden. (Takamatsu City, Kagawa Pref)

Below: In New York City, with Columbia University visible on the ridge and the Hudson River wedged in between, is the Chinzanso Retreat Garden. The rock arrangement pictured here seems to be in communication with the iconic buildings on the skyline across the expanse, accentuating the stone arrangement. (Designer: Kunie Ito, New York City, New York)

上：磯庭園の借景は海に浮かぶ桜島山がメイン（鹿児島市）

Above: Mt. Sakurajima rising out of the sea is featured as the main scenic element in Iso-teien Garden, though it is well outside of the garden, in this classic example of *shakkei*. (Kagoshima City, Kagoshima Pref)

山縣有朋と植治の合作、無鄰菴（**左**）と真々庵（**下**）共に東山を借景している

In both the gardens of the Murin-an Villa (**left** - created in a collaboration between former prime minister Aritomo Yamagata and garden designer Ogawa Jihei) as well as that of the Shinshin-an Villa (**below** - former villa of Konosuke Matsushita - founder of Panasonic), Mt. Higashiyama just outside of Kyoto is used as a focal point in yet another example of *shakkei*.

（４）樹藝 – 緑とつき合う樹木文化

　自然の樹形に人の手を加えて人間の思いを表現することを「樹藝（じゅげい）」という。人間は自分の生活を守り豊かにするために、自然のままの樹木を屋敷周りに植栽したり、樹形などに手を加えたりして、屋敷林や生垣を造成したり、果樹を仕立てて実を大きくしたり穫り易くしたり、美しく整姿して庭木に利用してきた。樹藝には、風土性（地域性）や文化性があり、国によってちがう。たとえば日本では「作り木」「刈込み」、ヨーロッパでは「トピアリー」という。

　著者は日本庭園の樹種別の植栽本数を調査したことがあるが、圧倒的に常緑樹が多く植えられ、緑濃い落ちついた背景づくりを重視していることがわかった。そのような緑の地に、点景としてカエデなど紅葉、椿など花木、モクセイなど香りの木を植え庭景とした。日本は温暖多雨で植物の生長が旺盛なため、生長が遅い松、槙

樹藝／海の大波の造形
頼久寺の大刈込。小堀遠州作
（岡山県高梁市）

Jugei - **Giant ocean waves**
A giant *karikomi* piece done by the famous Enshū Kobori, emulating a giant ocean wave in the garden of Raikyu-ji Temple. (Takahashi City, Okayama Pref)

4. Jugei - Arboriculture: Maintaining a Relationship with Greenery

In Japanese *ju* means "trees" and *gei* means "art" and the two words combined, *jugei*, suggests how nature can be sculpted to express human ideas or artistic aesthetics. To protect and enrich their lives, humans have planted trees in their natural habitat, modified trees by pruning them into different forms, planted and pruned trees to form

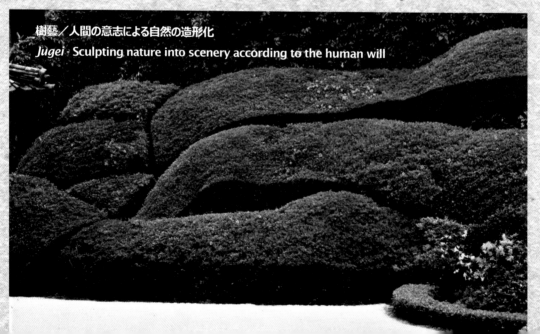

樹藝／人間の意志による自然の造形化
Jugei - Sculpting nature into scenery according to the human will

（まき）、梅などを庭木にとり入れたり、生長が速い樹種の場合は大胆に刈り込むことで、造形意志を工夫した。

　日本の樹藝のすばらしさは、小堀遠州作庭の頼久寺（高梁市）のサツキの大刈込（大海の波の表現）や修学院離宮上のお茶屋の混ぜ垣の大刈込、そして桂離宮の笹垣をみればわかる。桂離宮の東、桂川との間の境界に長さ250メートルの生きた竹の枝葉を編んだ笹垣がある（第6章「桂離宮」参照）。縦に繊維が通り逆V字に曲げても生きている竹の性質を生かした美事な竹藝である。

樹藝／樹形・樹姿を仕立てた主景木、「千代の傘松」（香川県丸亀市）

windbreaks and hedges, selected, propagated and pruned fruit trees so that they will bear larger and more easily picked fruits, and selected trees with more beautiful appearance for use as garden trees. These are all examples of *jugei* (arboriculture). Climate, local conditions, as well as culture are all a part of *jugei*. As a consequence, the traditions of arboriculture differ from country to country. *Karikomi* (shearing or shaping) in Japan for example is naturally different from topiary in Europe.

　　Based on tree surveys done by the author, evergreens are the most common kind of tree found in Japanese gardens by an overwhelming margin. Evergreens are important because they create a subdued, dark green background, against which other trees serve as features, such as maples, with colorful autumn foliage, flowering trees such as camellia, and fragrant trees such as Osmanthus are planted. Japan's temperate climate and abundant rainfall promotes vigorous plant growth thus measures to assure the maintenance of the designer's original intentions are essential. For example, trees such as pines and Japanese apricots, which grow slowly, need minimal pruning but azalea that grow quickly, must be pruned much more aggressively to maintain proportion and balance in the garden design.

Jugei - Creating a main character tree

A great example of this is found in the Nakazu Bansho-en Garden where a giant pine has been sculpted by *karikomi* in an umbrella-like shape and is known as the Thousand Ages Umbrella Pine. (Marugame City, Kagawa Pref)

樹藝／植物の成長抑制による植栽の造形美

盆栽：動かないもの、変化しないものの美を味わう目は、人生経験豊かな大人のもの。樹種樹形が多種多様の盆栽。樹齢、四季、愛情の美しさ。（昭和記念公園、日本庭園の盆栽苑、東京都立川市）

Jugei **- Bringing out the beauty of a tree through growth suppression**

Bonsai - While children are impressed by the beauty of a moving goldfish in water, a mature adult is more attracted by stable or slowly changing forms such as *bonsai*. Many different varieties of trees can be used for *bonsai* to convey the beauty of age, the seasons, and care. (Japanese Bonsai Garden in the Showa Memorial Park, Tachikawa City, Tokyo)

The excellence of Japanese arboriculture is demonstrated by the large-scale pruned Satsuki azaleas which emulate big ocean waves, in the garden of Raikyū-ji designed by Enshū Kobori, and the mixed species large-scale pruned hedge of the upper Teahouse Garden of the Shugakuin Detached Palace. The *sasagaki* ("bamboo hedge") of the Katsura Detached Palace is another outstanding example. The 250 meter eastern boundary of Katsura Detached Palace is defined by a bamboo hedge whose living branches have been woven into a dense wall in an A-shape that lies between the palace and Katsura River and acts a flood mitigation barrier. This kind of manipulation of bamboo is made possible only by intimate familiarity with the botanical characteristics of bamboo; namely the vertical alignment of its fibers and its ability to survive bending.

（５）然び（さび） − 時間変化（シークエンス）と
時間美（エイジングの美）を味わう

　樹木の根張りの盛り上がりや一面の苔、石の風化、また
御影石表面の錆び色は十分に永い時間の経過を感じさせる。
その深い味わいは、苔寺（京都、西芳寺）でよく知られる。
　日本庭園の美をいうのに「わび・さび」という言葉があ
る。合理的に説明するなら、これはアジア・モンスーン気候
では高温多湿のゆえに、樹木も庭石も建物も石灯籠や蹲踞も
「時間・歴史の美」がかなりの速さで醸成される。風化し苔
むすまでの長い時間的積み重ねの表出を「然び（さび）」と
いう。ちなみに、「さび」は時間的経過によってモノの本質
が表面に顕われるという時間美の概念とされる。新しく造成
した庭も、五年、十年経つと根張り苔むして、天然自然ソッ
クリになってゆく。これを「庭然び（にわさび）」という。

5. Sabi: Appreciating the Beauty of Time and History

The spreading and heaving roots of trees, moss-covered ground, weathered stones, and oxidizing granite are eloquent reminders of the passage of time. The appeal of such features is evident, for example, in Kokedera (literally "Moss Temple" - also known as Saihō-ji) in Kyoto.

　The terms *wabi* and *sabi* are inevitably brought up in discussions of the beauty of Japanese gardens. As a consequence of the Asian monsoon climate, with its warm temperatures and high humidity, trees, garden stones, buildings, sculptures, lanterns, and stone basins show evidence of time's passing fairly quickly.

　Wabi is the nostalgic beauty of modesty, simplicity and frugality. This humble and non-ostentatious character is highly prized and closely aligned with many values of Japanese culture. This aesthetic aspect sets Japanese garden design apart from other garden styles.

　Sabi is the character acquired over time by weathering and decay. It is an aesthetic concept that values the

下：比叡山延暦寺（滋賀県
／京都府）

Bottom: Enryaku-ji Temple at Mt. Hiei - a mountain northeast of Kyoto.

	Jan.	Feb.	Mar.	Apr.	May.	Jun.	Jul.	Aug.	Sept.	Oct.	Nov.	Dec.
FUKUOKA												
OSAKA												
KYOTO												
TOKYO												
SAPPORO												
NEW YORK												
CHICAGO												
LOS ANGELS												
LONDON												
PARIS												
BERLIN												

E. N.   ▨▨▨▨ moldy season（黴の世界）   ▬▬▬▬ decay season（腐朽世界）

passage of time, where the "essence" of an object is eventually revealed. Over time, a newly created garden becomes rooted in the earth, covered with moss, and indistinguishable from what is there naturally. That is *sabi*.

Wabi sabi was the guiding value for the establishment of the *Wabi-cha* style of tea ceremony founded by Juko Murata and Sen no Rikyū in which the use of simple tea ceremony utensils were favored over the expensive and fancy utensils that were the trend up to that point. This style valued the aesthetic beauty of lack, meagerness and simplicity, which was congruent with the perspective of ideal beauty that was emerging in garden design as well.

As a tree transforms with age, it can be said to represent the beauty of aging. What makes Japanese gardens unique is the way they gradually change; they are initially beautiful for their spatial design but eventually come to possess the more prized beauty of time and history.

The beauty of the passage of time is unique to Japanese gardens and it exists on many different levels: the changes from one moment to the next as the observer proceeds along the stepping stones of a tea garden; the changes that take place over

上表：アジア・モンスーン気候による、腐朽世界風土としての日本（大江新太郎、1934を進士調整）時間的経過によって、高温多湿モンスーン気候による植物生長美（根張）や岩石の風化美（わび・さび）がもたらされる。著者は、日本人が、上の表のような腐朽する環境で暮らしながらも、それを美しさとして受け入れ、共存してきたことと認識している。

While this original survey by Shintaro Ohe in 1934 measured mold and decay due to the monsoon climate, with its high humidity and temperatures, in a negative context, the author realized this was precisely what gave Japanese gardens their unique *wabi sabi* beauty and even explained cultural and societal attributes.

加齢することで木は大木となり、樹形の美も、若木のシンメトリーから老木のバランスに変化する。この時間の変化のもたらす味わいを著者は肯定的に評価し「Agingの美」と呼んでいる。著者は、日本庭園には空間造形の美から、徐々に時間美・歴史美に向かう点で独自性があると考えてもきた。

また、日本庭園固有の「時間美」としては、茶庭の飛石を一歩一歩すすむ分秒単位の変化、茶事茶会、朝日や夕日の時日単位の変化、新緑・深緑・紅葉・落葉や雪月花などの四季の変化、若松から老松に向かう百年単位の変化、数千年に及ぶ風土の重み等々、多段階の「時間の変化と味わい」の意義を強調しておきたい。

時間美／庭然び：自然そっくりになること　時間の美(エイジングの美)

上：老木と苔が歴史を感じさせる、白山平泉寺(はくさんへいせんじ)(福井県勝山市)

下：Agingの美を醸成しやすい那須の芦野石を活用した滝(深谷光軌設計制作の東京九段下、元ホテルグランドパレス)

The progression of time - *Sabi* in the garden is the beauty of aging as the man-made garden becomes identical to nature

Left: Heisen-ji Temple, Hakusan-jinja Shrine (Katsuyama City, Fukui Pref)

Right: The beauty of aging intentionally developed by the use of easily eroded volcanic Ashinoishi (welded tuff stone) for this waterfall at the Hotel Grand Palace (designed by Kouki Fukaya 1926-1997). (Kudanshita area, Tokyo).

the course of a day, from morning to evening; the seasonal changes such as new foliage, dark foliage, autumn foliage, fallen leaves, snow, the moon, and flowers; the changes that a pine tree undergoes over a century; and the appeal of natural features with a millennium of history. The value that Japanese garden design places on "experiencing" these changes throughout a day, over a year, and over the centuries, cannot be emphasized enough.

第五章　日本庭園の構成要素と細部技法

「自然に順_{したが}う」・「自然から学_{まな}ぶ」

世界最古の作庭書『作庭記』（橘俊綱/1028-1094）
The world's oldest text on gardening, the Sakuteiki ("Records on Garden Making") by the aristocrat, Toshitsuna Tachibana (1028-1094)

Chapter 5

Compositional Elements and Detailed Techniques of Japanese Gardens

Fundamentals of Garden Design: Abiding by Nature and Learning from Nature

日本庭園の技術指針は、「自
然に順う・自然から学ぶ」だとい
える。これを本文のように自然主
義の視点から植栽、水、土、石
のデザイン、垣根、橋、建物、そ
して風水、季節感。地球環境
時代の生物多様性へと、およ
そ、現代造園においても必要な
事柄を事例を入れて説明した。
日本庭園を自らのイメージと気
持ちで創作してみようという方々
に参考になるように編集した。

作庭（地割）の根本 ―「自然に順う」と「自然に学ぶ」

　日本の庭園は、6世紀ころ飛鳥時代には存在していたこ
とが、遺跡の発掘調査から明らかだ。ただ誰がどのように
作庭したかは不明である。著者の考えでは、稲作のための
溜池や用水路造成の農業技術が既にあり、農作業に従事し
ていた農民たちが工事に動員されたと思っている。

　平安後期から鎌倉期にかけては「造園のプロ」が存在
し、いわば「職能としての作庭家」が出はじめたようで
ある。世界最古の作庭書『作庭記』は貴族（橘俊綱1028-
1094）によって書かれたものだが、作庭の根本は思想的
に「自然に順う」こと、技術的には「自然に学ぶ」こと
だと記されている。

　8世紀平安京には「寝殿造形式の建築と庭園」が数多
くつくられており、その担い手として、構想（計画）で
は貴族や僧侶が、その施工（土木や植栽、利水や石組工
事）では「山水河原者（せんずいかわらもの）」と呼ばれ
る職人集団があげられる。作庭指南を得意とする僧侶も

The most fundamental
principle of Japanese
garden design is "learn
from nature and obey
nature." From such a
naturalistic perspective,
trees, water, earth, rocks,
fences, bridges, buildings,
feng shui and even the
change of seasons are
mindfully integrated into
design. The understanding
and embracement of such
a philosophy is particularly
relevant in this age of
global environmentalism
and biodiversity
awareness, as well as to
modern garden design.

Fundamentals of Garden Design: Abiding by Nature and Learning from Nature

Excavated remains attest to the existence of Japanese
gardens in the Asuka period (593- 710 AD), but it is not
clear how they were designed or by whom. However, the
author believes that such construction work involved
applying the agricultural technology normally used for
building ponds and irrigation channels for rice
cultivation to garden construction, as well as employing
the workforce who were already skilled in such
earthworks.

　Professional garden designers and builders
appeared between the late Heian period (794-1185) and
the early Kamakura period (1185-1333). The world's oldest
text on gardening, the Sakuteiki ("Records on Garden
Making") was written by aristocrat Tachibana Toshitsuna
(1028-1094). He explains that the fundamentals for
philosophy of Japanese garden design are based on
submission to nature while the fundamentals for the

輩出し、彼らを「石立僧（いしだてそう）」という。

　作庭最大のポイントは、立地・場所の選定であり、その土地の環境や眺望・水利等の好条件を発見し、地形の変化を最大限に景観構成に活用した。もしも市街地内の平坦地で、地形の変化に乏しい敷地に「作庭・築庭」する場合は、人為的に土を掘り、その土を盛り上げて「山」を築き、堀った場所に「水」を引き「池泉」を設ける。そのため作庭を『築山林泉』と呼んだのである。

六本木ヒルズ毛利庭園の植栽デザイン。日本の自然に順う、学ぶ思想を継承している榊原八朗設計の現代作品（東京都港区）

techniques used in garden construction are based on learning from nature.

According to the Sakuteiki, there must first be a clear, overall image or concept for the garden. There is usually a natural landscape that is to serve as a model for the garden which must be contemplated, then the garden layout is composed, taking into account the specific natural attributes of the site, such as its topography and what gives that particular spot its charm, while deciding how these natural attributes can be used in recreating the desired scenery. Respect for nature is the first rule of garden design in Japan.

Numerous *Shinden*-style buildings and gardens were created in Heiankyō (present day Kyoto - the ancient capital of Japan from 794 to 1868). These were designed in a style of domestic architecture developed for palatial or aristocratic mansions. The gardens were conceived and planned by members of the aristocracy and priesthood. Among priests, so called *ishitatesō* (rock placement monks) were also active in the garden design during these periods.

Tree placement design in the Mohri Garden in the Roppongi Hills area. The principle of obeying or listening to nature is applied in this modern design piece by Hachiro Sakakibara. (Minato Ward, Tokyo)

延養亭などの間取図
Vintage map of the plan view of the Enyo-tei House complex

「備前国岡山後楽園真景図」（池田家文庫所蔵）明治16年(1883)

Vintage, bird's eye view, scaled survey map, with pictorial representation of features, of the Okayama Kōrakuen Garden from when it when the area was still known as Bizen Province from 1883 (Ikeda Family Library).

ところで『作庭記』には、その基本はまず「大旨(たいし)を心得るべき」とある。すなわち『全体像・根本』(concept)をしっかりもつこと、地形など敷地の自然条件を踏まえ、場所の風情を描写するモデルとして『生得(しょうとく)の山水(さんすい)』すなわち大自然の風景を踏まえて、いかにもここはこのように作庭すべきであろうとイメージしつつ、滝や流れ、池や島のパターンを細部構成すべきだと述べている。日本の作庭は「自然の尊重」が第一であり、また「縮景」で事例紹介したように、本物の自然風景を深く観察し、これから造形を学習することが第一であったのである。

左頁の岡山後楽園の絵図は、測量が発達した1883年の作であり、地割りの様子が正確にわかる。江戸初期作庭の後楽園は当初、後園や菜園場とも呼ばれていたように、城の後ろにある庭、または菜園という意味合いをもっていた。封建制下の大名家の財政の基盤である稲作(水田)や、茶畑、梅林や竹林など、「農」の風景が基調となっていることがよくわかる。

The illustration on the opposite page shows Okayama Korakuen in the early Edo Period when it was often referred to as a "backyard vegetable garden" because of its inclusion and emphasis on agricultural landscape features. In the feudal era, the daimyō's power and finance was measured largely by agricultural output or assets whether it be rice yields, tea groves or Japanese plum orchards. This pictorially representative, bird's eye view map made in 1883, when survey techniques were becoming well established, gives a very realistic representation of the garden structure and nature. The plan view of the Enyou-tei House complex (upper left) shows the daimyō's *zashiki* tatami sitting room, as well as a Noh theater among other structures. The expanded view of the garden afforded from the *zashiki* sitting room demonstrates advanced design planning and coordination of both the landscape and architectural design.

The actual construction work, such as moving and shoring up earth, planting vegetation, supplying water, and arranging rocks, was performed by groups of craftsmen called *senzui kawaramono* literally meaning "mountain and river people". These were highly skilled laborers, who generally lived by the rivers and belonged to the bottom caste strata of Japanese society. They conducted work considered to be "unclean" to the upper classes.

The most important decision in the design of a Japanese garden is the selection of its location. It must make the most of what gives a particular spot its charm, such as its surrounding environment, views, or access to water, and the utilization and dramatization of changes in its topography. If the garden is to be created on a flat, topographically uniform site, located in an urbanized area, soil must be dug, the displaced soil piled into "mountains," and water channeled to the place where the soil was excavated to create a pond. That is why designing a garden traditionally is referred to as *tsukiyama rinsen* ("mound and pond").

（1）植栽術

①自然風景らしさ・自然樹形の尊重

　日射要求上の陰樹・陽樹、気候帯と関連して常緑・広葉・落葉・針葉のいずれかを基調とし、個々の樹種の生理生態上の特性を踏まえるのが植栽の根本であるが、日本庭園が重視してきたのは「より自然に（ナチュラルに）」という考え方である。

　したがって、日本庭園では「自然樹形」を尊重する。刈込には、丸形や方形もあるが、全体としてそれらを非対称や七五三くずしに組み合わせ、より自然風に見せようと工夫する。

1. Planting Techniques

① Semblance of a Natural Landscape / Respect for Natural Tree Forms

Opposite page top: The magnificence of the Iide mountains leave a deep and profound impression of the beauty of nature. (On the borders of Fukushima, Yamagata, Niigata Pref's)

Opposite page bottom: The beauty of a larch forest at the Minebea Mistumi Inc.'s guest house, designed by Ken Nakajima in the resort town Karuizawa. (Nagano Pref)

The physiological and ecological characteristics of individual species of trees are taken into account in the selection of trees for a garden. For example, a distinction is made between "shade trees" (*inju*) which demand relatively little exposure to sunlight and "sun-loving trees" (*yōju*) which require more sunlight. The climatic zone of the site has a bearing on which tree group - evergreen, broadleaf, deciduous, or conifer - is chosen to be the "keynote" of a garden. Importance is placed in Japanese gardens on making trees appear as natural as possible. Consequently, "natural tree form" is emphasized. Plants are sometimes pruned into rounded or square shapes but they are arranged for the most part, in a naturalistic manner in an asymmetrical configuration or grouping of seven, five or three that is the traditional aesthetic ratio in Japan.

飯豊（いいで）連峰の雄大さと深遠さを感じさせる自然風景（福島県、山形県、新潟県境）

カラマツ林をいかしたミネベアミツミ株式会社の軽井沢ゲストハウス庭園（中島健作品、長野県）

②東西南北を象徴する樹種（風水地理説）

　風水説では、中国由来の「四神相応（しじんそうおう）」という都にふさわしい立地選びの考え方がある。平安京の場合、鴨川・山陰道・巨椋池・北山とそれぞれ東西南北に河川、大道、大池、山が存在した。この考え方を作庭の場合にも適用し、敷地内の東西南北に流水・道・池・築山を配置する。もしそれが無理なときは、樹木を植えればよいとする。東に流水なければ柳９本、西に大道なければ楸（きささげ）７本、南に池なければ桂９本、北に山なければ檜３本、を植えればよいとする。

② Relationship Between Location and Tree Species (*Feng Shui*)

According to *feng shui* geomancy, which originated in China, the topographical arrangement known as *shijin sōō*, or congruence with the four gods of the cardinal directions, was considered ideal for the location and layout of projects. This is of particular importance for the site and layout of a capital city. In accordance with the *shijin sōō* geomancy, Heiankyō

方位にふさわしい樹種を選んで敷地全体としての「自然らしさ」を醸成するためだ。

③生長抑制型植栽術と「庭木の五木」

日本庭園は基本的に「縮景」で、敷地も広くないので常緑樹でなるべく成長しない樹木モッコク、モクセイ、マツ、カシワ、マキを「庭木の五木」と呼んで活用した。常緑（エバーグリーン）は、永続性。不老長寿への願いとも重なる。

もちろん、日本庭園全体に占める本数では常緑樹本位であったが、現代造園では立地や目的に合わせて多様な樹種が活用されている。

(the ancient capital and present day Kyoto), satisfied these requirements in that there is a river to the east (Kamogawa), the main traversing road to the west (San'indō road network), a lake to the south (Oguraike Pond) and a mountainous region to the north (Kitayama Range).

These principles are also applied to layout planning for smaller scale projects like a garden, where these features can be created in a scale-appropriate size. In instances where creating these scaled *shijin sōō* geomantic features is unfeasible, the planting of appropriate species of trees was said to compensate for any shortcomings in these dictates. For example: nine willows to the east in the absence of a river; seven Chinese catalpa to the west in the absence of a major road; nine katsura trees to the south in the absence of a pond; and three Japanese cypress to the north in the absence of a mountain. These dictates were meant to preserve the appearance of naturalness by taking location and orientation into account with the selection of tree species.

③ The Use of Slow-growing Trees - The Five Garden Trees

Japanese gardens are basically worlds in miniature and the sites are of limited size. Evergreen trees that do not grow prolifically are therefore desirable. Japanese cleyera (*mokkoku*), fragrant osmanthus (*mokusei*), pine, Japanese emperor oak (*kashiwa*) and Chinese podocarpus (*maki*) are considered the Five Garden Trees. These trees are deeply respected as they represent eternal youth, all being evergreens.

Opposite page: In f*eng shui*, certain trees have particular importance in bringing balance and a sense of naturalness to a landscape and can be used in substitute for geographic features thought necessary for proper balance. One of these is pictured here, the Chinese catalpa (Catalpa ovata) with its fruit gracefully hanging. (Kameoka City, Kyoto Pref - Omotohanameisan Botanical Gardens, Tanba Kameyama Castle Ruins originally built by famous samurai-would-be-*daimyō*, Mitsuhide Akechi)

73

生け花の構成：天地人が基本形

Ikebana flower arrangements are guided by the *ten-chi-jin* (lit. heaven, earth, human) principle which identifies primary roles of each component in its basic form. This is more specifically described as *shin-ryu-uke* or center, flowing and receiving elements.

④平面立面ともに不等辺三角形で配植

　日本庭園では、同一樹種、同一樹高を直線的に列植することを避ける。自然界には樹種統一や直線はないからである。そこで平面図的にも立面図的にも「不等辺三角形」を基本とする自然風植栽法「真（しん）・副（そえ）・対（たい）・控（ひかえ）・前置（まえおき）・見越（みこし）」の植栽形式を生み出した。

　マツやマキの高木を植栽ユニットを中心木とし、「真」とする。「真」の木の枝振りが片側に偏していたり、欠けている場合、これを補うように別のマツなどを「副（そ）え」る。「真」と「副」を引き立てコントラスト効果を演出するのが「対」。マツの緑に対してカエデの紅葉が「対」、「真・副・対」のユニットの前景を引きしめ根締め役を果たすのが「前置」のツツジ、「控」はキャラボク。

④ Arranging Scalene Triangles in Plan View and Elevation View to Achieve an Appearance of Naturalness

Japanese gardens avoid planting trees of the same species or trees of the same height in a straight alignment as there are no straight lines in the natural world. It has therefore been a basic precept of planting design in Japanese gardens to employ scalene triangles in plan view or elevation view. In garden planting, trees are generally designated by their forms and locations as *shin* (main), *soe* (supporting), *tai* (contrast), *hikae* (fill-in), *maeoki* (foreground), or *mikoshi* (background).

If a tall pine or Chinese podocarpus is the central tree of a planting unit, it is referred to as the *shin* (main) tree. If the branches of the *shin* tree are biased or are missing on one side or the other, a slightly smaller tree of the same variety is used to

奥行き感を出す明るいサクラが「見越」となる。

　なお、華道では、生け花を構成する3本の役枝を「真・副・体」や「天・地・人」という（**左頁写真**）。「真」は中心となる直立した枝を指し、「副」がそれを助け、「体」は下部に置かれ、「真」「副」の上に向かう力との均衡を図る。3本の役枝が平面、立面ともに不等辺三角形を描くようにすると落ち着く。役枝の関係性は造園においても同様である。

compensate for or to supplement it, and this is referred to as the *soe* (supporting) tree. The *tai* (contrast) tree provides contrast to the combination of the *shin* and the *soe* (supporting); for example, the autumn foliage of a maple contrasts with the green of the pine.

　Azalea can serve as the *maeoki* (foreground) tree and dwarf Japanese yew as the *hikae* (fill-in) tree, enhancing the foreground of the *shin/soe/tai* unit, grounding it in the composition. A cherry tree can serve as the *mikoshi* (background) tree, setting off the dark green of the pine of the *shin* (main) by its lightness and endowing the unit as a whole with a sense of depth.

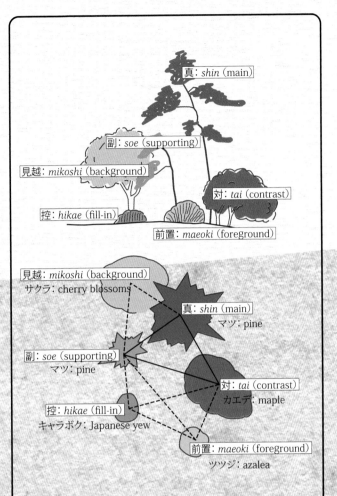

真: *shin* (main)

副: *soe* (supporting)

見越: *mikoshi* (background)

対: *tai* (contrast)

控: *hikae* (fill-in)

前置: *maeoki* (foreground)

見越: *mikoshi* (background)
サクラ: cherry blossoms

真: *shin* (main)
マツ: pine

副: *soe* (supporting)
マツ: pine

対: *tai* (contrast)
カエデ: maple

控: *hikae* (fill-in)
キャラボク: Japanese yew

前置: *maeoki* (foreground)
ツツジ: azalea

日本の樹藝の極意は、天地人・真副対で自然風景を構成すること。　1グループの不等辺三角形のユニットを広い土地に繰り返しで配植すれば、大面積にも自然風景にできる。

　The secret to the beauty of Japanese arboriculture is the application of *ten-chi-jin* or *shin-soe-tai* (main, supporting and contrast actors) which guides the creator on how to achieve a natural-looking and balanced design.
　Even when landscaping very large areas, the landscape can be made to look natural by using these same scalene triangle groupings treated as a single unit in larger scalene groupings. It is said that to make a landscape look natural, groupings need to be random as opposed to orderly.

75

⑤効果的景観構成のための「役木」

　日本庭園では、スポット的な scene 構成上 key 的効果のための定形技法がある。植栽技法では「役木（やくぼく）」、石の使い方では「役石（やくいし）」である。たとえば次の場面にふさわしい景観効果のための樹木（＝役木）がある。

・橋本（はしもと）の木
橋と陸をつなぐ役目を担っており、橋挟み石近くの橋際に植えられるもので、シダレヤナギなどが似合う。

・垣留（かきどめ）の木
垣根の最後のところにアクセントとして植えられる。

・飛泉障（ひせんざわり）の木
滝の前方に枝がかかるように植えて、流れ落ちる瀑布を

飛泉障の木の例（京都市、梅小路公園朱雀の庭、井上剛宏作庭）

A *hisenzawari-no-ki* (waterfall-screen tree) is planted so that its branches partially obscure the cascading water and sway from the effect of the spray and movement of the air. (Suzaku-no-niwa, Umeko-ji-kouen, Kyoto City - designed by Takahiro Inoue)

⑤ Use of Yaku-boku (Role Trees) for Effective Scenic Composition

Trees and stones play specific roles in certain formulas of scenic composition of Japanese gardens. In the case of trees, they are referred to as *yaku-boku* or role trees, and in the case of stones or stone groupings, they are called *yaku-ishi* or role stones. Some examples of *yaku-boku* trees planted to serve certain scenic functions or creating a certain mood, include:

- ***Hashimoto-no-ki* (bridge-end tree)** serves to connect a bridge to land. A tree such as a weeping willow is planted at one end of a bridge, near a *hashibasami-ishi* or "bridge-flanking rock".

一部隠してチラチラと見せるためと、瀑布のしぶきと風を受けて枝が揺れる動きを演出する。（前頁下写真）

・灯障（ひざわり）の木

灯籠の火袋の前に植えて、灯影をぼんやりさせ奥行き感を演出する。ダイレクトな照明を避ける工夫である。

・門冠り（もんかぶり）の松（中国の迎客松の意か。本頁下左写真）

日本の民家の門の脇きににマツやマキを添え、歓迎来福と風格を感じさせる。枝張りが「ようこそ」と手招きしてウエルカムを表現する。

・中国では送客松といって手を振って「さようなら」もある。

- *Kakidome-no-ki* **(hedge-stop tree)** is planted at the end of a hedge as a visual terminus.

- *Hisenzawari-no-ki* **(waterfall-screen tree)** is planted so that its branches partially obscure the cascading water and sway from the effect of the spray and movement of the air.

- *Hizawari-no-ki* **(light-screen tree)** is planted in front of the firebox of a stone lantern to obscure the light and suggest a sense of depth; the aim is to produce indirect lighting.

- *Mon-kaburi-no-matsu* **(gate-crown)** is a pine or Chinese podocarpus (*maki*) planted on either side of the gate of a residence to lend it dignity, welcoming guests and inviting good fortune. In China, this is known as a welcoming pine (*geikyaku-sho*) with branches spread to suggest welcoming arms while a seeing-off pine (*soukyaku-sho*), is a pine with branches that suggests an arm raised in farewell.

樹姿からのイメージを造園にする。迎客松(**左**)と送客松(**右**)(中国)

The shapes of trees can be used to convey imagery or play a part in a narrative. A welcoming pine (**left**) and a seeing-off pine (**right**). (China)

上：大徳寺孤篷庵（こほうあん）布泉（ふせん）の手水鉢（京都市）**下**：うちぬき井戸（愛媛県西条市）

Top: A *fusen* (ancient coin) shaped *chozubachi* purification basin, where one washes their hands and face. (Koho-an Hermitage, Daitoku-ji Temple, Kyoto, Kyoto Pref)
Bottom: One of the Uchinuki artesian wells in Saijyo City in Ehime Prefecture, which are rated as one of the 100 famous water sources of Japan, known for their purity.

（2）水工法（すいこうほう）水景 4 態・水系のデザイン

　E. Zubeはあらゆる景観資源のなかで、「水」は最高のものだと言う。どんな場面でも「水」が加わると、景観評価がより高くなる。だから古今東西、水のない庭園はない。

　庭園の水デザインでは、落水（滝）、流水（流れ）、湛水（池）、湧水（噴水）の4態があり適宜活用する。日本庭園では、「滝」から「流れ」そして「池」へと重力に順い、山から海へ水系ともいえる連続する風景づくりをめざすのが基本である。

　滝の後には山、流れに沿って園路、池には島と橋が架けられる。滝石はふつう三尊石組様に組む。中心にひときわ大きく安定感のある立石が組まれ、「不動石」と

2. Water Techniques: Four Modes of Waterscaping and the Design of Water Ecosystems

Ervin H. Zube, a renowned American landscape architect in the field of environment-behavior research, stated that water is the ultimate scenic resource and the addition of water enhances every landscape. Water has been an integral part of gardens in all ages of history and in every corner of the world.

　　There are four basic forms of water design - falling water (waterfall), flowing water (stream), brimming water (pond), and welling water (fountain) - and the use of water in a garden is a matter of integrating those forms. The waterscape of a Japanese garden mimics nature where water flows due to gravity, from its source high in the mountains in a continuum from waterfall to stream and then to a lake and eventually making its way to the ocean. All scenic components are organically connected by the water course. The general pattern of Japanese garden landscape starts with a mountain behind a waterfall with the garden path following the water course to the pond where there are islands and connecting bridges.

　　The stones at the head of a waterfall are typically arranged in the shape of a triad of Buddhist images. The

もいう。不動明王が滝の形で現世に姿を見せたものとされる。

　滝水を受けるのは「滝壺」で、壺の底には「水受石」（波受石ともいう）が置かれ、壺から流れ出た水は「水分石」で左右に分けられ「流れ」に入る。

　流れのはじめは寝殿造庭園の「遣水（やりみず）」である。自然主義で浅くさらさら流れる。流れの魅力は、蛇行の具合、護岸材料、瀬と淵のつくり方など。自然の清らかな流水の有無が最も重要である。

　池や島は「にわ」と同義であった。神社にも池が多い。仏教以後「曲水の池」（日本最古の平城京宮跡庭園）、阿弥陀堂前の「阿字池」、禅僧の感性から名づけ

東京都豊島区東池袋中央公園、荒木芳邦設計の落水（滝）作品

Falling water feature
designed by Yoshikuni Araki
(East Ikebukuro Central Park,
Toshima Ward, Tokyo)

large upright rock in the center of this grouping suggests stability. It is called the *fudō-ishi* which references Fudō Myōō, one of the Five Kings of Wisdom in Buddhism and makes the viewer feel his austere presence. The water falls into the plunge pool, at the bottom of which a *mizuuke-ishi* "water receiving rock" is laid flat. It is also referred to as *namiuke-ishi* or "wave receiving rock." The water flowing out of the pool is split by the *mizuwake-ishi* "water dividing rock" and enters the stream.

　The best-known type of stream in Japanese gardens is the *yarimizu*, a gentle brook devised for the *shinden* style garden in the Heian period. The murmuring streamlet, wide and shallow, is naturalistic. There are many ways to make this simple stream attractive whether by constructing a meandering course, by the selection of the materials of its banks or by how the succession of rapids and pools are laid out, but the availability of pure, natural, flowing water is the most important factor.

　Ponds and islands were once synonymous with a garden. There are many ponds in Shinto shrines and Buddhist temples accordingly. Since the introduction of Buddhism into Japan, ponds of many shapes have been created including: an S-shaped pond, traces of which have been found in the remains of Heijōkyō Palace (today's Nara); the *aji-ike* pond created in front of Amida Buddha halls shaped like the Sanskrit character for the

られた「心字池」、その他「九字池」「半月池」などいろいろな形がつくられた。

　島にもいろいろあり、『作庭記』には、山島、野島、杜島、磯島、雲形、霞形、片流、干潟、松皮様があげられ、日本人の自然学習性の証明になっている。その後は象徴的な三神仙島（蓬莱－ほうらい島・方丈－ほうじょう島・瀛州－えいしゅう島）、さらに大衆化して鶴島・亀島となるが、根底には人々の不老長寿を願う祈りがある。日本庭園で水工法の見られない庭園はない。

"a" in Amida; the *shinji-ike* pond shaped like the kanji ideogram for heart (心 - *shin*), an expression of Zen sensibility; as well as the *kuji-ike* pond shaped like the kanji ideogram for the number nine (九 - *ku*) considered the ultimate number, and the *hantsuki-ike* (half-moon pond). These shapes were not necessarily the basis for the design, but rather describe the organic shapes created by the designers who were endeavoring to make the ponds look as natural as possible.

The islands in the ponds also take diverse forms and carry meaning. Ten types of island designs are mentioned in the Sakuteiki (Records of Garden Making): *yama-jima* (mountain island), *no-jima* (field island), *mori-jima* (sacred forest island), *iso-jima* (beach island), *kumo-gata* (cloud-shaped island), *kasumi-gata* (fog island), *suhama-gata* (sandy beach island), *katanagare* (narrow flow island), *higata* (beach at ebbing tide), and *matsukawa* (pine bark-like beach).

In time, these ten island patterns evolved into three basic patterns named after three Chinese Taoist immortals: Hōrai, Hōjō and Eishyuu. These then simplified into two basic archetypical island patterns *tsuru-shima* (crane island) and *kame-shima* (turtle island), which are animals that were considered messengers of the gods and therefore had implications of immortality and thus associated gardens with the realm of the gods. Though the archetypal shapes changed through the ages, they all were intended to imply prayers for longevity.

A：対龍山荘（たいりゅうさんそう）の湧井の池泉（京都市）　B：真々庵（しんしんあん）の流れ（京都市）　C：蛇篭護岸と野川、対龍山荘（たいりゅうさんそう）　D：慶澤園（けいたくえん）（大阪市）　E：短冊形の石垣積で滝を表す。右上に吐水口。江戸時代の城の石垣で滝を見せる、めずらしい手法である（金沢城玉泉院丸庭園内、金沢市）

A: Artesian well, stone basin in the Tairyu-Sanso Garden. (Kyoto City, Kyoto Pref)　B: Flowing stream in the Shinshin-an Hermitage Garden. (Kyoto City, Kyoto Pref - Panasonic founder, Konosuke Matsushita's villa)　C: Woven bamboo with stones placed inside to form a decorative revetment to prevent stream bank erosion. The design emulates the appearance of snake skin. (Tairyu-Sano Garden, Kyoto City, Kyoto Pref)　D: Keitaku-en Garden (Osaka City, Osaka Pref)　E: In the Gyokusen'inmaru Garden within the Kanazawa Castle, this castle wall is a rare instance where a functional wall was built decoratively, in this case using distinctive, tall vertical stones in a pattern, which also featured a waterfall. The outlet spout for the waterfall can be seen in the top right of the wall. (Kanazawa City, Ishikawa Pref)

（3）土の造形　築山（つきやま）と地（ち）の構成

　園内に築かれた人工の山は、古代では「仮山（かざん）」と呼ばれた。「築山林泉」は、作庭、造庭、造園と同義に使われた。日本庭園では、「築山」のみならずそれより低い「地瘤（ぢこぶ）」、低い丘を重ねたような「野筋」など土の造形デザインボキャブラリーがある。

　縮景基調の日本庭園が、平坦な敷地を広く深く見せようとすれば、池を掘り、山を築き、谷をつくり、岬を出すのは当然。作庭の基礎は「土」を動かし「地形（ぢぎょう）」をつくること。「盛土」「切土」、そして「むくり」と「てり」を組合せる。草花や植栽、亭榭（ていしゃ）や灯籠など細々と配置されるが、庭園全体の、いわばランドスケープのボディを決定づけるのは、築山・地瘤・地形（ぢぎょう）づくり（＝土のデザイン）にほかならない。

無機的な建築線を、土のやわらかい築山デザインがやわらげる（日本科学未来館、東京都江東区）

The austere, straight lines of the architecture are softened by rounded, earthen mounds. (The National Museum of Emerging Science and Innovation, Koto Ward, Tokyo)

3. Earthen Forms: Composition of Mounds and the Creation of Landmarks

In the ancient period, artificial hills built in a garden were called *kazan* (temporary mounds). The expression *tsukiyama rinsen* which literally translates as "mounds, groves, streams and ponds," once meant garden design. Various earthen forms such as *tsukiyama* (man-made "mountainous" mound), the slightly lower *jikobu*, (earth "lump" mound) and the *nosuji* ("field" mound) are all components of the design vocabulary.

Japanese gardens are based on the idea of reduced-scale scenery where mountains and rivers are represented and small sites are made to appear larger and deeper than they actually are; ponds are dug, mountains and ravines created, and headlands extended. Simply put, the foundation of garden design is the movement of earth and the creation of topography. Earth is dug and mounded, and

池泉空間の骨格は盛土と切土でつくられる。敷地内で等量の土を移動し、景観に変化を与える。土に張芝すれば明るくなるし、苔ならしっとり静寂にできる。

　回遊式庭園は、敷地が変化のない平坦地につくられ、しかも数十ヘクタールにおよぶ大面積を造園することから、高めの築山を設けて園景のランドマークとし、その上を展望台にした。

　今後は現代都市のグレーと剛の建物を引き立て気分を柔げるためにも、土の造形や風にそよぐ萩などの植栽、さらさら流れる遣水は大きな効果を発揮するだろう。

中国の廬山(ろざん)をオカメザサで覆った築山で象徴(小石川後楽園、東京都文京区)
This mound planted with ruscus-leaf bamboo, emulates the famous Mount Lushan in Jiujiang, China. (Koishikawa Kōraku-en Park, Bunkyo Ward, Tokyo)

its surface is designed to follow a slightly convex or concave curve. In a garden, flowers are planted, gazebos, lanterns, stairs, and steppingstones are carefully arranged, but it is the creation of topography (the design of earthen forms such as *tsukiyama, jikobu, nosuji* and ponds) that determines the overall body of a garden. The spatial framework is created by this excavation and mounding to create scenic diversity. The earthworks when covered by lawn become cheerful and bright; when covered by moss, it conveys a peaceful, quiet atmosphere.

　　As *kaiyū*-style (pond-strolling) gardens of the Edo period were flat and without variety and often covering tens of hectares in area, mounds were created to serve as landmarks in the landscape and teahouses were built on top where they afforded panoramic views of the entire garden. Hard-edged buildings were set off by the soft earthen forms, Japanese bush clover swaying in the breeze, and the murmuring water of the *yarimizu* stream.

瀬戸内海のマサ土、マサ砂を盛り上げた島づくり(岡山後楽園、岡山県)
Islands made using decomposed granite soil emulate the typical scenery found in the Seto Inland Sea of Japan found between Honshu, Kyushu and Shikoku. (Okayama Kōrakuen Garden, Okayama City, Okayama Pref)

地瘤風に盛土し、野筋の景を創る（井上剛宏作庭、梅小路公園朱雀の庭、京都市）
Small earthen mounds with a path between evoking the image of a mountain path. (Suzaku-no-niwa, Umekoji-kouen, Kyoto City, Kyoto Pref - Designed by Takahiro Inoue) *

上：中庭の陶製灯籠、平櫛田中(ひらぐしでんちゅう)彫刻美術館（東京都小平市）

中：子孫繁栄を祈念する陰陽石（男性、女性を象徴する石組、岡山後楽園）

下：韓国、昌徳宮の不老門（ソウル市）

Top: Fired clay *tōrō* lantern in the inner court of Kodaira Hirakushi Denchu Art Museum. (Kodaira City, Tokyo)

Middle: A *ying* and *yang* stone arrangement intended as a prayer for the prosperity of descendants. The rock arrangement symbolizes the male and female forms. (Okayama Kōrakuen Garden, Okayama City, Okayama Pref)

Bottom: The Eternal Youth Gate in Changdeokgung Palace. (Seoul, South Korea)

（4）石組・石造物　不動性・永遠性のシンボル

　西洋庭園と日本庭園の違いはひと目でわかる。それは「石組（いしぐみ）」の有無による。日本庭園は、自然のままの石を活用するのが特徴。彫刻や加工石の西洋とは全く異なる。日本人は自然石に霊性を感じるアニミズムをもつ。自然の巨石は、つい見上げて拝んでしまう。大きな石に注連縄（しめなわ）をめぐらした「天津磐座（あまついわくら）」には神が宿ると考え、後、神社が祀られたことも少なくない。

　自然石に神仏が宿ると思える感性をもつ日本人の精神文化の下でこそ、「石組」が発達したのである。3つの石を立てて「三尊石」という。高い真ん中の石が阿弥陀如来、右の石が観音菩薩、左が勢至菩薩である。三尊

4. Rock Grouping: Design of Permanence and Solidity

The difference between Western gardens and Japanese gardens is immediately obvious in the absence of rock groupings (*ishigumi*) in the former and its presence in the latter. Japanese gardens are characterized and distinguished by the use of rocks in their natural state and are very different from Western gardens that make abundant use of stone sculptures and rocks that have been cut and worked on.

The Japanese with ancient animistic beliefs ascribed sacredness to certain and often huge natural rocks. They could not help but look up at and worship such objects. There are many examples of "heavenly rock seats" or *iwakura* rocks with distinct shapes, which are marked off by *shimenawa* rope. It was precisely because the Japanese sensed divine presence in these impressive natural rocks, the art of rock groupings was born. Three usually upright rocks are juxtaposed and referred to as *sanzon-seki* symbolizing the three bodhisattvas. The tallest rock in the middle is the Amida Nyorai (Amitābha), the rock to the right is Kannon Bosatsu (Avalokiteśvara), and the one to the left is Seishi Bosatsu (Mahāsthāmaprāpta). There are gardens where three

石を3組並べて「九品曼荼羅（くぼんまんだら）」を
あらわす庭園もある。

　力強い石組は、いかにも大地からの露頭のよう
に見せなければならない。そのためには、昔から
石の三分の二以上は地中に埋めるべきだといわれ
てきた。大地性、永遠性を象徴し、不動、不変を
体現する石組には安定感が最も重要だからであ
る。

　緑や水の「柔」との対比において、「剛」の石
の存在感は極めて大きい。その点で石の利用は石
組のみならず、実用的な飛石、延段、石橋、敷砂
利、さらには修景的な石灯籠、蹲踞。そして信仰
的な陰陽石、不老門など、いずれも庭にとって大
切な添景であり景観上のフォーカス・ポイントで
ある。

sets of *sanzon-seki* are arranged to represent the
nine ranks into which believers of Amida were
divided on arrival in Paradise.

　　A stone grouping symbolizing a mountain is
suggested by rocks embedded in the soil. From long
ago, it has been common practice for at least two-
thirds of a rock in a Japanese garden to be buried in
the ground which gives the rock an appearance of
permanence and stability. The aesthetic hardness of
rock offers superb contrast to the soft aesthetic of
trees and water.

近代日本の哲学者、井上円了（1858-1919）の計画した哲学堂公園77場の一つ、たぬき灯籠（東京都中野区）

The devious Japanese *tanuki* racoon dog-shaped lantern is one of the 77 sites in Tetsugaku-dō Park, designed by modern Japanese philosopher Enryō Inoue (1858-1919). (Nakano Ward, Tokyo）

（5）庭灯籠（にわどうろう）プロポーションの美と場所性

　庭園の景観構成は、ひとつの視野をひとつの風景としてまとめること。「絵になる風景」をつくること。「創景」「造景」だ。ひとつの scene は、ひとつのモデル、ひとつのテーマで表現される。

　灯籠には２種類ある。ひとつは「献灯」。東大寺大仏殿の真正面に大きな金灯籠（かなどうろう）がある。平等院鳳凰堂の真正面の石灯籠も同様で古代の献灯は真ん中に一基据えたもの。もうひとつ古い形として、春日型がある。奈良の春日大社に列状に奉納された。後世には、左右一対を献灯したり、左右に対列したりするようになる。はじめはこうした神仏への献灯に供された灯籠が、茶道の物を大切にする心から茶庭の照明や点景として再利用されるようになった。

5. Use of Stone Lanterns: Proportional Beauty and Character of Place

Japanese gardens are often composed in such a way that each view forms a scene. The intention is to create picture-perfect landscapes. A scene is typically composed so that it suggestively mimics the famous landscape on which it is modeled or expresses a particular theme.

There are two types of uses of lanterns. The first is the use as a votive or prayer lantern. There is a large metal votive lantern directly in front of the Great Buddha Hall of the Tōdai-ji Temple in Nara that is a good example of this type. The light given off by this lantern is offered, as flowers are, in prayer to the Buddha. The stone lantern placed directly in front of the Amida Hall of the Hōō-dō (the Phoenix Pavilion) of the Byōd-ōin Temple in Kyoto is another example of a votive lantern. These lanterns are placed in front and center of the hall or temple.

Another style of votive lanterns are the Kasuga-type named such after the many lanterns arranged in a row along the covered walkway of Kasuga Shrine in Nara. In shrines and temples of later periods, other arrangements of this style of lantern came to be used wherein lanterns were arranged in pairs, one to the right and the other to the left, or where lanterns were arranged in rows on either side of a walkway.

それが近世に入ると、桂離宮で典型的だが、庭園の縮景構成上の演出装置、オーナメントとして、庭灯籠がオリジナルにデザインされるようになる。

照明施設であった灯籠が、日本庭園で不可欠の景観要素になったのはなぜか。その理由の第一は、石灯籠や層塔（そうとう）など各部の形態とプロポーションが、黄金分割・無理数の比で構成される石造美術品として評価されるほどに美しいデザインであったこと、第二は、桂離宮の岬や船着場の灯台、水蛍、また三角、六角の雪見灯籠をはじめ、他の庭園の渓流に咲く花の蘭（らん）を象徴する蘭渓灯籠のように庭園のあるシーンの場所性を表現するため等、多様な工夫がなされたからである。

石灯籠、宗像大社の迎賓館（福岡県宗像市）
Stone lantern at the guest house in the Munakata Taisha Shrine. (Munakata City, Fukuoka Pref)

既存の笏谷石の大型置灯籠を生かして、桂離宮の岬灯籠の写しをアクセントにした、笈田邸
（20代の進士五十八設計施工、福井市若杉町）
Working around the focal point of the existing volcanic tuff stone lantern, this garden design emulates the cape and lantern in the famous Katsura Rikyu garden to accentuate the existing lantern in the Oida residence private garden. (Designed by the author Isoya Shinji while still in his twenties, early in his career. Wakasugi Town, Fukui Pref)

87

Stone and metal lanterns were of great value and were often salvaged from old temples, shrines and gardens, especially those from famous sites. These votive lanterns were repurposed in gardens as focal points of scenic compositions and provided night-time lighting.

The second type of lantern usage was the ornamental use in gardens. These lanterns were specifically made for this purpose as opposed to being repurposed. In the feudal period, as can be seen in Katsura Detached Palace in Kyoto, such ornamental lanterns were designed at an appropriate scale to be able to be used in compositions of reduced scenery or as forms of artistic design expression appropriate to particular places.

Why did stone lanterns (*tōrō*) which had simply been lighting apparatuses become indispensable scenic elements of Japanese gardens? First, stone lanterns were beautifully designed and highly appreciated as objects of art, with overall forms and proportions often based on the golden ratio. Second, they were often carefully designed to express the character of a place. For example, the *rankei tōrō* suggests an orchid blooming by a mountain stream, while a *tōrō* at the tip of a rock or earthen projection into a pond emulates a lighthouse on the tip of a peninsula in the ocean.

大河内山荘／名俳優大河内
伝次郎の石造美術品コレクショ
ンを配置した現代の日本庭園
（京都市）

A collection of stone art pieces are displayed throughout the garden of the Ōkōchi Sansō, Mountain Villa which is the former home and garden of the Japanese *jidaigeki* (period film) actor Denjirō Ōkōchi. (Kyoto City, Kyoto Pref)

A *yukimi-dōrō* (snow-viewing lantern) is placed close to the water and due to its large brim or *kasa*-type roof, beautifully catches snow on this roof brim while at the same time casts light downwards onto the water, much like lighting along a harbor would show the water level indicating safe landing for boats.

上：兼六園の徽軫(ことじ)灯籠（石川県金沢市）

Top right: The Kotoji stone lantern in Kenroku-en Garden. This beautiful two-legged lantern is a very rare and famous design which emulates the movable bridge in the Japanese *koto* harp. (Kanazawa City, Ishikawa Pref)

雪見灯籠（東京都、浅草、浅草寺本坊の伝法院、小堀遠州作の庭園）
The *yukimi* "Snow Viewing" stone lantern in the Dembō-in Temple garden (head temple of Sensou-ji Temple) designed by the famous landscape architect, Enshū Kobori. (Asakusa, Tokyo)

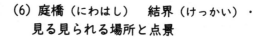

（6）庭橋（にわはし）　結界（けっかい）・
　　見る見られる場所と点景

　庭園には、形態別に平橋・反橋、材料別に木橋・石橋
・土橋などがあって、庭のシーンにふさわしい橋が活用
されている。庭園の橋は、"渡る"機能だけでなく、
"眺める"場所、眺められる景観要素として、また家橋
で"楽しむ"とか、"休憩する"ところとしても造られ
た。寝殿造や浄土庭園の島には、木造朱塗りの平橋と反
橋がかかり、擬宝珠つきの欄干で飾られ、歩面は板張り
であった。江戸の大名の回遊形式では、回遊路に変化を
与え、園内各所の場所性を演出すべく、材料もいろい
ろ、大小さまざまな橋が組合わされた。

6. Garden Bridges: A Connection Between Two Realms As Well As a Scenic Element and Viewpoint for Scenic Elements

There are diverse types of bridges found in Japanese gardens; level, arched, wooden, stone, earthen; depending on the desired effect. Garden bridges are not simply structures to be crossed over but places from which to view the garden as well as elements of scenic composition to be looked at. They are also built as places for entertainment and rest. In a *shinden*-style garden of the Heian period, islands were accessed by straight and arched wooden bridges, painted vermilion and equipped with parapets ornamented with onion-shaped finials called *giboshi*. Their floors were made of wood planks. In the *kaiyū*-style gardens of the Edo period, bridges of diverse materials and different sizes were combined to give variety to the strolling path and to produce distinct character of place.

上：桂離宮　園林堂前の土橋
（京都府）
中：自然石の橋(京都御所)

Top: The earthen bridge in front of the Onrindo Family Memorial Hall in the Katsura Rikyū Detached Palace Garden

Middle: Natural stone slab bridge at the Kyoto-Gosho Imperial Palace (Kyoto Pref)

下左：琉球庭園の円月橋、識名園（沖縄県那覇市）　**下右**：山田真山（しんざん）画伯の識名園の西湖橋

Left: Moon bridge in the Okinawa-style Shikina-en Royal Garden. (Naha City, Okinawa Pref)
Right: Painting of the famous moon bridge in West Lake in China. (Artist - Shinzan Yamada from Okinawa)

特に杭州の西湖堤を縮景した大名庭園では、中国スタイルの石造アーチ橋を再現し、橋名まで西湖と同じ跨虹橋と名づけた広島「縮景園」の例もある。

反橋、太鼓橋は、象徴的で目立ち、庭園の主景となる。屋根のある「家橋」は、親水性や展望性に富み滞留場所として有効で庭園の主景となる。

庭橋には、木橋、石橋が多いが、野の風景を演出するには土橋が効果的であり、桂離宮の土橋は背が高く、下を舟が通れるよう水運にも配慮されていた。

縮景庭園での架橋には自然石をそのまま倒せばよい。荷重に耐えるか構造計算をする必要もない。ただ見かけ上の安定感と景観効果のために左右に橋挟石（はしばさみいし）を2ないし4石配置すればよい。「橋本の木」を添えて立体的に修景することもある。

Arched stone bridges were the bridges with the most recognizable symbolic character and most often emulated after famous Chinese arched bridges. A well-known example of such imported but reduced scenery is the Kokō-kyō Bridge in Shukkei-en Garden in Hiroshima. The garden is not only modeled after the scenery of the causeways of West Lake in Hangzhou, China but the bridge also shares the name of the original bridge in China that it emulates. Whereas an arched bridge has a conspicuous, symbolic form and is a feature to be looked at, a roofed bridge spanning a pond or a stream is a place to linger and view the garden from a unique viewing point that enables one to better sense the presence of the water.

While most bridges are made of either stone or wood, bridges made of clay are also found in gardens and effective in suggesting a field or meadow. The earthen bridge in front of the *shoin* in Katsura Detached Palace is built high enough to allow boats to pass under it.

As the streams and ponds in reduced scenery gardens are of a smaller scale, accordingly, so are the bridges. While full-scale bridges need engineering, a reduced scale bridge which is intended for a limited number of people on foot, a slab of natural stone, tipped over a stream, or a large plank, is sufficient. One or two so-called "bridge-flanking stones" (*hashibasami ishi*) on either side of the end of a bridge anchor its visual appearance.

上：広島空港前の三景園の反橋（広島県、伊藤邦衛設計施工作品）
下：薨(いらか)の道のコンクリートの橋は、楽しい印象を与える（世田谷区用賀、象設計集団作品）

Top: Arched bridge in Sankei-en Garden, in front of the Hiroshima airport designed and constructed by Kunie Ito. (Hiroshima Pref)
Below: A cheerfully patterned concrete bridge on the Iraka road in Yōga, Setagaya Ward, Tokyo (Designed by AtelierZo Design)

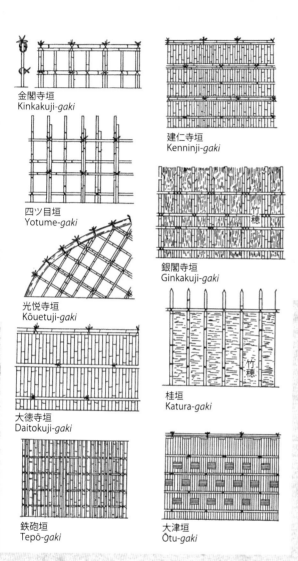

金閣寺垣
Kinkakuji-*gaki*

建仁寺垣
Kenninji-*gaki*

四ツ目垣
Yotume-*gaki*

竹穂

銀閣寺垣
Ginkakuji-*gaki*

光悦寺垣
Kōuetuji-*gaki*

竹穂

桂垣
Katura-*gaki*

大徳寺垣
Daitokuji-*gaki*

鉄砲垣
Tepō-*gaki*

大津垣
Ōtu-*gaki*

竹垣のいろいろ
日本の垣根は多様な竹垣の種類で、場所性を極立たせているが、茶庭の発達と共により洗練された。すぐれた参考書に、北尾春道著『露地・茶庭』（彰国社1956）がある。

（7）垣根術 美しい季節変化の生垣と日本独特の竹垣文化

　空間を囲んで保護し敷地を区画するのが、垣根（かきね）。庭園をミクロコスモス（小宇宙）として独立世界を構成するには、遮蔽、囲繞目的で、築地塀や境栽、常緑高木の高生垣が有効である。こうした機能はもちろん、さらに新芽や花が生垣に季節感を与えたり、庭園に個性を与えようと職人が工夫した多彩な竹垣が、庭園に固有の魅力を与える。

　生垣は外からの視線を遮蔽するが、竹垣には透視できて内外を区切りながらつなぐ四ツ目垣、また完全目隠しの

7. Fence Techniques: Enclosing and Dividing Space

The fence on the periphery of a garden encloses the space and demarcates and protects the site; it also turns the garden into a microcosm. Trees planted along the border, an earthen perimeter wall, a high hedge of tall evergreens or a bamboo fence is used as a screen to create an enclosure. These fences or hedges are more than just barriers though. The craftsmanship apparent in the fence construction and changes in the colors and seasons of skillfully pruned hedges are in and of themselves a garden feature and part of the unique beauty of Japanese gardens. While hedges provide complete and generally opaque barriers, bamboo fences, such as the *yotsume-gaki* (lattice-style) allow for only partial screening with glimpses of the scenery beyond it, used as devices to articulate and separate space.

There is a wide array of fences used in Japanese garden design; the most diversity of any of the world's landscape styles. Many of the famous temples of Kyoto have

建仁寺垣もある。

　日本庭園の垣根ボキャブラリーは豊富で、庭垣、竹垣、生垣のバリエーションは世界一だ。京都の有名な寺院では、建仁寺垣はじめ金閣寺垣、銀閣寺垣、龍安寺垣、大徳寺垣、光悦寺垣などオリジナル竹垣がいろいろある。

　垣根の種類は、材料、設置場所、目かくしか否かなどの機能、形状によるが、囲繞機能のみならず美的な意匠上の工夫を重ね創意を凝らそうとする職人精神が認められる。材料の種類では、柴垣、竹穂垣、くろもじ垣、木賊垣（とくさがき）、篠垣、檜皮垣、萩垣、鶯垣が、また地名では沼津垣、大津垣、桂垣が、形態では鉄砲垣、茶筅垣、御簾垣（みすがき）、蓑垣、松明垣（たいまつがき）、なまこ垣、四つ目垣がある。

Previous page：**Various style of** *takegaki* **bamboo fences** which reflect the regional style of architecture where they were established and named after and evolved simultaneously with roji teahouse approach path design developments.

their original bamboo fences named after them; Kenninji-*gaki*, Kinkakuji-*gaki*, Ginkakuji-*gaki*, Ryoanji-*gaki*, Daitokuji-*gaki* and Kouetsuji-*gaki* are a few such examples.

　　Differences in the materials used, the places where they are installed, the functions they serve (e.g., whether they are screens or not) and the forms they take, account for the enormous variety of fences. The Japanese spirit of craftsmanship is evident in the many inventive ways that have been devised to simply enclose a space. Fences are named for materials, places or forms. Fences named after the materials they are made from include: *shiba-gaki* (brushwood fence), *takeho-gaki* (bamboo branch fence), *kuromoji-gaki* (spicebush fence), *shino-gaki* (shinodake [Simon bamboo] fence), *hiwada-gaki* (Japanese cypress bark fence), *hagi-gaki* (Japanese bush clover fence), and *uguisu-gaki* (woven brushwood fence). Fences named for places include Numazu-*gaki,* Ōtsu-*gaki*, and Katsura-*gaki*. Fences named for their shape include *tokusa-gaki* (rough horsetail fence), *teppō-gaki* (gun fence), *chasen-gaki* (tea whisk fence), *misu-gaki* (rattan blinds fence), *mino-gaki* (straw raincoat fence), *taimatsu-gaki* (torch shape fence), *namako-gaki* (arched bamboo slats arched), and *yotsume-gaki* (four-grid fence).

　ここここで桂離宮の笹垣（**写真右頁**）について特に付言しておく。地に生えたまま竹の真ん中あたりに鉈（なた）を入れて逆V字型に二つ折りし、敷地境界線へ引っぱり、先端の竹穂を編み込む。裏側から見ると竹があちこちから引き寄せられて曲げられ修羅場のようだが、外見は青々した竹の葉が逆さになびいて輝いている。綿密な編み方で猫の子一匹もぐり込めない頑丈な垣根でもある。

　この桂垣は桂川氾濫時の水制工の一環で、勢いよく書院建築を襲う洪水をこの竹生垣が受けとめ、水勢を削ぎ、実質的に水屋造となっている高床式の書院には、水はひたひたと浸るだけですむ。防御と囲繞と水制という「用」と、生き生きした緑の外観の「景」が調和した日本的美の好例といってよい。

上：住宅で使われている建仁寺垣
Above: Kenninji-gaki fence used in the landscape of a private residence

左上：漁村民家の間垣（まがき）（石川県輪島市）、**右上**：透けた垣、丸竹製の矢来垣、**左下**：昭和記念公園内の日本庭園を囲む生垣、**右下**：本阿弥光悦の考案した光悦寺垣
Top left: Tightly picketed timber bamboo, *ma-gaki* style fence in a fishing village (Noto Peninsula, Wajima City, Ishikawa Pref) **Top right**: See-through fence made in the *yarai-gaki* style (arrow tip fence) constructed from unsplit bamboo rounds. This style originated as a fence used to help defend a position. **Bottom left**: *Ike-gaki* (living) fence surrounding a Japanese garden in Showa Kinen Park. **Bottom right**: The Koetsuji-*gaki* fence originally designed by Hon'ami Kōetsu (1558 - 1637) was a famous Japanese calligrapher, craftsman, lacquerer, and potter.

The Bamboo Hedge of Katsura Detached Palace

Stalks of *hachiku* or henon bamboo (*phyllostachys nigra var. henonis*) growing out of the ground are bent over in half with their tips pulled down to form an inverted V; the tips are then woven together at ground level. From the back, it appears as a snarl of bamboo pulled from different directions, but from the front, the leaves create a luxuriantly green hedge wall that can be trimmed into a flat surface. The hedge is so carefully woven and so dense that not even a cat can get through it.

    This Katsura-*gaki* hedge was in fact part of the construction work carried out to control flooding of the nearby Katsura River. The bamboo fence was meant to head off and reduce the force of floodwater heading for the *shoin* (study) buildings and consequently the water would at most just reach the raised-floor buildings of the *shoin*, which were designed in the *mizuya* style (elevated ground floor style). This is a well-known example of a Japanese hedge that combines the function of not only protection and enclosure but flood control with the scenic beauty of a manicured hedge.

洪水対策ともなった生きた真竹の笹垣（京都、桂離宮）

Woven, living bamboo hedge for flood control at the Katsura Imperial Villa.

上：船小屋（福井県若狭町）**中**：広島県三景園の水上四阿（あずまや）**下**：対龍山荘（たいりゅうさんそう）の茅葺東屋（京都市）

Top: Boat house (Wakasa Town, Fukui Pref) Middle: Azumaya gazebo over water in Sankei-en Park. （Hiroshima Pref）**Bottom**: Kayabuki thatched roof style azumaya gazebo in the Tairyu Sanso Mountain Villa (Kyoto City, Kyoto Pref)

（8）庭園建築物　ランドマーク・場所性と格式のデザイン

　日本の空間文化の基本には、「庭屋一如」（ていおくいちにょ）の思想がある。外（Outdoor）と内（Indoor）にはそれぞれの良さがあり、この両方がひとつになって快適な生活をおくることができる。「家庭」（Home）の文字も House（家）and Garden（庭）である。木造の日本家屋では、縁（えん）・庇（ひさし）・庭の連続感が重要視され、近代以前の日本建築では「庭無し」はあり得なかった。

　江戸の大名庭園など大面積の場合は、全園に広がる自然風景地の点景として、それぞれの場面にふさわしい規模とデザインの茶屋（ちゃや）や亭榭（ていしゃ）が配された。

8. Garden Pavilions: Design of Landmarks and Expressions of Character of Place and Status

Ordinarily, a house is built first, and a garden appropriate to that house is then created. However, in spacious gardens such as the *daimyō* gardens of the Edo period, that order was reversed. The house or any other structure was incidental to the landscape of the garden and built to the scale and design appropriate to the place.

「お茶屋」や「園亭（えんてい）」は、４本の柱で方形寄棟の屋根を支えるだけの簡素な四阿が一般的だが、東屋（あずまや）、亭（てい・チン）・庵（アン・いおり）、閣、楼、数寄屋（すきや）など格式や意匠上、いろいろ活用される。造園上、樹林など緑の風景を引き締めるランドマーク（点景）となり得る明快な図の建築物は有効である。園亭は、高台や築山の上につくられ、景や遠景を眺め、休憩食事、待ち合いの実用に供される。屋根材で茅葺、形で傘亭（かさてい）、座席配置で卍亭（まんじてい）等姿形は、庭園の格式やテーマと一致しなければならない。

The palace was the main building in such a garden. Subordinate to it were teahouses and garden pavilions. The latter were variously referred to as *azumaya* and *tei* (also pronounced *chin*). The simple *azumaya* gazebo, with four posts supporting a hipped roof, is the type of pavilion commonly found in a Japanese garden. Pavilions are fairly diverse and make each garden distinct. Such three-dimensional, straight-line structures with a clear form are effective in endowing a garden space characterized by the organic softness of trees and grass with a framework and formality as well as a focal point (i.e. a landmark).

Built on a rise or mound that affords a view of the landscape, such pavilions provide a place to rest, partake of a repast or meet others. The different styles of pavilions had different names appropriate to their purpose, designation and status or formality The appearance of the pavilion and the material and size of its roof are decided in accordance with the theme or image of the garden landscape.

上：哲学堂公園の六角堂（東京都中野区）**中**：清風荘（せいふうそう）の茶室（京都大学）**下**：茶道美術館の茶室の躙り口（福井市足羽山愛宕坂）

Top: The hexagonal Rokkakudo Temple in Tetsugakudo Park. (Nakano ward, Tokyo) **Middle**: Seifu-so Teahouse at the Kyoto University **Bottom**: *Nijiriguchi* (crawling entrance) at the teahouse in the Atagozaka Tea Ceremony Museum. (Fukui City, Fukui Pref)

（9）園路（えんろ）　スラロームの線形とレジャーウォーク

　近代都市計画では馬車や自動車のスピードにふさわしい直線道路、直角格子道路網が一般的だ。しかし造園における園路は、やさしくおだやかな気分にさせたり、園路の醸成する風致が樹林や池を巡る変化や奥行感を演出するものでなければならない。早く移動するための街路や鉄路とは大違いなのだ。

　「人間にとって最短距離は曲線だ」といわれるが、園路にふさわしいのは歩きやすく疲れないスラローム曲線である。右に左に曲折する典型的日本庭園の園路パターンである。

　カーブする園路の曲がり方を曲率というが、それは、敷地が広く開放的な庭園ではゆったりと曲がり、小

9. Garden Paths: Slalom-like Courses Followed at a Leisurely Pace

Modern city planning is invariably characterized by a grid of straight roads. Unlike urban streets and railways, garden paths must have ambiance, charm, scenic beauty, and style. "Nature abhors a straight line," said William Kent (English landscape gardener that was revolutionary in his style of "natural" garden design), and the easiest curving course to take is slalom-like. That is why paths in landscape gardens follow gently curving lines.

　　There are two entirely different zones to Shinjuku Gyoen in Tokyo, a Japanese garden that has existed, at least in part, since the area was part of the Naitō clan estate (1591) and an English landscape-style garden that was

面積で閉鎖的な庭園ではわずかな起伏や周囲の植栽に合わせて細かに曲折する。

　園内の歩行者動線は、小砂利を敷きつめた園路や飛石、延段など多彩な舗装で飽きないように工夫される。園路はただの通路ではなく、園路の舗装材、アップダウン、曲折、分岐、幅員の変化などすべての細部デザインによって「道すがら（シークエンス）」を「庭園の愉しみ」に転換してしまう。著者は園路の環境や幅員の違いと歩行速度の関係を計測したことがあるが、造園空間の質が高いほどゆっくりと歩く。これを「そぞろ歩き（leisure walk）」といい、歩行速度0.8メートル/秒 以下である。

　なお、車道幅とちがって園路幅は一定である必要はまったくない。視点場部分の園路幅は少しゆったり広くとった例もよくある。平面図を見ると、庭園の性格や雰囲気がわかる。園路パターンや園路密度をみると一目で全体像が直感できる。園路デザインは、造園空間の骨格づくりといえる。

created in the modern period. The former is a closed space centered on a pond and surrounded by dense foliage, and its paths are typical of Japanese gardens, constantly twisting to the right and the left. The latter is an extensive open space of lawns and large Liriodendron trees with wide paths that curve gently in a way typical of Western gardens. Path curvature and path width affect the walking pace. The higher the quality of space, the slower the desired pace. As one walks slower, they are better able to appreciate the view or environment.

One can make a rough estimate of the atmosphere or character of a garden by looking at a drawing, even in plan view, because the pattern and number of paths and their density gives a good idea of the garden's overall image. In that sense, the design of the path of a garden can be said to be the construction of the garden's spatial framework. Paths need not have contiguous homogeneous paving materials, they can change to create an effect just as they can have a sudden shift from curves to a straight segment that extends as a tangent to the curve up to that point which makes the garden visitor want to pause.

上：対龍山荘（たいりゅうさんそう）（京都市南禅寺界隈）

中：新宿遊歩道公園「四季の路」（伊藤邦衛設計、東京都新宿区の緑道）

下：井上敏宏邸（自作、京都市右京区）

99

（10）敷砂（しきすな）術　枯山水・神聖性のデザイン

　西洋では舗装材やコンクリートの骨材でしかない砂や砂利が、日本庭園では立派に造景の主役を演じている。花崗岩系の白川砂を山型に盛り上げたものを「盛砂（もりすな）」、皇居南庭や書院の前庭などに敷きならす「敷砂（しきすな）」、敷砂の凹凸につけた紋様を「砂紋（さもん）」という。粒径が大小さまざまの、また産地のちがいで色合いも多様な砂利や砂をそれぞれ粒を揃えて使う。

　庭の地表面のグランドカバーは、植物が一般的だが、日本の寺院や書院の庭園では白砂が主役である。京都では白川砂が大量に供給でき、その色あいが清浄無垢、神聖、転じて正義、権威を連想させること。盛砂や砂紋など、多彩な表情を引き出すのに砂の可塑性が効果的であること等、枯山水の主役ともなっている。

仁和寺の敷砂（京都市御室）

Shikisuna pattern raked
sand bed at the Ninna-ji
Temple (Omuro, Kyoto City)

10. Use of Sand: Kare Sansui and a Groundcover Expressive of Purity

Sand or gravel, which is normally nothing more than aggregate in paving material or concrete, plays a main role in the creation of scenes in Japanese gardens. Shirakawa gravel is a form of granite containing mica which comes from the region of Shirakawa in Kyoto, which when crushed retains a somewhat round shape no matter its aggregate size. It is referred to as morizuna (molded sand) when shaped into conical forms but when used as ground cover in an open area such as the south court of the Imperial

100

Top: The *kare sansui* garden in the courtyard of the guest house in the Munakata Taisha Shrine, built in ancient times and home to more designated national treasures than any other single site. This courtyard was a collaboration between garden designer Baili Higashi and Uchiyama Landscape Construction Co., Ltd. in 1938. (Munakata City, Fukuoka Pref)

上：日本で最も国宝の多い古代創建の宗像大社(むなかたたいしゃ)の貴賓館の中庭、枯山水。福岡県宗像市、作庭家・東梅里(ひがし　ばいり)と内山緑地建設施工の1938年作。

下：宗像大社の祈願殿の神籬(ひもろぎ)。葦津敬之(あしず　よしゆき)宮司構想により2022年作庭。大社のご祭神(3女神)の3島が大海に並んでいる。

Bottom: *Himorogi* sacred trees, designated by the distinctive rope and white folded paper *shide* in this prayer spot (*kiganden*) within Munakata Taisha Shrine. This area was made under the initiative of chief priest Yoshiyuki Ashizu in 2022. The three rock islands in a vast sea, represent the three goddess deities of the shrine. (Munakata City, Fukuoka Pref)

Palace or the forecourt of a *shoin* residence, it is called *shikizuna* (covering sand). The linear patterns created by raking *shikizuna* are called *samon* (sand patterns). The gravel is sorted into different aggregate sizes before use.

The ground surfaces of gardens were usually covered with grass or moss, but white gravel was the main ground cover in the palaces, *shoin* and temples of Kyoto. The *kare sansui* dry garden arguably would not have come into being, had there not been this large local supply of white gravel. The white gravel suggested virtue and authority and whose

ホテルオークラ オークラプレステージタワー（岩城造園作、東京都港区）
Garden at the Okura Prestige Tower hotel created by Iwaki Landscape. (Minato Ward, Tokyo)

　日本人の白砂敷へのイメージは「神聖」で、それゆえに深遠な精神的世界に通底するところがあり、これが日本庭園イメージに重なる結果になった。岩と砂の構成の枯山水が、広く受容されたのは、日本人の深層心理と共振したからだと思われる。

　なお、砂紋には、青海波、渦巻、網代、井桁、流水、曲水など日本伝統の紋様が使われる。京都鹿ヶ谷、流水落花の趣の法然院の花紋は庭師、植治の創意でおもしろい。ところで園池の護岸に玉石敷の「洲浜」を導入したのは、日本庭園のオリジナルで、陸上から水中へ汀（みぎわ）を斜面で連続させる技法で、親水デザインとして有効であり、一方でEcologicalにはエコトーン（遷移帯）の機能を果たす点で、現代性をもつ。

plasticity made possible different forms of expression such as *morizuna* mounds and *samon* line patterns. This gravel alone can suggest the flow of a stream or the surge of a waterfall.

A space covered with white gravel was subconsciously associated in the Japanese mind with sanctity, with a magical, supernatural power. The profound, mysterious world it conjured up, overlapped with the image projected by the Japanese garden. The enormous appeal of the *kare sansui* garden, composed only of natural rocks and gravel, has roots deep in the Japanese psyche.

Samon makes use of patterns traditional to Japan such as *seigaiha* (overlapping waves), *uzumaki* (whirlpool), *ajiro* (wickerwork), *igeta* (double cross), *ryūsui* (stream), and *kyokusui* (meandering stream). An unusual example is the *ryūsui rakka* (stream and fallen blossom) pattern in the sand at Honen-in temple in Shikagaya District in Kyoto.

The idea of introducing a sandy beach *(suhama)* on the shore of a garden pond is believed to have originated in Japan. Having a sloping beach, instead of an abrupt vertical drop, mediate between land and water is not only aesthetically more elegant but also provides for a more organic and functional transition.

玉石敷きの洲浜（京都御所小御所の庭）
Tamaishi (cobblestone) beach (Kogosho Palace Garden, Kyoto-Gosho Palace)

大徳寺塔頭瑞峯院枯山水（重森三玲作庭、京都市柴野）

Kare sansui in the garden of the Zuiho-in sub-temple within Daitoku-ji Temple.
Designed by famous landscape architect Mirei Shigemori (Shino, Kyoto)

（11）風水（ふうすい）術　安心安定の環境計画

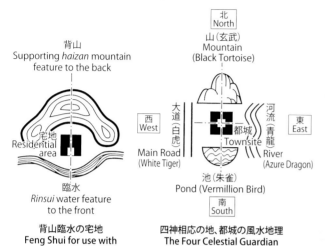

背山
Supporting *haizan* mountain
feature to the back

宅地
Residential
area

臨水
Rinsui water feature
to the front

背山臨水の宅地
Feng Shui for use with
residential development

北
North
山（玄武）
Mountain
(Black Tortoise)

西
West
大道（白虎）
Main Road
(White Tiger)

都城
Townsite

東
East
河流（青龍）
River
(Azure Dragon)

池（朱雀）
Pond (Vermillion Bird)

南
South

四神相応の地、都城の風水地理
The Four Celestial Guardian
Animals of Feng Shui and its
application for municipal planning

日本庭園は、塀や垣で囲まれた狭い敷地の中で完結しているように見えるが、バードアイで上空から眺めれば町並、水辺、農地、里山、また鎮守の森や菩提寺、そして盆地をつつむ山並みなどとの関係性（座標軸）によって位置づけられていることもよくわかる。こう考えると、与えられた敷地の中で庭園デザインを考えるだけではなく、本来は住居をどのような地域や場所に立地させるか敷地選択を優先すべきだということになる。古人はこれを「風水」と呼んだ。

　平安京の庭園立地の分布の特徴は、都城の周辺部、都を包み込む東山、北山、西山の山辺（やまのべ）の山麓斜面地に多い点だ。緑豊かな環境の山の斜面では、清水が得られ都への眺望にめぐまれ名園の条件を充たすからである。平安京の立地選定は、中国の都城の条件とされる「四神相応（しじんそうおう）」の地であったからとされ

中国の風水説による宅地や都市の立地選択の図解（王其亭編『風水理論研究』天津大学出版会、1992）より抜粋）左の図には、背山、臨水、右図には、山（玄武）、大道（白虎）、河流（青龍）、池（朱雀）。ひとは背後に山を背負い、前方に平地が広がるような場所で落ち着く。左は住居の敷地レベル、右は都城、都市レベルの風水、背山臨水の自然地理をいかした空間構成。

11. *Feng Shui*: Power to Read the Land to Achieve Peace of Mind

While some people have an image of a garden being limited to a small, enclosed space entirely man-made, it can be much more than this. Large captured natural scenes can also be included. Examples of this would be the natural scenery surrounding an old temple or a spacious Zen monastery. The aesthetic satisfaction and profound spirituality that one experiences when viewing this scenery can be said to be "garden-like" in character. A Japanese garden is not limited to the confines of garden walls but is inclusive of connected scenery and cognizant of natural harmonic scenic compositions. An enclosed garden, a lowland surrounded by mountains, a small island in the ocean: each is a microcosm. Any spot in the natural world where one discovers such a place and senses a place or shelter for oneself can be called a garden.

A temple or shrine built in the mountains of Japan was a product of landscape planning, as evidenced by its strategic location in a mountainous space as well a product of site planning, as

る。中国では東・青竜に（大河川）、西・白虎に（大道）、南・朱雀に（大池）、北・玄武に（山）の地形が、末永く繁栄する城市といわれ、日本ではこの考え方を庭園の地割にも適用して、敷地の北に築山か樹林を、南に大きな池泉を配置し、東に遣水や流れを配置。方位と土地や家屋の使い方の原則は「風水地理説（ふうすいちりせつ）」とも呼ばれ、単的に「背山臨水（はいざんりんすい）」の敷地選定といわれた。

　文明の力で快適な人工環境を構成することができる以前の人々は、「自然地理の安全安心感覚」にもとづいて、都市や住居や作庭の設計規範として生きてきたのである。正に古人は、安心できる土地や場所を見抜く目をもっていた。

　たとえば日本の山中に構えられた社寺建設は、①ランドスケープ・プランニング（景観計画）的には山辺空間に立地し、②サイト・プランニング（敷地計画）的には山辺の襞（ひだ）のような微地形（びちけい）を上手に生かしながら堂宇を配置し、③ランドスケープ・デザイン（景観設計）的には、アプローチ（参道）を長くして奥への期待感をもたせ、急な石段を昇ってゆく変化を演出し、鳥居や門の結界で気分を転換させ、本殿や本堂の前の斎庭で信仰心を充たし、塔を見上げて宗教的荘厳を感得させるような環境計画であった。

evidenced by the skillful use made of small-scale topography such as the folds in mountains. These places were also powerful products of landscape design, as witnessed by the anticipation created by means of an extended approach, the drama produced by the introduction of steep steps, and the transitions created by the effect of boundaries, such as gates. The use of a formal courtyard (*yuniwa*), combined with a place of worship enclosed by a main hall, where visitors reaffirmed their faith, and the placement of a tower in the background, whose soaring structure inspired solemnity, all contributed to the contemplative experience. This skillful composition of space and landscape is surely proof that the receptive and attuned Japanese of old were the early "garden" masters.

Many of the famous gardens of Kyoto are located in the mountainous areas on the periphery of the city such as Higashiyama, Kitayama and Nishiyama. No doubt, the Japanese of old possessed the power to identify land or places in which they could feel peace of mind.

Previous page:
Diagram from a Chinese *feng shui* text indicating where both cities and residences are best positioned for proper energy flow. In *feng shui* tradition, a city should have a mountain to the north, and a water element to the south of it. For residences, similarly, there should be a mountain to the north which is identified as a black turtle, to the east there should be a flowing river or a green dragon, to the south a pond or a red phoenix, and to the west a large road which is identified as a white tiger. These guidelines were applied in both Japanese garden design as well as in ancient municipal planning. Humans feel reassured with a mountain guarding them in the back and a clear and expansive view in front of them to the bright south, revealing very primal and fundamental, natural principles that allow us to feel safe, settled and at peace in our minds, which can be effectively applied universally in design.

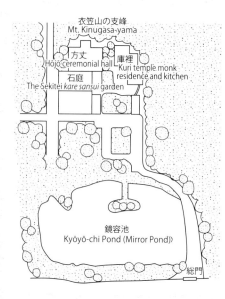

衣笠山の支峰
Mt. Kinugasa-yama

方丈
Hōjō ceremonial hall

庫裡
Kuri temple monk residence and kitchen

石庭
The Sekitei *kare sansui* garden

鏡容池
Kyōyō-chi Pond (Mirror Pond)〉

総門

龍安寺庭園　石庭で有名な龍安寺ではあるが、①背山臨水の地形構成、②土地利用多様性で生物多様性が担保された庭園により、広大な敷地のほとんどは**生態系**の豊かな生物生息空間だとわかる（京都市）

Diagram of a species biodiversity survey done of the Ryōan-ji Temple garden. Even though the garden is famous for being a rock garden, this map shows the incredible diversity of species that this expansive area hosts, which is credited to the naturalized traditional layout of the garden, with a mountain behind and pond in the front. (Kyoto City, Kyoto Pref)

（12）生き物術　生物多様性・庭園は美しいビオトープ

　日本の空間文化の特色は、「庭屋一如」といい、内の人工的建築と外の自然的庭園のバランス感覚にある。人工と自然、無機と有機のバランス、囲繞と眺望のバランス感覚、その知恵と技術が総合化されていたのだ。日本庭園では、山から海までの自然環境が、狭い敷地に築山から流れ、池へ、また、林、芝原へと連続した生態系として縮景されている。現代地球社会の重要課題である「生物多様性（Bio-diversity）を特別に意識したわけではないが、日本庭園は元来、立地上も豊かな自然にあり、テーマも自然（山水）の縮景であり、材料も自然、施工も透水性、通気性が担保されて、生き物が生息し易い建設技術であった。

　実に「生物多様性に富んだ美しいビオトープ」が日本庭園であった。中でも龍安寺は外国からの観光客で賑わうが、そのお目当ては「石庭」で、およそ生物多様性とは対極のイメージの名園だ。しかし、改めて龍安寺を訪ねてみよう。南

12. Organisms: The Japanese Garden Is a Biotope Rich in Organic Diversity

A Japanese garden, though it seems natural, is actually an artificial space. At first glance, everything about it, from the plants to the flow of water, may appear to be natural, but the landscape has in fact been thoroughly and deliberately constructed and manipulated. On the other hand, a *kare sansui* garden or a rock garden while it may appear to be an inorganic space, with little about it that is natural, feels organic because of its surroundings. Observe, for example, the famous garden of Ryōan-ji in Kyoto. Today, it is crowded with tourists. They are all there for the rock garden. Passing through the main gate, then the inner gate, one finds a large pond on the left. If one circles around the pond and walks north, the hillside becomes steep. Stone steps take one to higher ground, occupied by the *kuri*, the main hall of the temple. To the west is the *hōjō* (main ceremonial hall). The south garden of the *hōjō* is the rock garden. Behind the *hōjō* is a mountainous area that is an extension of Mt. Kinugasa.

面する総門、中門を入ると左手に鏡容池と名づけられた大池、池を巡って北上すると急斜面で山になり、石段を上った台地上には庫裡、その西に方丈、そして方丈の南庭が「石庭」になっている。方丈の裏は衣笠山の支脈で山地である。本堂は「背山臨水」の地にあって、背山は野生的大自然、臨水の池とその周囲は家畜的中自然、石庭は半自然、建築物は人工と、多段階のランドスケープ構造となっていることがわかる。

　一般には「石庭」のみが有名な龍安寺庭園であるが、全景的ランドスケープは、美しい景観であるだけでなく、生物多様性に富んだビオトープ（Biotop）でもあることを著者ら研究室の調査が明らかにした。龍安寺境域調査では、鳥類・爬虫類・両生類・魚類・甲殻類・蛛形類、貝類・昆虫類など59科90種の多様な生物の生息が確認されている。

右：ボタニカルガーデンアートビオトープ『水庭』石上純也設計、櫻井淳施工（静岡グリーンサービス）、北山ひろみ総合プロデュース（オーナー）の現代アート。320本の落葉樹と160の池の人為的ビオトープ(Bio-top)（栃木県那須高原）

The overall landscape, with its back to the mountains and a body of water to the south, as prescribed by *feng shui*, satisfies the need for tranquility and a view. Within it lies a multi-tiered structure: wild nature; domesticated half-nature; half nature such as the rock garden; and man-made, in the form of buildings. Although the rock garden is the part of the garden of Ryōan-ji, the overall landscape is not only scenic and effective but is a natural space rich in organic diversity and full of many kinds of life. The phrase *teioku ichinyo* (exquisite harmony between the building and the garden) describes how, ideally, architecture and the garden are inseparable; the inside and the outside must be integrated and in balance. Moreover, the Japanese have sought to achieve balance between the artifice of the garden and the natural elements of the garden, between enclosure and view, between the man-made and the organic. Japanese gardens, diverse compositions of mounds, streams, ponds, woods, and fields on small sites, are biotopes rich in organic diversity that also happen to be beautiful.

The Botanical Farm Garden Art Biotop "Water Garden" is a modern art project, designed by Junya Ishigami and constructed by Jun Sakurai, Shizuoka Green Service Co., for the owner and producer of the project, Hiromi Kitayama. It features 320 deciduous trees among 160 pondlets forming a man-made biotope. (Nasukougen highlands, Tochigi Pref)

　日本庭園のグラウンド・カバー・プランツ（地被植物）は、苔がメインの感がある。実際、亭々と立つスギの林床をしっとりとおおうスギゴケのやわらかさとのコントラストは、それだけで名園の趣きを醸しだす。

　スギとコケが似合う日本の風土で生きる日本人には、その反対の明るく快活なイメージの芝庭を歓迎する気持ちも強い。もとより、十分な日照時間を要求する芝生を活用するには、十分な広さの敷地が必要だ。したがって古代宮廷の庭、近世江戸の大名庭園、そして都市公園が芝生活用の舞台であった。

　芝生とは、芝草が一面に生えた原っぱ状の場所をさす。大昔、人間が樹林を伐り拓き、放牧したり、野焼きしたり、また芝刈りして低いターフ状態を維持した場所

清風荘（せいふうそう）の芝庭
（京都大学、植治作、京都市）

Lawn garden with organically curved paths in Seifu-so Villa within the Kyoto University campus designed by famous landscape architect Ueji. (Kyoto City, Kyoto Pref)

13. Use of Lawns: An Invitation to Engage in Outdoor Recreation

Moss is the main ground cover plant used in Japanese gardens. The contrast in softness between towering Japanese cedars and the moist bed of juniper hair-cap moss (Polytrichum juniperinum) that covers the ground around them is a feature of many well known gardens.

Notwithstanding that the Japanese climate is perfectly suited to cedars and moss, or precisely because it is so suited, the Japanese yearn at times for the complete opposite, grass and a lawn, and the cheerful image they project. A site of sufficient scale is a prerequisite for the use of grass, which demands enough sunlight and daylight hours. Lawns have therefore played a major role in the open

を芝生と呼んだ。奈良の若草山がよく知られているが、芝焼きと放鹿によって、絶えず草丈は抑えられ芝生状態が風景として定着した。

　古代人の野遊びや歌垣を遊んだアウトドア・レクリエーションの場所が芝生地で、その雰囲気は江戸の花見や大名庭園の宴遊にもつながる。苔と違って芝生では、そのなかに入り野遊び、蹴鞠（けまり）、弓、馬、野点（のだて）を楽しめる。

　また芝生地の景観的意味として、明るく宏大でモダンな景観表現をあげなければならない。たとえば岡山後楽園の場合、大芝生園地が厚みのある樹叢を背後に控えつつも、それ以上に存在感を示し、大芝生地が岡山後楽園の明るくモダンな名園イメージの象徴になっている。

spaces of ancient courts, the *daimyō* gardens of feudal Edo, and gardens of the modern era.

Long ago, in places where humans had cut down or burned away trees for their own use, wild grass would grow. Such fields of wild grass, maintained as low turf through the burning of dead grass in early spring or cutting, came to be called *shibafu* (lawn). A well-known example is Wakakusa-yama mountain in Nara, where the height of grass has always been controlled through *noyaki* (controlled burns) and deer let loose on the grounds and subsequently a lawn has formed.

Since ancient times, such lawns have been places for outdoor recreational activities referred to as *no-asobi* (field-play) and *yama-asobi* (mountain-play). Similarly, lawns in *daimyō* gardens of Edo were the sites of banquets. The difference between areas of lawn and beds of moss is that lawns get used for *no-asobi* (field-play), *kemari* (a ball game played by Heian period aristocrats), archery, horseback riding, and other open-air activities.

A spacious lawn has a powerful presence, even more impactful than the deep thicket surrounding the garden. There is enclosure and expanse. Three-dimensional and two-dimensional. Male and female. Darkness and light. The contrast, though simple, is quite effective. This is a lawn garden at its finest.

（14）季節術　フェノロジー・花札風景と四季の変化

　日本庭園の美は、四季の美として説明される。日本は四季の変化に恵まれているからだという。しかし「四季の変化」は日本の専売特許ではない。むしろカナダの紅葉などは遥かに劇的でさえある。したがって、日本庭園の技術が、意図的に四季の変化を強調したり演出したり、花見、月見、虫聴き、雪見などの年中行事化などソフトウエアを充実した成果であるというほうが正しい。これを著者は「季節術」と呼びたい。

　日本の名所には、梅、桜、萩、楓などがテーマの「花の庭や花の寺、山紅葉」は少なくないが、日本庭園の実際の樹種と本数を分析すると、植栽構成の骨格的要素として常緑樹が圧倒的に多いことがわかった。

　欧米のガーデニングではカラフルな草花が主役だが、日本庭園では中国伝来のボタン、シャクヤクが花壇

14. Phenology - The Study of the Cyclical Events of the Seasons: Greenery Plays the Main Role; Flowers Are Subordinate

In the West, over ninety percent of gardening has to do with flowers, or so it seems. Well known "flower gardens" and "temples of flowers" do exist in Japan, but flowers are rarely used as the foundational elements of Japanese gardens. Flowering plants rarely take center stage and when they do, flowering trees are generally used. Even such, flowering trees are generally not the main elements of gardens, with Japanese plum tree gardens and groves being the exception. The Japanese plum tree, which flowers before most other plants do, are highly valued, and while the flowers are certainly important, the main attraction of Japanese plum tree groves is their scent.

　Aside from Japanese plum trees, flowers are not deliberately used as components of gardens. Oftentimes, when a garden becomes famous for its flowers, it is the result of happenstance. Seeds that somehow found their way into the garden led to the blooming of a few flowers

に使われた以外、花菖蒲園やつつじ園が目的的に設けられる場合はあるが、園景の中に意図的に配植することはない。ただ自然の種がこぼれてなにげなく咲いてしまい、それが緑濃い樹木や砂と石組の園景に「紅一点」のアクセントとなったというぐらいである。重要なのは日本庭園の主体はあくまで緑の樹木だということ。草花のカラーではなかったことだ。

左：春の桜、城門と調和する春の桜（福井城址、福井市）
中：秋のススキ（著者邸屋上、神奈川県大和市）
右：桜は春だけでなはない秋の桜　緑葉から紅葉にかわる桜葉の味わい（著者自宅の庭、神奈川県大和市）

that set off the green of the trees or the rock grouping.

In any case, the greenery of trees, rather than flowering plants, accounts for most of the color in Japanese gardens. Flowering plants are embellishments that symbolically convey a moment in time or the passing of the seasons. They are not resplendent elements occupying prominent positions.

A study of the various proportions of tree varieties in historic Japanese gardens found the ratio of evergreen trees to deciduous trees, to be nine to one. Evergreen trees dominate by an overwhelming margin. They stabilize human vision and the image of the landscape, creating a world of calm rather than restlessness. Flowering trees, autumn foliage, and deciduous trees are mixed in to give a garden just enough piquancy to avoid monotony, without threatening stability.

In this way, flowers are limited to a subordinate role as embellishments in Japanese gardens. Dark green therefore provides the basic background tone. Similar to that of backdrops to *ikebana*; the more peaceful or subdued the backdrop, the more a flower arrangement

Left: Spring cherry blossoms harmoniously placed at the gate of the Fukui Castle ruins. (Fukui City, Fukui Pref)
Middle: Quintessential fall *susuki* or Japanese pampas grass scenery in the author's rooftop garden. (Yamato City, Kanagawa Pref)
Right: Beautiful, not just in the spring, these fall cherry trees in the author's garden with their leaves changing from green to their autumn colors, are vividly beautiful. (Yamato City, Kanagawa Pref)

著者らの（史的名園の植栽樹種別本数）分析結果、常緑樹と落葉樹の使用本数比率は9対1で、常緑樹が圧倒している。日本庭園は、常緑樹の濃い緑が人の視野と風景イメージを安定させ、庭園を落ちついた風景世界として性格づけた。ただこれではあまりに安定して退屈になるので、安定を壊さぬ程度に花木や黄葉、紅葉、落葉樹をアクセントとして1割ほど混ぜたのである。日本庭園は、「市中の山居」で空間の安定性が第一で、そのためには濃い緑が基調でなければならなかった。紅葉で真っ赤に染まる大自然の山と、市中の庭は違うのである。

　ちなみに日本人の自然観は、カードゲーム「花札」に表れている。花札には、樹木でいえば1月の松から12月の桐まで、それぞれの季節にふさわしい昆虫や鳥、小動物、そして花見、菊見、雪見などの大名庭園での年中行事と共に、花鳥風月と季節が登場する。花札に季節を彩る動植物と催事がワンセットであること、その舞台が大名庭園である点で、生物多様性と自然共生型自然観が「日本庭園」の本質であると著者は確信している。

comes to life. While mountain forests in autumn colors may be beautiful and glorious to view, this is not a typically desired or appropriate aesthetic for the modesty and humility imbued in Japanese garden design. If such color does exist, it is thought to be a seed that by chance sprouted in that spot.

Translation of Traditional Themes of Natural Beauty into Garden Design

Japanese "flower cards" (*hanafuda*), feature traditional themes of natural beauty. The set of forty-eight cards are arranged by season, from the pine of January to the paulownia of December, and depict both animals and plants from which pairs or combinations are made. The landscapes depicted by *hanafuda* reveal the flora and fauna, a sense of the different seasons, and the character of the culture of Japan. The same aesthetic expressions manifest in the design and use of *daimyō* gardens during the Edo period, and they are superb expressions of the Japanese view of the ideal environment that is characterized by both organic diversity and human coexistence with nature.

1月(松)
January (pine)

2月(梅)
February (plum)

3月(桜)
March (cherry blossoms)

4月(藤)
April (wisteria)

5月(菖蒲)
May (iris)

6月(牡丹)
June (peony)

7月(萩)
July (bush clover)

8月(薄)
August (moon)

9月(菊)
September (chrysanthemum)

10月(紅葉)
October (maple)

11月(雨)
November (rain)

12月(桐)
December (paulownia)

日本固有のカードゲーム、花札。四季12か月を代表する動植物や太陽、月、年中行事を描いている

上：冬の風物誌、雪吊り（金沢城内玉泉院丸庭園、石川県金沢市）**下左**：清澄庭園の冬の牡丹と防寒（東京都江東区）
下中：稲わらによる防寒対策、日蓮宗北陸本山妙成寺(みょうじょうじ)(石川県羽咋市)。雪や寒さから植物、石灯籠などを守るための実用性
とともに、藁で美しく包むことで、冬らしい季節感を演出している。**下右**：雪景色の紫式部庭園、借景日野山 (森 蘊設計)(福井県越前市)

Top: The quintessential winter scenery of traditional and artistic *yukitsuri* (ropework and bamboo support poles) which give garden trees support and protection in heavy winter snows. (Gyokusen'inmaru Garden, Kanazawa Castle, Kanazawa City, Ishikawa Pref) **Bottom left**: Peonies protected from snow and cold by rice straw covers in Kiyosumi Garden. (Koto Ward, Tokyo) **Bottom Middle**: Aesthetic and practical, cozy rice straw snow protection wrapping in the Myojo-ji Temple garden that invokes winter imagery and beauty. (Hakui City, Ishikawa Pref) **Bottom Right**: Winter scenery of Murasakishikibu Park with Mt. Hino forming a borrowed scenery *shakkei* element in the background. (design by Osamu Mori) (Echizen City, Fukui Pref)

天体観察さえも日本文化の延長として捉える写真家の杉本博司、
江之浦測候所の冬至光遥拝隧道（小田原市）
写真：小田原文化財団

Winter Solstice Light-Worship Tunnel, Enoura Observatory
Odawara, Japan - Designed by Hiroshi Sugimoto
Photo credit: Odawara Art Foundation

第六章　現代に生きつづける日本庭園

仏寺貴族の古代、大名の近世、日米の近現代：用と景の調和・地方色・エコアート

Chapter 6

Japanese Gardens that Survive to and Exist in the Present

*Ancient Aristocratic Era, Daimyō Era,
Modern Era of Japan and the US:
Yin and Yang Harmony / Regional
Flavoring/ Eco-Art*

第6章では、日本へのガーデン・ツアーを予定にしておられる方や、多様性に富んだ日本庭園の実態を知りたい方に向け、庭園形式の代表的名園を30庭園紹介する。著者進士が計画したプロジェクトも含め、観光者のためだけでなく、ガーデンデザイナーにとってのキーポイント、さらには今後の庭園制作上の留意点も記述した。

Chapter 6 is intended to give a deeper understanding of the breadth of diversity in Japanese Gardens by looking at thirty renowned gardens of different styles and examining how they differ. This overview includes projects that the author has been involved in and delves past a tourist's perspective and into the rationale of the various garden designers.

（1）仏寺・貴族の庭園

I. Gardens in Buddhist Temples and Aristocratic Gardens

1，平等院鳳凰堂庭園 （1052年：京都府宇治市）

末法から救われたい平安貴族の「阿弥陀来迎世界（あみだらいごうせかい）」

宇治平等院鳳凰堂と浄土庭園の造園術は、平安貴族の住居、寝殿造形式に則（のっと）り、舟遊式池泉に荒磯、洲浜、島、橋、松を活用したもので、来世を描いた「浄土曼荼羅図（じょうどまんだらず）」を地上に再現した形となっている。

父の関白藤原道長から別業を譲られた藤原頼通（よりみち）（992-1074）は、1052年、これを仏寺、平等院にし、翌年阿弥陀堂（鳳凰堂）と阿字池を配置し、現世に極楽浄土を再現しようとした。

表門である北の御門から入ると、北小島があって、ここに平橋、反橋が架かり、鳳凰堂の建つ中島にいたる。大池の西側の中島中央には阿弥陀堂が立つ。棟の上には雌雄一対の鳳凰がのるので鳳凰堂と呼ばれる。南北 2方向には翼廊、西裏側には尾廊、浄土院、最勝院（さいしょ

ういん）とつながっている。

庭園は、宇治川の旧河床の水溜まりを利用し金色丈六の阿弥陀如来のお顔を水面に映す阿字池とし、砂洲上に盛土して主建築を建てている。青空や雲を背景に、朱塗りの阿弥陀堂の美しさが阿字池にうつるよう工夫されている。

中堂の中心線上には存在感のある平等院型灯籠が置かれる。灯籠の基壇は四石で組み合わされた円形、その上に蓮の花と格狭間（こうはざま）が刻まれた基礎石が置かれ、さらには高々と平等院型灯籠が阿弥陀仏に対し献灯されている。

なお平等院鳳凰堂は昔から人々に知られ、10円硬貨や一万円札にも描かれている。庭園は日本を代表する浄土庭園として、1922年いちばん早く国指定の史跡・名勝となっている。指定面積は6,100坪。

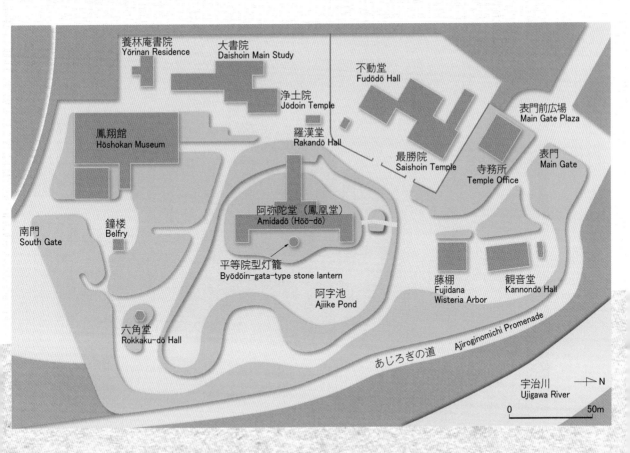

養林庵書院 Yōrinan Residence
大書院 Daishoin Main Study
不動堂 Fudōdō Hall
浄土院 Jōdoin Temple
表門前広場 Main Gate Plaza
鳳翔館 Hōshokan Museum
羅漢堂 Rakandō Hall
最勝院 Saishoin Temple
寺務所 Temple Office
表門 Main Gate
阿弥陀堂（鳳凰堂）Amidadō (Hōō-dō)
鐘楼 Belfry
南門 South Gate
平等院型灯籠 Byōdōin-gata-type stone lantern
阿字池 Ajiike Pond
藤棚 Fujidana Wisteria Arbor
観音堂 Kannondō Hall
六角堂 Rokkaku-dō Hall
あじろぎの道 Ajiroginomichi Promenade
宇治川 Ujigawa River
0 50m
N

1. Garden of Hōō-dō, Byōdō-in Villa

(Uji City, Kyoto Prefecture, 1052)

In 1052, Fujiwara Yorimichi, a court noble and regent to the Emperor, made his villa into a Buddhist temple, which he named Byōdō-in. The following year, he completed the Amida Hall (popularly known as the Phoenix Hall - Hōō-dō). The garden design appropriates the *shinden*-style of Heian aristocrats including wild shores, beaches, islands, bridges and pine trees arranged around and within the main feature, a large pond in the *chisen shūyū / funa asobi* or "leisure boat" style and was intended to be an earthly re-creation of a mandala depicting the Pure Land. The temple was created in the hope of countering the anticipated decline of the world as prophesied by Mahayana Buddhism, which was a widespread concern of the time.

The front, north gate leads by way of a straight horizontal bridge to a small north island. An arched bridge gives access to the middle island on which the Amida Hall stands. The building sits in the middle of the island on the west side of Aji Pond. On top of its roof is a pair of phoenixes, male and female. To the south and north are "wing" corridors (*yoku-rō*), and on the west, back side is the "tail" corridor (*bi-rō*) that provides access to both the Jōdo-in and Saishū-in temples.

写真提供：平等院

The garden features a pond created in the flood plain of the Uji River, and the main buildings, including the central hall where the statue of a seated Amida is enshrined, constructed on what had been a sandbank. The two wing corridors extend from the hall like the spreading wings of a phoenix, which along with the sky and clouds behind, are designed to be reflected in the pond in front of the buildings, creating a beautiful composition.

Standing in front of the hall is what is now known as a Byōdō-in-type stone lantern, made from four stones. Its circular podium or "stem" sits on a base decorated with carved lotus flowers. The stone lantern is intended for votive offerings of light to Amida.

The temple of Byōdō-in has a special place in the heart of the Japanese people and thus is featured on the front of the Japanese 10 Yen coin and the back of the 10,000 Yen note. The garden of Byōdō-in is the best known and most recognized Jōdo-style garden in Japan and was the first garden to be designated a Historic Site and a Place of Scenic Beauty by the government in 1922, amazingly surviving from it creation in 1052 to the present.

2，毛越寺庭園（伝850年創建、1117年頃浄土庭園完成：岩手県平泉町）

世界文化遺産の奥州平泉に「仏の国」，「極楽浄土」を地上に再現

　世界遺産の平泉は、11世紀末の東北武士団をひきいた奥州藤原氏の初代清衡が、肉親まで殺しあう戦さを止めさせ、地上に平和な佛の国を実現しようと支配地の中心に中尊寺金色堂（1124）を建立。2代基衡（もとひら）は大金をかけて毛越寺の金堂円隆寺（1157）と本格的な浄土の庭を造成した。3代秀衡（ひでひら）は毛越寺に隣接して宇治の平等院鳳凰堂にならい無量光院を造営した。本堂は極楽の宮殿を、また庭園は極楽世界そのものの表現であったのである。

　藤原3代はこの世を、美しく平和な佛の国：極楽浄土にしようとしたのである。なかでも毛越寺は、建物は残っていないが浄土の庭の景観構成の基本がよくわかり、来訪者に浄土とはこういう雰囲気かという気分をよく伝えてくれる。

　敷地の北側には塔山、南側には東西に長い大泉が池。かつては庭園の正面には山を背に水に臨んで阿弥陀如来を祀る金堂が立ち、その前の大池には中島、島には平橋と反橋が真っすぐ架けられていた。

　浄土の池の面積は広く、汀線のカーブもゆったりして、周囲を囲む杉木立の

2. Garden of Mōtsu-ji Temple

(Hiraizumi Town, Iwate Prefecture: The temple was founded in approx. 850, the Jōdo-style garden completed in approx. 1177)

The town of Hiraizumi was an ancient center of the Tohoku region in northern Japan, built around the residence of the governing Fujiwara Clan, in the frontier province called Ōshū. Hiraizumi is home to the prominent temples Chuson-ji and Mōtsu-ji, which feature a *Jōdo*-style or Pure Land garden and other sub-temples, which were built around the early 12th century. Occupying an area of approximately 14.85 hectares, Hiraizumi is a designated National Special Place of Scenic Beauty and became a UNESCO World Cultural Heritage site in 2011. The garden of Mōtsu-ji was once lost to sedimentation and abandonment but later was carefully uncovered and restored to what was believed to be its original form.

Its location in the idyllic and beautiful region of northern Japan, far removed from the capital Kyoto, made the creation of this impressive Pure Land garden of unprecedented scale and authenticity, possible.

The original temple buildings no longer exist, but this representative Pure

垂直線に対して水平線の安らぎ感が、人々の心を癒してくれる。もちろん池中には、自然の柔しさのアクセントとして、荒々しい海岸風景の荒磯や立石組み岩嶋で剛の景観ポイントが構成されている。

毛越寺庭園の荒磯の石組み（**右**）と優しい曲線の池汀線（**下**）。日本庭園には剛と柔・垂直と水平のバランス感覚が存在する

Notice the contrast between the emulation of a rugged ocean shoreline created by the stone arrangement featuring vertical and austere elements (**upper right**) and the gentle, sweeping shoreline (**left**) in the pond at Mōtsu-ji Temple Garden. Japanese garden design balances hard and soft, vertical and horizontal.

Land garden of the Heian period is still centered on the Ōizumi Pond which opens out to the southeast and stretches east to west. The hills of Tōyama rise in the background on the north and west of the garden. The shoreline of the center island with its round stones and pebbles, which just emerge above the water line, make it appear as if the island is floating. The edge of the pond with its sweeping, beautiful curves, lined with round rocks, are what is referred to, in the garden treatise the *Sakuteiki*, as the "tidal flat" style.

A peninsula suggesting a rugged coast, an islet with a distinctive upright rock grouping, and a mound, contrast with the broad expanse and the gentle curves of the pond shoreline. An exquisite, pond-feeding *yarimizu* stream, that has been restored to its original condition after archaeological excavation, offers a fine example of what such a feature was intended to look like according to the *Sakuteiki*.

The garden designer is unknown, though the garden design suggests a possible involvement of someone from Kyoto. Inasmuch as the garden is a reflection of not only the skill of its designer, but also the sensibility of its owner, the creation of this garden serves as a reminder of the power of the religious faith and artistic character of the Fujiwara clan that ruled the Tōhoku region.

3, 称名寺庭園 （伝1258年：神奈川県横浜市金沢文庫）

鎌倉幕府執権の北条実時、貞顕の浄土庭園と禅院伽藍

金沢八景の一つ「称名（しょうみょう）の晩鐘（ばんしょう）」で知られた横浜市金沢の古刹。称名寺には「結界図（けっかいず）」が残り図面に忠実な苑池や庭園の復元整備事業が推められ、往時の「浄土庭園」の姿を見ることができる。

史跡指定面積は、約52,000坪、うち約2,000坪が園池部分である。1971年から発掘調査、その後10年をかけて整備事業を進め、朱塗り木造の反橋、平橋が復元された。

称名寺は、鎌倉幕府の執権で金沢北条氏の祖となる北条実時（ほうじょうさねとき）が建立、その境内に「金沢文庫」も設置した。その孫貞顕（さだあき）（1255-1333)が1319年苑池造成に着手し、人足を延1000人も使役して約1年半で完成。1323年『称名寺絵図並結界記』（**右頁**）を制作している。

貞顕は後に幕府執権となるが、約十年間京都の六波羅探題（ろくはらたんだい）をつとめ京都の浄土庭園や寝殿造住宅を熟知していた。よって称名寺は平安期の浄土庭園を基調にしている。ただ建築は　鎌倉後期の主流であった禅宗様式の伽藍配置となっている。庭園と建築のミスマッチは移行期のためであろう。作庭家は、性一法師（しょういつほうし）とされる。

3. Jōdo-Style Garden of Shōmyō-ji Temple

(Yokohama, Kanagawa Prefecture, founded in approx. 1258)

The Shōmyō-ji Temple built by Hōjō Sanetoki, a military general and a seasoned Shogunate regent of the Kamakura period. Shōmyō-ji is known as the temple depicted in "Evening Bell at Shōmyō," one of the classic "Eight Views of Kanazawa," a series of woodblock prints by Andō Hiroshige.

The Shōmyō-ji complex of temples and the garden has been designated a Historical Site, covering approximately 17.2 hectares, of which 6.6 hectares is accounted for by the pond. Archaeological excavation began in 1971, and the restoration of the garden and pond was carried out over a ten-year period. The vermilion arch bridge and the vermilion straight, horizontal bridge, both characteristic of a Jōdo Pure Land style garden, have also been restored.

Sanetoki, after retirement, was also known for building an impressive library in this compound. He treasured learning and books so much, he built the dedicated library building separate from other buildings. This library continued to be expanded by his son, grandson

122

この絵図は元亨（げんこう）3年（1323年）に称名寺の境界を明確にするために作られたもの。絵図を見ると、称名寺は園地を中心とした浄土教寺院の特徴を持つ。庭園の池には中島があって南北に橋がかけられている。南の仁王門を入り、橋を渡ると、中心に本尊の弥勒菩薩（みろくぼさつ）をまつる金堂（こんどう）、講堂（こうどう）、両界堂（りょうがいどう）、護摩堂（ごまどう）などが建つ。池の西方には南から新宮（しんぐう）、寝殿造風の称名寺、三重塔（さんじゅうのとう）が並ぶ。池の東方には雲堂（うんどう）、庫院（くいん）、無常院（むじょういん）などが並び、この構成は、鎌倉期に始まった禅宗寺院の伽藍配置であって、庭園がそれ以前の平安期に一般化した浄土形式であるのと時代を異にしている点に注意。重要文化財称名寺絵図並結界記、1323（出典：称名寺所蔵、神奈川県立金沢文庫保管）

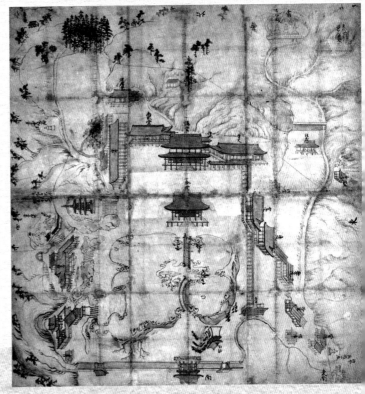

The Shōmyō-ji Ezu narabini Kekkaiki ancient temple and grounds overhead map diagram drawn in 1323, on loan from the Shōmyō-ji Temple to the Kanazawa-bunko Museum. This diagram shows the transition of garden styles between historic periods. The garden is typical of the Jōdo-style garden from the Heian period (794 - 1185) with a large pond and central island connected by symmetrically aligned arched and flat bridges, while the buildings and how they are laid out on the grounds, is typical of the Kamakura period's (1185 - 1333) Zen Buddhist Shichido Garan (lit. seven halls) arrangement.

and great-grandson. After their deaths the library survived and was maintained by the Shōmyō-ji Temple that became a seminary. The library has had assets removed and restored over time but in 1930 the place became the Central Library of Kanagawa Prefecture and in 1954 became the Kanagawa Prefectural Kanazawa-Bunko Museum specializing in historical documents and artifacts. The library continues as a valuable information center for researchers of the Japanese Middle Age and has active ties to the research community.

The site plan shows the main hall (*kondō*) dedicated to the bodhisattva Miroku, the principal deity of the temple, in the center. The pond lies in front of the main hall; the straight, horizontal bridge, island, a vermilion arch bridge and the main gate were arranged in a straight line. The lecture hall (*kōdō*) was situated on the opposite, north side of the main hall. To its left and right were the abbot's residence (*hōjō*), a pond, and the mandala hall. On the east side were a meditation hall, kitchen, and bath house. On the west side were arranged the priests' quarters, a three-story tower, Amida (Skt: Amitābha) hall, Shinto shrine, and shrine steward's quarter. This arrangement conforms to the organization of Zen temple compounds and diverges from the earlier Jōdo-style temple complexes.

4，西芳寺庭園（伝729年-749年、中興1339年：京都府京都市）

苔と池の浄土の庭・枯山水の禅境

夢窓の書『西芳遺訓（さいほういくん）』では、黄金池を中心とした浄土宗の西方寺と山畔の指東庵（しとうあん）を中心とする穢土寺（えどじ）とに2分されていた。これを夢窓国師が開基の臨済宗の寺院、西芳寺とし、永い歴史の中で無住の廃園同様になったこともあったが、現在は苔寺として有名である。洛西松尾大社（まつおたいしゃ）の南で嵐山、松尾の嶺つづきの最南端にある国指定特別名勝で、境内は北の洪隠山（こういんざん）を背に、西芳寺川に南面する。現在の寺域は約5,000坪である。

浄土的な下段、禅的な上段の2段で構成される。下段、つまり黄金池を中心とする平坦部には、かつて本堂の西来堂（さいらいどう）、礪精亭（れいせいてい）、瑠璃殿（るりでん）、池をへだてて対置する潭北亭（たんぼくてい）と湘南亭（しょうなんてい）、僧寮としての釣寂庵、環中庵、貯清寮、方丈、庫裡などの諸建築、橋亭付きの家の邀月橋（ようげつきょう）が展開していたようだが、いまは無く現在はただ苔の美しい池庭が広がるばかりだ。向上関をくぐって上る上段はまったく趣を異にする。山の頂きに縮遠亭、四十九折の小道、坐禅堂

4. Garden of the Saihō-ji Temple

(Kyoto, Kyoto Prefecture, originally founded in 729-749 and restored in 1339)

Saihō-ji, a Zen temple of the Rinzai sect founded by Musō Soseki, is known today as the Moss Temple (*Kokedera*). Located in western Kyoto, south of the Matsuo Shrine, it is at the southernmost end of a series of peaks stretching from Arashiyama to Matsuo. It has been designated a Special Place of Scenic Beauty by the Japanese government. Today, the compound, situated between Mt. Kōin to its north and Saihō-ji River to its south, is approximately 1.65 hectares in area.

The lower level of the compound is said to have been like a Jōdo-style garden centered around a pond in an intricate form, and the upper level is a dry cascade or *kare sansui* garden. The lower level of the garden was once crowded with many structures that were a collection of bridges and pavilions such as the Moon Welcoming Bridge (Yōgetsu-kyō). Walking up and through Kōjōkan gate, the upper level had a very different and contemplative atmosphere with the Shukuen-tei pavilion at the top of the hill as well as Shitō-an, a hall for Zen meditation.

The character of this upper garden of Saihō-ji is best expressed by Ryōgakutsu,

としての指東庵（しとうあん）
（後の開山堂）、その東側の
楞伽窟、上中下３段の力強い
枯山水石組が構成された。

　禅の修行者は、樹下、巌
穴、露地に住すべしといわれ
るからである。西芳寺を筆頭
に、天龍寺、永保寺、瑞泉
寺、恵林寺など、禅僧で作庭
家の夢窓疎石（むそうそせき）
（1275-1351）の庭園観は『夢
中問答集』（1344）に詳しく述
べられている。

a three-staged rock grouping
located east of the Shitō-an
meditation hall. According to
the Laṅkāvatāra Sūtra, a person
training in Zen practices needs
to live under trees, in caves or
huts, in the grass or on the bare
ground. The *kare sansui* rock
grouping on the promontory of
Mt. Kōin was composed to
suggest just such an environment. It shows the aesthetic

sensibility and mastery of garden design of
Musō Kokushi in his later life.

　Saihō-ji, or the "Moss Temple", today
is a beautiful archaeological ruin. The moss
for which this temple is known was not
part of Musō's original design however. The
moss grew profusely after periodic floods
when the monastery lacked sufficient funds
to maintain the temple grounds. The
garden grounds covered by the lush
blanket of moss then became the primary
beauty and fame of Saihō-ji today.

5，鹿苑寺金閣庭園　（1397年：京都府京都市）

貴族性と武家性、密教様と禅宗様が一体の足利義満の北山文化

室町幕府3代将軍足利義満（1358-1408）は、37歳のとき長子義持に将軍職を譲り大政大臣となるが、翌年これを辞し、出家して天山道義と号す。その居所として元の西園寺（さいおんじ）家本邸であった「北山第（きたやまてい）」を譲り受け、1397年「北山殿」を着工、翌年完成した。その中心として禅僧天山道義が住持の鹿苑院（ろくおんいん）の本堂、仏殿として「金閣」をつくった。

義満は、応永6年から亡くなるまでの10年間を北山殿に居住した。

北山第以来の池、鏡湖池（きょうこち）の北岸に建てられた金閣は、三重の舎利殿（しゃりでん）で、屋根の上の露盤に鳳凰、最上階が究竟頂（くっきょうちょう）、中が潮音洞（ちょうおんどう）、下が法水院（ほうすいいん）と名づけた。

金閣の南正面、鏡湖池の中央には、日本国を象徴する横に長く大きい葦原島豊葦原（とよあしわら）の瑞穂の国、その右手（西）には半島状の出島、葦原島と金閣の間には中国の名石、太湖石（たいこせき）で宇宙をあらわす九山八海石（くせんはっかいせき）、鶴島、亀島が浮かぶ。どの島も、金閣に向け護岸石組、マツの植栽など正面性を見せている。

池の全景は平安以来の寝殿造系の雅びを感じさせるが、葦原島正面の護岸な

5. Garden of the Golden Pavilion, Rokuon-ji Temple

(Kyoto, Kyoto Prefecture, 1397)

Yoshimitsu Ashikaga , third Ashikaga shogun, ceded his position to his son Yoshimochi and became Grand Chancellor of State. He retired from this position the following year and entered the priesthood. On land which included the former residence of the aristocratic Saion-ji family, Yoshimitsu constructed Kitayama-dono, a residential compound. Its central structure and the main hall of Rokuon-in, the Rinzai Zen temple of which he was a priest, was the Golden Pavilion (Kinkaku-ji). Yoshimitsu began construction of Kitayama-dono in 1397 and completed it the following year. He lived there from 1399 until his death ten years later.

The Golden Pavilion was built on the north shore of Kyōko (mirror) Pond, which had existed since the days of the Saionji family. The pavilion is a three-story Relic Hall (Shari-den) with an iconic golden statue of a phoenix on the roof. The top floor is called the *Kukkyō-chō* (Cupola of the Ultimate), a private space for Yoshimitsu, the middle floor is the Chōon-dō (Tower of the Sound of

どには、垂直線水平線が明快な立石や横石が禅院らしく力強い石組がなされている。北山殿は義満がすすめた対明貿易での収益もあって、北山文化の拠点となっていく。史跡名勝指定面積は28,200坪。

左：再建された金閣寺と鏡湖池　右：龍門瀑（りゅうもんばく）。ここの水分石は鯉魚石といい、鯉が滝を上り龍に成る登龍門（とうりゅうもん）の故事を伝える。写真提供、左右とも：鹿苑寺 蔵

Left: The rebuilt, gold-leaf covered Kinkaku-ji Temple (Temple of the Golden Pavilion). with the Mirror Lake Pond in front of it.
Right: Ryumonbaku Waterfall at the Kinkaku-ji Temple . It was fabled in China that carp climbed a waterfall in hopes of becoming a dragon which served as inspiration for monks to persevere in their discipline with hopes of reaching enlightenment. This waterfall is incorporated as an expression of that teaching in garden form.

Waves), and the lowest floor is the Hossui-in (Chamber of Dharma Waters).

South of the Golden Pavilion, in the center of Kyōko Pond, is a large and laterally-extended Ashiwara-jima island, symbolizing the archipelago of Japan; to its right (i.e. west) is the Dejima peninsula; between Ashi-wara-jima island and the Golden Pavilion is a *Kusenhakkaiseki* rock brought from China by Shogun Yoshimitsu. The *Kusenhakkaiseki* emulates the Buddhist cosmic view of the world symbolically expressing the sacred five-peaked Mt. Meru (*Shumisen*), the center of all the physical, metaphysical and spiritual universes. This central island is accompanied by a crane island and a tortoise island with century-old pine trees.

The pond possesses the refinement of a *shinden*-style garden of the previous Heian period. Unlike other gardens of the period, the shoreline of the islands at the Golden Pavilion are powerful and distinctive groupings of rocks, keeping with the austere tradition of a Zen temple.

6，慈照寺銀閣庭園　（1490年：京都府京都市）

茶華道東山文化へ、日本の空間文化の原形・露地とユニークな盛砂造形

慈照寺は、室町幕府の8代将軍足利義政（1436-1490）の晩年の邸宅、東山殿で、死後臨済宗相国寺塔頭として維持される。作庭は、夢窓国師の西芳寺十境にならい、「東山殿（ひがしやまどの）十境」として構想した。東山山系の月待山を前に、敷地約7,000坪を、義政の構想と善阿弥（ぜんなみ）（1386-1482）の山水河原者（せんずいかわらもの）の技で名園が完成した。

銀閣寺へのアプローチの第一段階は「銀閣寺道（ぎんかくじみち）」。道の突き当りの石畳を経て総門をくぐると、長さ約50mの高生垣の鍵形空間が中門まで続く。これこそ銀閣に向う象徴的でシンプルで力強く効果的な第二段階のアプローチ構成である。石垣を腰まで積み、その上に通称「銀閣寺垣」と呼ぶ低めの建仁寺型竹垣を通し、その上にはツバキやカシの常緑樹の高垣がより高くのる。

高垣が終わり左折すると中門で第三段階、庫裡の前庭にいたる。こうしてゴールの銀閣の庭になる。方丈と国宝東求堂（とうぐどう）（義政の持仏、阿弥陀如来像を祀るお堂）の前方にひときわ目立つ白川砂の造形は銀沙灘（ぎんさだん）と向月台（こうげつだい）である。銀沙灘の盛砂は厚く大胆な広さとボリュームを誇る。月の光を堂内に反射して灯りとしたともいわれる。また、めずらしい正円錐台形盛砂の向月台は、地上に満月を映す。

龍背橋を渡った左の「洗月泉（せんげつせん）」、月の光に中国西湖が浮かぶとされる

6. Garden of the Silver Pavilion, Jishō-ji Temple

(Kyoto, Kyoto Prefecture, 1940)

Ashikaga Yoshimasa, the eighth Ashikaga shogun of the Muromachi Period (1336-1573), made Jishō-ji temple his villa and residence in his later years. The villa is called Higashiyama-dono or present day Ginkaki-ji, the Silver Pavilion. Inspired by the Ten Views of Saihō-ji (Moss Temple), Yoshimasu created the Ten Views of Higashiyama-dono. As women were not allowed into temple gardens such as Saihō-ji, Yoshimasa wanted to re-create this famous scenery in this garden so his mother could enjoy it.

Ginkaku-ji occupies a site of 23.1 hectares near Mt. Tsukimachi in the Higashiyama mountain range, east of Kyoto. This garden includes many famous features including Ginkaku-ji Road, Ginkaku-ji (bamboo) Fence, Ginshadan, Kōgetsudai (see next page) and Ginkaku (Silver Pavilion) which form a magnificent sequence. This garden was a collaborative work by Zen'ami, a *kawaramono* of the emerging garden craftsmen under the directive of the shogun Yoshimasa.

The first stage in the approach to Ginkaku-ji Temple is Ginkakuji Road. The road ends at stone steps that lead to the first gate. Passing through it, one arrives at an L-shaped space bordered on

銀沙灘、庭をつつむ月待山、月にたとえられる銀閣と、東山は夜と月にをテーマとする。

この庭のシークエンス（移動景観）は、幾つもの結節点を設け、奥へ奥へと人々を誘う点で「奥の思想による日本の空間文化」の好例である。

また、茶華道をはじめ、東求堂の茶座敷「同仁斎（どうじんさい）」、蹲踞（つくばい）の原形「相君泉（そうくんせん）」など、後に日本の住宅文化の基本形を形成したといわれる東山文化の象徴的舞台でもある。国指定特別名勝。

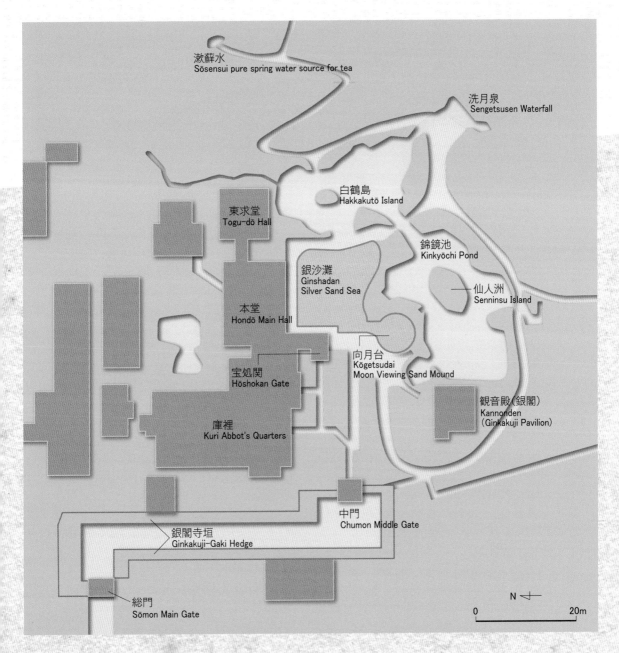

漱蘚水
Sōsensui pure spring water source for tea

洗月泉
Sengetsusen Waterfall

白鶴島
Hakkakutō Island

東求堂
Togu-dō Hall

錦鏡池
Kinkyōchi Pond

銀沙灘
Ginshadan
Silver Sand Sea

仙人洲
Senninsu Island

本堂
Hondō Main Hall

向月台
Kōgetsudai
Moon Viewing Sand Mound

宝処関
Hōshokan Gate

観音殿（銀閣）
Kannonden
(Ginkakuji Pavilion)

庫裡
Kuri Abbot's Quarters

中門
Chumon Middle Gate

銀閣寺垣
Ginkakuji-Gaki Hedge

総門
Sōmon Main Gate

N

0　　　　　　20m

左：銀閣寺名物の袈裟（けさ）型手水鉢　右：白川砂の盛砂による銀沙灘（ぎんしゃだん）と向月台（こうげつだい）。中国の西湖ともいわれる。

Left: Gingaku-ji Temple's *kesa-gata* (monk robe pattern shaped) *chozubachi* purification basin.
Right: The Ginshadan striped gravel bed and Kōgetsu-dai conical shaped mound made from Shirakawa white granite gravel, which are said to emulate the scenery of West Lake in China.

both sides by a high fence - this is the second stage in the symbolic approach to Ginkaku (Silver Pavilion). The approach is structured in a simple and effective way. A stone wall rises to waist level; above it is a low bamboo fence that is commonly referred to as a Ginkakuji fence (Ginkakuji-gaki); and rising up from behind and over that is a tall hedge of evergreen (camellia and evergreen oak) trees.

At the end of the high hedge, one turns left and arrives at the second gate, that is the third stage of the approach, and enters into the front yard of the *kuri* or the abbot's quarters. One then proceeds to the destination of the sequence: the garden of the Silver Pavilion. The most conspicuous features of the garden are Ginshadan and Kōgetsu-dai. These are molded forms of Shirakawa white granite gravel, which are widely used in gardens of Kyoto, but these are unique for their large scale, volume and boldness. Ginshadan is a striped pattern on the ground created by raised and flattened lines of the gravel and Kōgetsu-dai is a

perfect conical shape made of the same material. Perhaps because they are made of natural gravel, the striped patterns and conical mound, though obviously man-made and geometric, do not seem out of place in the Japanese garden. One exits the garden, impressed by the graceful contours of Mt. Tsukimachi-yama (Moon Waiting Mountain) which rises up to form the background of the garden while the loveliness of a red pine backdrop encompasses the entire garden. This garden is one of the best-known examples of Japanese garden view-sequencing.

Ginkaku-ji is an outstanding example of the aesthetic traditions of Japanese architecture and garden design, often referred to as the Higashiyama Culture. The *zashiki* (tatami mat sitting parlor) in the complex's Tōgū-dō Hall where tea was served, became a prototype for tea ceremony houses. The Sōkunsen spring for the *tsukubai*, the water basin at which guests ritually cleanse themselves before a tea ceremony, also served as another significant prototype.

深山幽谷から大河、そして大海へ、写景式枯山水の代表的庭園

大仙院は、室町期1513年大聖国師古岳宗亘（こがくそうこう）（1465-1548）が開創の大徳寺でも主要な塔頭（たっちゅう）である。

大仙院庭園は、国指定、史跡特別名勝の庭園で、面積約200坪。方丈（ほうじょう）と南庭東南隅には、国宝建築、廊下形式の「玄関」がある。

南庭は、西南角に1本の沙羅双樹（さらそうじゅ）が植わるだけの白川砂敷平庭である。平庭の南と西側は2重2段の刈込み生垣で、築地塀との間の植栽背景とをやさしく区切る。方丈建築の東側、庫裡（くり）との間から方丈裏にかけた鍵形空間が、大仙院の主景、枯山水（東庭）である。

東庭の左中心に観音石、不動石と名づけられた大きな立石を組んで深山とし、その奥から枯滝を3段に落とし、手前には自然石の橋が架かる。立石組の背後にはツバキの大刈込が遠山を形づくる。前の2石以外にも姿形に秀でた石が配石されている。ほとんどは阿波の青石で、一石一石に名がつけられた銘石である。

7. Garden of the Daisen-in, Daitoku-ji Temple

(Kyoto, Kyoto Prefecture, 1509 AD)

Daisen-in is a prominent sub-temple within the Daitoku-ji temple complex, which was founded in 1513 by Kogaku Sōkō, a Japanese Rinzai Zen priest and poet. The total area of the Daisen-in garden is approximately 660 ㎡.

In the southeastern corner between the *hōjō* priest living and meditation quarters and the south garden is a *rōka*-style *genkan* entrance hall, which is the oldest extant *genkan* in Japan and has thus been designated a National Treasure.

The south garden facing the *hōjō*, is a spacious garden covered in Shirakawa gravel with a single tree (Stewartia japonica) in the southwestern corner. On the south and west sides of this garden are double-layered, double-tiered pruned hedges, that separate the space from the line of background trees which stand in front of permimeter clay wall. The *kare sansui* (east garden) of Daisen-in is in an L-shaped space on the east side of the *hōjō* and extends between the *hōjō* and the kitchen (*kuri*) to the rear of the *hōjō*.

Two large upright rocks at the left center of the east garden are referred to as the Kannon (Buddha of compassion) and Fudō (cosmic Buddha). The stones are arranged to represent a distant mountain scenery. From the crevasse between the two rocks, a dry waterfall cascades in three stages

滝から流れ出た水は、石橋をくぐり、7寸の高さの堰を落ち、1段下の大河に出る。なお堰の真上には、後、渡廊橋が架けられていた絵が見つかり、これをもとに現在は廊橋が復元されている。ここには釣船石、霊亀石、宝山石があり、宝船も亀も具象的で誰にもわかる。この東庭の大河が、いよいよ南庭の大海に向かうのである。

大仙院の庭は、造景が明快である。深山幽谷から堰、大河、海へと砂紋の波形は水がいかにも流れているかのようにイメージさせていてわかりやすい。具体的でよくわかる写景式枯山水の典型。禅味に欠け、古岳作庭とは考えにくく、桃山期の四条流、山水河原者の作との久恒秀治の説もある。

大仙院東庭の枯山水。枯滝石組で遠山を表現し、手前には深い渓谷から流れ出た水の上に橋がかかり、橋の手前の3つの石からは、水しぶきさえ感じられる。 写真提供：大徳寺大仙院

The dry waterfall in the east *kare sansui* garden of the sub-temple Daisen-in at Daitoku-ji Temple. The camellia hedge behind this rock arrangement suggests a distant mountain while the three rocks in front of the stone bridge over the dry stream emulate the boils of rapids in the river. Photo credit: Daisen-in, Daitokuji Temple

with a bridge of natural rock in the foreground. A large camellia hedge behind the upright rock grouping suggests a distant mountain.

Other superbly shaped rocks are arranged in the garden as well. Most are green stones from the island strait of the Awa region between eastern Shikoku and Honshu and each rock is of such excellence that it has its own unique name.

The dry cascade suggests water passing under the stone bridge and flowing into a dry stream bed. Here are arranged three impressive feature rocks named *tsuri-bune-seki* (fishing boat rock), *reiki-seki* (spirit-tortoise rock) and *houzan-sek*i (treasure mountain rock). The imagery of the boat and tortoise is quite realistic and easy to identify. The large river of the east garden finally reaches the (dry) "ocean" of the south garden.

Sacred scenes are clearly expressed in the garden of Daisen-in. The raked patterns on the gravel show the flow of water from the deep mountains, to the river, then into the ocean. This is a representational work of *kare sansui* at its best.

8，桂離宮庭園 （桂御所、1615年：京都府京都市西京区）

かつらのごしょ

洪水対策と観月の「用と景」が調和した、遠州好みの回遊式庭園の初まり

　平安貴族が花見や月見に遊んだ桂川西岸、下桂の里は、藤原道長の山荘桂殿もあった郊外の別業地帯で、古来"月の桂"というように"月の名所"であった。

　桂山荘の創建者は、後陽成天皇の弟で一時、豊臣秀吉の猶子（ゆうし）になったこともある八条宮智仁（はちじょうのみやとしひと）親王（1579-1629）であり、その子智忠（としただ）親王（1619-1663）との2代40ヵ年にわたり、総面積5.8ヘクタール（農地0.7ヘクタール、表門緑地0.4ヘクタールを含む）の日本初の本格的回遊式庭園を創出した。2代は

共に、武家政権の幕府と対比的な王朝文化への憧れをもち、皇族ならではの幅広い教養人として俗を離れ風流と美の世界を求めて、茶の湯（露地）の空間化を大成しようとした人物であった。

　智仁親王は中国、白氏文集の「池亭記」に作庭の心を知り、また同年生まれの小堀遠州とも深い関係があったこともあり、空間構成から、書院と庭、茶亭と露地の関係性、直線や斜めの意匠にいたるまで、桂の御所にはいわゆる「遠州好み」が展開されている。

　舟運や舟遊びに好適の桂川だが度々

8. Katsura Detached Palace Garden

(Katsura-Misono, Nishikyō Ward, Kyoto Prefecture, 1615)

The Shimokatsura region on the west bank of the Katsura River in Kyoto was a place where Heian period aristocrats engaged in cherry blossom and moon viewing. An outlying area of villas, which included at one time, the Katsura villa of Fujiwara Michinaga (966-1028), has been famous since ancient times for the views it afforded of the moon.

　The Katsura Detached Palace was first built by Prince Toshihito (1579-1629) of the Hachijō family, the younger brother of Emperor Go-Yōzei and who was at one time, the adopted son of

Toyotomi Hideyoshi (Japanese samurai and *daimyō* of the late Sengoku period regarded as the second "Great Unifier" of Japan). Over a period of approximately 40 years, Prince Toshihito and his son, Prince Noritada (1619-1663), created on a site of 5.8 hectare, the first full-scale *kaiyū*-style (circuitous strolling) garden.

　Both father and son cherished the aristocratic culture of the Heian period as opposed to the culture of Samurai warriors. The cultivated members of the imperial family with wide-ranging

氾濫することもあり、庭園の周囲を竹林で囲ったり、桂川沿いには桂垣とも呼ばれる笹垣（ささがき）（生きた竹を逆V字に折り曲げて穂先を美しく編み込んだめずらしい生垣）を250メートルにわたり設け洪水防止（用）に意を用いながら、アプローチ道路の美と品格（景）を演出している。また洪水に備え高床式（水屋形式）を工夫して実用性（用）を発揮しながら、それゆえに白壁と柱のコントラスト、書院建築の立面のプロポーションに独自の美（景）を与えている。

一方、月の名所・桂らしく観月と日照通風を考慮して古書院・中書院・新御殿の書院群が北東から南西に向かって19度の角度で後ずさりする雁行型配置にするとか、池に映る月を賞でるために月波楼の地盤を高くしたり、竹の縁の月見台を前面に張り出すなど工夫している。

敷地の過半を占める池水面は、それぞれの茶亭に食事を運ぶ舟の通路ともなり、賞花亭のような高所からの眺望もあれば、土橋の下をくぐりながら水面近くから変化に富んだシークエンスを楽しむ見えがくれの景を演出してもいる。「用と景」の両面が完璧なバランスある点でも日本の代表的名園といえる。

tastes, in the pursuit of elegance and beauty, sought to realize *chanoyu*, the way of tea, in a large-scale landscape.

Prince Toshihito became acquainted with the essence of and passion for garden design through classic literature of the Herian Period. Further influence came from his close relationship with Enshū Kobori, the tea master, connoisseur, and artist, who was born in the same year as the prince. There are various aspects of the Katsura Detached Palace: the spatial composition and relationship between the *shoin* architecture and gardens; between the teahouse and the tea garden (*roji*); and the prolific use of straight and diagonal lines in the design, that reflect Enshū's taste.

Although the Katsura River is suitable for boat transportation and recreational boating, it is also subject to flooding. The garden is surrounded by groves of bamboo and has a unique 250m-long bamboo hedge along the east side facing the river. Known as the Katsura hedge, it consists of living henon bamboo stalks which have been bent into upside-down V's and whose tips have been woven together to form a fence-like hedge. This unique bamboo hedge was created along the Katsura River to protect the palace from floods, and it provides a beautiful and elegant approach to the palace entrance. The *shoin* buildings are constructed in the raised floor *mizuya*-style in anticipation of flooding. While this is a practical architectural feature, the contrast between the white stucco walls and the slender posts, and the proportion of the building's elevations, form the distinctive beauty of the Katsura Detached Palace.

To facilitate the viewing of the moon as well as to allow in more daylight and ventilation, the Old Shoin, Middle Shoin and the New Palace are staggered in a layout called *ganko* or *"flying geese"* pattern, from the

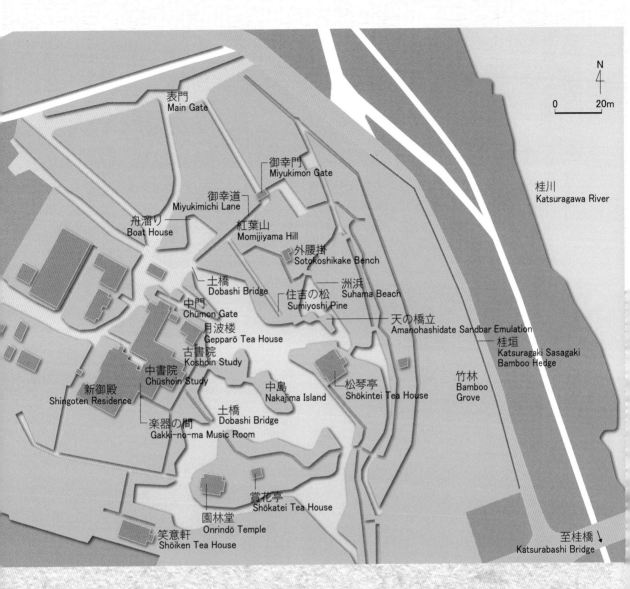

表門
Main Gate

御幸門
Miyukimon Gate

御幸道
Miyukimichi Lane

舟溜り
Boat House

紅葉山
Momijiyama Hill

外腰掛
Sotokoshikake Bench

土橋
Dobashi Bridge

住吉の松
Sumiyoshi Pine

洲浜
Suhama Beach

中門
Chūmon Gate

天の橋立
Amanohashidate Sandbar Emulation

月波楼
Gepparō Tea House

桂垣
Katsuragaki Sasagaki
Bamboo Hedge

古書院
Koshoin Study

竹林
Bamboo
Grove

中書院
Chūshoin Study

中島
Nakajima Island

松琴亭
Shōkintei Tea House

新御殿
Shingoten Residence

土橋
Dobashi Bridge

楽器の間
Gakki-no-ma Music Room

賞花亭
Shōkatei Tea House

園林堂
Onrindō Temple

笑意軒
Shōiken Tea House

桂川
Katsuragawa River

N

0   20m

至桂橋↘
Katsurabashi Bridge

northeast to the southwest. The foundation of the pavilion known as the Geppa-rō Pavillion teahouse is elevated so that the reflection of the moon on the pond can be better appreciated. The moon viewing platform, made from bamboo, extends out from the Old Shoin building.

The pond, which occupies over half the site, provides access for boats carrying meals to the various pavilions and creates an intriguing sequence of ever-changing scenery: views afforded from high places such as Shōka-tei contrasted by views from various locations closer to the water such as the passage beneath an earthen bridge. The Katsura Detached Palace demonstrates a perfect balance of utility and scenic beauty and it is a true representative garden of Japan.

135

笹垣（桂川堤上の外観）

Sasa-gaki (Japanese *sasa* broadleaf bamboo) style hedge-fence viewed from the Katsura River embankment side.

竹垣（表門付近）

Take-gaki style fence which features large bamboo posts with matted, horizontal, small diameter bamboo infill between the posts, as seen from near the front gate.

御幸門

The Miyuki-mon Gate featuring posts made of *abemaki* cork-tree rounds and a reed thatched roof.

御殿玄関前の広場修景・織部灯籠と苔

Entrance to and landscaping in front of the Goten villa with the Oribe-*dōrō* stone lantern and moss scenery in the left foreground.

御幸道（真黒石を敷詰めた園路、霰こぼし）

The Miyukimichi Path is a path paved using small black stones. This stone laying pattern is reminiscent of scattered hailstones and is thus called *ararekoboshi* or "scattered hailstones".

住吉の松　池への眺望、アイストップ

The Sumiyoshi Pine Tree acts as a focal point as well as a screen that blocks the view of the pond.

茅葺門とクロモジ垣

Kuromoji spice bush hedge and the thatched roof covered, *chumon* middle-gate.

御輿寄せに向かって切石を打った真の飛び石

Shin-no-tobi-ishi stepping stones laid in *nobedan* style (characterized by long, rectangular milled stones laid in a straight edged pattern), orientated directly towards the *mikoshi-yose* stone in front of the entrance. *Mikoshi-yose* literally means the stone where the divine palanquin or hand carried litter, in this case for the Emperor, is boarded or disembarked from.

舟溜りと舟屋（舟遊、食事運搬用の舟の収納）

Boat house which stored watercraft used for pond-touring boats and for boats used to transport food by water to the teahouses surrounding the pond.

御殿（手前から古書院、中書院、新御殿へと雁行に配される）

The Goten complex of *shoin* palaces, including the Ko-shoin (Old Shoin Palace), Chu-shoin (Middle Shoin Palace) and Shin-goten (New Palace) of the Katsura Imperial Villa are laid out in a flying geese, staggered pattern.

月波楼（池に映る月を賞でるため石垣で高くしている）

The Geppa-rō Pavillion is a teahouse which sits on an elevated stone-walled site beside the pond which gives it a perfect vantage point for observing the reflection of the moon in the water.

石垣上の月波楼（池面に映る月を見る）

The Geppa-rō Pavilion from which visitors viewed the moon and its reflection in the pond.

松琴亭に到る外腰掛の蘇鉄山（ソテツヤマ）

Cycad Mountain on the way to the Shokin-tei teahouse which was traditionally used for tea ceremonies.

外腰掛、二重桝形手水鉢と石灯籠

Old purification basin emulating one *masu* sake drinking box / rice measuring cup stacked inside another, and a stone lantern in the Soto-koshikake arbor bench in the waiting area outside Shokin-tei pavillion where tea ceremonies were held.

大池泉への給水口だが約10cmの落差の小さな水音を「鼓の滝(ツヅミノタキ)」と名づける妙技

10 cm high waterfall at the inlet of the large pond, designed to create the Tsuzumi-no-taki soundscape which references the sound made by *tsuzumi*, traditional hourglass-shaped hand drums.

月見台（古書院から丸竹床が張り出される）

The Tsukimi-dai moon-viewing veranda attached to the Kosho-in has a deck floor made of round stock bamboo.

月波楼前庭の月型手水鉢

The moon-shaped *chozubachi* purification basin in front of the Geppa-rō Pavilion.

日本三景の一、天橋立の縮景と茶室・松琴亭

A *shukkei* emulation of what is considered one of the three most scenic spots in Japan, Amanohashidate Sandbar and the Shokin-tei Teahouse.

139

桂の岬灯籠（本歌）

A uniquely designed Misaki-*tōrō* (or cape-style) stone lantern

松琴亭への石橋

Slabbed stone bridge to the prestigious Shokin-tei Teahouse

峠の茶屋ふうの賞花亭は園内外への展望地点

The Shoka-tei Teahouse located on the highest point in the garden offering views within and outside the garden

左：賞花亭の額と土壁と天井 **中**：賞花亭木舞の袖壁 **右**：小石散らしのたたきペーブメントは近景と足元を楽しませる

Left: "Shoka-tei" in a wooden frame atop a clay plastered earthen wall and the beautiful underside of the teahouse's thatched roof **Middle**: A *komai* bamboo latticed partition wall at the Shoka-tei Teahouse **Right**: A close up of the *koishi-chirashi* (scattered small stones) compacted earth and lime floor, a delight to the feet.

左から、松琴亭軒内の飛び石、茅葺屋根、室内の市松模様の床の間とふすま

From left to right: *Tobi-ishi* stepping stones at the Shoka-tei Teahouse, its thatched roof underside, and the *fusuma* sliding interior door and *tokonoma* alcove decorated in *ichimatsu moyo* (Indigo and white checkered pattern)

賞花亭から京都の名山、比叡山方面への遠望

The famous Mt. Hiei of Kyoto visible in the background as seen from the Shoka-tei Teahouse

左：園林堂（おんりんどう／えんりんどう）への大胆な飛石 **右**：園林堂の額

Left: The bold pattern *tobi-ishi* stepping stone pattern leading up to the Onrin-do family ancestral memorial hall. **Right**: "Orin-do" in a decorative wooden frame

上左：雪見灯籠と笑意軒の全景　上右：笑意軒の額（笑：わらうの意の文字、ひとが笑っているように見える）と丸壁

Top left: A *yukimi-dōrō* (snow viewing lantern) with the Shoi-ken Teahouse in the background

Top right: "Shoi-ken" in a decorative frame, and six round windows with intricate bamboo and wood lattice with rice paper backing in an earthen plastered wall in the interior of the teahouse. The third character in the name Shoi-ken is "laugh". The calligraphic character for laugh in this sign is thought by many to literally look like the embodiment of "laugh".

左：笑意軒への飛び石。桂御所の飛石は、歩きやすく美しいので有名である

Left: Tobi-ishi stepping stones leading up to the Shoi-ken Teahouse. The stepping stones at the Katsura Imperial Palace are renowned to be both beautiful and delightfully easy to walk on.

142

9，修学院離宮庭園 （1655年－1659年：京都府京都市）

天皇（上皇）自らが立地選定、造園構想、模型による検討までして完成した雄大な借景庭園

　桂離宮は後陽成天皇の弟、八条宮智仁（としひと）親王の構想であるが、修学院離宮は後陽成天皇の第三皇子で後の後水尾天皇(後、上皇、法皇、1596-1680)によるもので、立地選定、数度にわたる実地踏査を、さらには模型制作までを自ら試みられ、上皇60歳で工事に着手、3年後の1659年に完成した日本を代表する雄大な自然風景式の名園である。又、天皇自身が構想を立てられそれを実現した造園としてもめずらしい。

　徳川幕府の干渉に反発して退位した後水尾上皇は、京都御所から東北に6km離れた比叡山の西南麓、音羽川がつくった扇状丘陵地に俗塵を離れて隠棲すべく総面積54.6ヘクタール(約165,000坪)の「雄大な眺めのある田園の中の幽邃境」の実現にこだわったのであった。

　京の都から離宮の入口に当るのが傾斜地の麓の「下の御茶屋」。上皇の御座所、寿月観(じゅげつかん)がある。

　海抜150mの高台には隣雲亭(りんうんてい)と洗詩台(せんしだい)、音羽川の水を落した雄滝の水を湛えた浴龍池、その中島に

9. Shūgaku-in Detached Palace Garden

(Sakyō Ward, Kyoto, 1655 -1659)

The Shūgaku-in Detached Palace was created by Emperor Go-Mizunoo (1596-1680) who abdicated and subsequently joined a Buddhist order. It is a magnificent garden in the natural landscape style and one of the best-known gardens of Japan. Go-Mizunoo was the third son of Emperor Go-Yōzei, whose younger brother, Prince Toshihito of the Hachijō no Miya family, conceived the Katsura Detached Palace. Go-Mizunoo himself selected the site, made a number of surveys and even created a model to study the design and construction of the Shūgaku-in Detached Palace. The retired emperor at age sixty began its construction and work was completed three years later in 1659. It is a rare example of a garden conceived and realized by an emperor.

　Go-Mizunoo, who had abdicated in response to interference by the Tokugawa shogunate, chose a hill site of 54.6 hectares on an alluvial fan of the Otowa River at the southwestern foot of Mt. Hiei. There he realized a place of seclusion with magnificent *shakkei* (borrowed scenery) that enabled him to lead a life in the country. The Shūgaku-in Detached Palace is characterized by its organization into three zones: the Upper; Middle; and Lower Gardens with each centered on a teahouse and their gardens. A path lined with pine

The three gardens are linked by two straight allées, each about 100 meters in length, lined by plantings of pine trees, that run through the surrounding rice fields and offer views of both the fields and the nearby mountains.

The opposite page top: The Upper Garden - The Yokuryū-chi Pond which was created by means of an earthen dam supported by a laid rock wall (**upper left**) which is hidden from view by the famous, rounded Okarikomi hedge comprised of tens of different tree varieties, 200m long and 15m in height, as well as a series of squared hedges below it. (**upper right**).

Opposite page middle: The Middle Garden - The garden as seen from the Rakushi-ken Pavilion. With the overhanging vegetation and unclear shoreline, the water looks deep and expansive in spite of its small size and contains a Hōrai-san-themed rock island.

The opposite page bottom: The Lower Garden - The Jugestsu-kan Pavilion (**bottom left**) and its approach path nestled into deep moss traversing Naka-jima island (**bottom right**).

は窮邃亭(きゅうすいてい)。浴龍池(よくりゅうち)では舟遊びもでき広々とした水景が演出され、堰堤(えんてい)の法面(のりめん)は石垣積だが、常緑樹33種、落葉樹36種を混植した大刈込(おおかりこみ)で修景した他に例をみない独特の風景を創出。それら全体を「上の御茶屋」と呼ぶ。

　その前面の傾斜地には離宮総面積の14%に当る棚田がつくられ修学院独自の「農」の風景が展開する。

　上と下の中間の位置に、上皇の第8皇女、光子内親王のための「楽只軒(らくしけん)」、後、出家され林丘寺の開山となるが、明治時代に宮内省に移管されてからは「中の御茶屋」と呼ばれている。

　修学院離宮庭園の特色は、上・中・下の3つの御茶屋を中心とした特徴的な庭園ゾーン(総面積の16%)を中核としていること、それぞれは棚田の中の松の並木道でつながっていること、その全体を樹林地(総面積の70%)が包んでいる雄大な借景を味わえる田園風景式造園である。

trees that cuts through the rice paddies and joins these three gardens.

At the base of the hill is the Lower Garden area with the emperor's villa, Jugetsu-kan. On a rise 150m above sea level are the Rin'un-tei (reaching clouds) Pavilion and below is the man-made Yokuryū-chi (wading dragon) Pond fed by a waterfall drawn from the nearby Otowa River. Yokury-ūchi Pond is large and can accommodate boating and provides for a spacious waterscape in the garden. The face of the dam holding the pond water consists of terraced stone walls densely planted with over thirty varieties of evergreen and decid-uous trees that are pruned to create a distinctive "hedge" at a massive scale. Terraced rice paddies below and in the foreground of the pond exemplify Shūgaku-in's unique "agrarian landscape" theme. This entire area is referred to as the Upper Garden.

Located between the Upper and Lower Gardens is the Rakushi-ken Teahouse, built for Princess Mitsuko, the eighth daughter of the retired emperor, who later joined a Buddhist order and founded Rinkyū-ji Temple. After half of the temple was moved to its current site from a site in Nara by the Imperial Household Ministry in the Meiji period (1885), the area has been referred to as the Middle Garden.

洛北の山を背に、前面に棚田や農地が広がる斜面に立地する開放的な田園的な環境を敷地とする風景式庭園。
上の御茶屋、中の御茶屋、下の御茶屋の3つの庭園ゾーンは、すべて樹林と水田と松並木でつながっている

上：上の御茶屋。石垣（石積み）と土堤で築いたダムで造られた浴龍池(上左)と、その石垣を隠す生垣とその上部の土堤に数十種類の樹木を混植した大刈込は、高さ15m、幅200m(**上右**)。そのスケールは雄大で修学院の独自性を表す。

中：中の御茶屋。楽只軒(らくしけん)の二の間からのぞく前庭。水面が深くくぼんでいるので小池が宇宙に見え、小さい岩島は蓬莱山に見まがう。

下：下の御茶屋。寿月観(**下左**)と寿月観に向かう中島の苔につつまれる園路(**下右**)

（2）大名の回遊式庭園

II. Daimyō Kaiyū-Style Gardens (Circuitous Strolling Gardens)

10，二条城二の丸庭園 （1626年：京都府京都市）

**壮大な御殿建築に匹敵する豪快な桃山時代風石組と
京にめずらしい南国のソテツによる蓬莱世界**

二条城は、慶長8年（1603年）に徳川家康が創建し、2代将軍秀忠が天守、矢倉などの造営に着手。二の丸庭園は、3代将軍家光が作事奉行（さくじぶぎょう）を小堀遠州（1579-1647)に命じ、1624年から3年かけて本格整備した。秀忠、家光が後水尾天皇の御幸を仰ぐためで、その当時の二の丸庭園が「寛永御幸御城内図」に描かれている。

二条城二の丸御殿が歴史の表舞台に再び登場するのは、15代将軍慶喜の「大政奉還」のとき。明治維新、1884年からは皇室別邸となり宮内省所管の二条離宮となり、1939年、宮内省から京都市に下賜、翌年「恩賜元離宮二条城」として市民に公開された。二の丸庭園の林泉部分の面積は1,400坪、国指定特別名勝である。

江戸初期の桃山風の豪快で大胆な石組の蓬莱世界が特色。深く掘り込まれた池泉には、立派な松が植えられた大きな蓬莱島が築かれ、その両側には典型的な羽石のある鶴島、亀頭石のある亀島が配され、右手奥には滝口、その手前には京都ではめずらしいソテツが植わる。

吉祥を願う意匠は単純明快であり、庭

10. Ninomaru Garden, Nijō Castle

(Kyoto, Kyoto Prefecture, 1626)

Tokugawa Ieyasu constructed Nijō Castle in 1603, and Hidetada, the second shogun, began construction of the inner tower. His successor, the third shogun, Tokugawa Iemitsu, Nijo Castle undertook significant renovations to accommodate the royal visit of Emperor Go-Mizunoo. The creation of a garden for the Ninomaru (the secondary enclosure) was carried out by Iemitsu and Enshū, Kobori, the shogunate samurai administrator in charge of construction.

Ninomaru construction began in 1624 and took three years to complete.

Nijō Castle, the Kyoto residence of the Tokugawa Shogun, took center stage later in history when the shogun issued the statement known as Taisei Hōkan (the Return of Political Rule to the Emperor) in 1867, marking the end of the shogunate. In 1939, the castle was donated by the Imperial Household Ministry to the city of Kyoto and renamed the "Former Detached Palace Nijō Castle."

石は派手な青石で、大振りの立石が目立つ。将軍家の威光をダイレクトに表出する庭園構成だ。

作庭は遠州配下の河原者・賢庭（けんてい）とされている。大きな石や三尊石など立石を多用、池を深くし、姿形を整えた大景観木を多用しているからこそ、大規模な御殿建築と対抗して、一歩も退かない力強さを持ち得ている。

なお二条城には、「二の丸庭園」のほか、明治半ばにつくられた芝生が広がる「本丸庭園」、また1965年完成の「清流園」がある。

二条城の鶴島、亀島　Crane and Tortoise Island pair

The lawn-covered Hommaru Garden (the garden of the main enclosure) was created in the middle of the Meiji period, and the Seiryū-en Garden, a facility for receiving official guests to the city, was created in 1965 also within Nijō Castle.

A bold rock grouping created in the early Edo period in the Momoyama-style, represented the world of Hōrai, an island in Chinese mythology inhabited by immortals. The large Hōrai island, planted with magnificent pine trees and built in a deep pond, is flanked by a pair of Crane and Tortoise Islands. Toward the rear, on the right side of Hōrai Island is a waterfall, and in front of it is a cycad (Cycas revoluta), an unusual choice of plant in this temperate region of Japan. The design, intended to symbolize good fortune, is simple and clear. The garden rocks, including large ostentatious green stones, the depth of the pond, and the use of large specimen trees, enable the garden to be congruent with the scale of the enormous palace building and the bold garden design symbolizes the authoritative power of the shogun.

11， 小石川後楽園　（1629年：東京都文京区）

「先憂後楽（せんゆうこうらく）」の儒教精神を表出、日本と中国の名所を写す

　徳川御三家の一つ水戸家の江戸屋敷（当初、88,000坪）で、書院（内庭）とともに、1920年復元された唐門（からもん）を結界として営まれた回遊式テーマパーク（現在残っている庭園面積は約20,000坪）で、江戸初期の代表的大名庭園である。

　水戸家初代頼房（よりふさ）（1603-1661）は3代将軍家光のアドバイスを受け、作庭家の徳大寺左兵衛に指図して造園を開始、2代光圀（みつくに）のとき完成した。造園の方針は「庭はつとめて自然のままとし、古木をきらず、凹凸の地形にまかせて山水を配置する。伊豆の山々から奇異なる大石をとりよせ、是をもつて荘厳に取りまとめる」であった。

　樹齢数百年の高木が生い茂っていた小石川台地が敷地で、その前方の沼を改良、家光の許可により小日向上水（こびなたじょうすい）を引いて大泉水をつくった。大泉水の中央には、徳大寺石と呼ぶ守護石（しゅごせき）が立てられ、弁財天祠がある中の島（蓬莱島）がつくられた。回遊式という庭園形式は、大泉水の周囲に多彩な景色や施設を配置し、これを経めぐり歩きながら景観変化を楽しむように工夫した形式である。

　園内には、大泉水周りに展開する"海の景"、通天橋から西湖にいたる"川の景"、小廬山（ルシャン）から円月橋（えんげつきょう）にいたる"山の景"、水田や菖蒲園などの"田園の景"など多彩な風景がつくられる。京都嵐山の大堰川と渡月橋、富士山麓の白糸滝、信州の木曽路などは日本の名所であり、廬山、西湖堤は中国の名所である。庭園建築には、儒教精神を表現する、涵徳亭（かんとくてい）、得仁堂（とくにんどう）がある。

11. Koishikawa Kōraku-en Garden
(Bunkyō District, Tokyo, 1629)

The Koishikawa Kōraku-en Garden was created in the northern Tokyo Koishikawa Plateau, at the former estate (originally 29 hectares in area) of the Mito clan, one of the three cadet branches of the Tokugawa family. This was the first garden laid out in the *kaiyū* or stroll style in Edo, in today's Tokyo. The surviving Kōraku-en is now reduced to approximately to 6.6 hectares.

With advice from the third Shogun Iemitsu, the founding head of the Mito clan, Yorifusa (1603-61) gave an order to the garden designer Tokudaiji Sahei to begin construction. The garden was completed by Mitsukuni, the second *daimyō* of Mito. The idea was "to keep the garden natural, retain old trees, and arrange the landscape using the undulations of the topography. Large, distinctive rocks were to be sent from the mountains (in the distant region) of Izu and arranged in an impressive manner."

In the forested site with centuries-old trees, water was drawn from the nearby Kobinata public aqueduct to expand a small existing pond and create a lake with the tress of the Koishikawa Plateau as a backdrop. Within this lake called, Daisensui Pond, a guardian stone was erected and an island of the immortals, or Hōrai-jima, created that was home to a building enshrining Benzaiten (Saraswati - the goddess of knowledge and learning).

大泉水から南に流れる竜田川は紅葉の名所を、西には古くからの松が残され近江八景の"唐崎の松"も写されている。北のほうには"松原"が広がり薫葺きの茶屋（九八屋）、

その他亭（丸屋）が点景となる。

小石川台地の自然地形の上に、儒教精神と日中の名所を縮景した大名の格式を感じさせるテーマパークといえる。

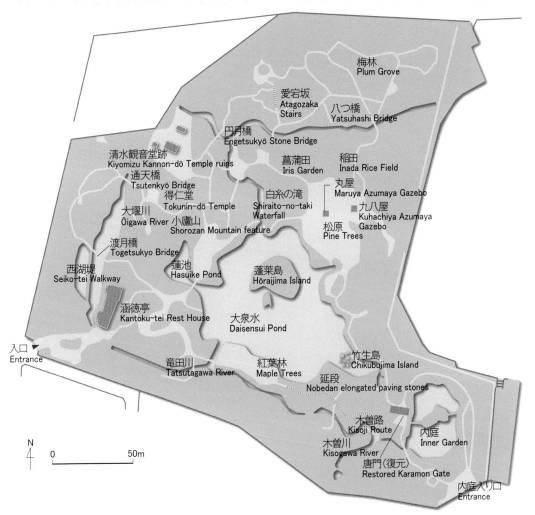

梅林
Plum Grove

愛宕坂
Atagozaka Stairs

八つ橋
Yatsuhashi Bridge

円月橋
Engetsukyō Stone Bridge

清水観音堂跡
Kiyomizu Kannon-dō Temple ruins

菖蒲田
Iris Garden

稲田
Inada Rice Field

通天橋
Tsutenkyō Bridge

得仁堂
Tokunin-dō Temple

白糸の滝
Shiraito-no-taki Waterfall

丸屋
Maruya Azumaya Gazebo

大堰川
Ōigawa River

小廬山
Shorozan Mountain feature

九八屋
Kuhachiya Azumaya Gazebo

松原
Pine Trees

渡月橋
Togetsukyo Bridge

蓮池
Hasuike Pond

蓬莱島
Hōraijima Island

西湖堤
Seiko-tei Walkway

涵徳亭
Kantoku-tei Rest House

大泉水
Daisensui Pond

入口
Entrance

竜田川
Tatsutagawa River

紅葉林
Maple Trees

竹生島
Chikubujima Island

延段
Nobedan elongated paving stones

木曽路
Kisoji Route

内庭
Inner Garden

木曽川
Kisogawa River

唐門（復元）
Restored Karamon Gate

内庭入り口
Entrance

N

0   50m

Within the garden, numerous celebrated natural scenes and landscapes in Japan and famous sites in China are referenced. Structures within the garden are designed and arranged formally to express the Confucian spirit and wisdom. Japanese maple trees were planted for fall color along the Tatsuta River flowing out from the Daisensui pond, and pine trees were retained on the west side of the garden to suggest Karasaki, one of the so-called Eight Views of Ōmi (Lake Biwa). The result is a complex and sophisticated "theme park" in which touches of history and philosophy have been added to the natural beauty and topography of the Koishikawa Plateau.

2020年に復原した唐門（写真左、右とも、撮影：菊池正芳）
The Karamon Gate rebuilt in 2020 (**left and right** - Photo credit: Masayoshi Kikuchi)

木曽路山中の山道（写真提供：菊池正芳）
Emulation of the famous Kisoji Road in the mountains of Nagano Prefecture. Photo credit: Masayoshi Kikuchi

竜田川と紅葉林（写真提供：菊池正芳）
Emulation of the famous Tatsuta River in fall colors. Photo credit: Masayoshi Kikuchi

涵徳亭前の園地にある陰陽石。陰石（**左**）と陽石（**右**）
Yin/female (left) and Yang/male (right) stone arrangement in the garden in front of the Kantoku-tei Teahouse

白糸の滝の写し
Emulation of the famously beautiful Shiraito Falls (lit. "white thread" falls) in the foothills of Mt. Fuji

屏風岩
The Byobu folding screen rock

中国杭州の西湖堤（せいこつつみ）の写し
Emulation of the famous West Lake Causeways in Hangzhou, China

通天橋の朱橋（京都、東福寺通天橋の写し）
Emulation of the famous vermilion Tsūten-kyō bridge at the Tōfuku-ji Temple in Kyoto

朱舜水設計の円月橋
The Moon Bridge, designed by the famous Chinese Confucius scholar and political refugee from the Ming Dynasty, Zhu Zhiyu, who contributed heavily to Japanese education and intellectual history while in Tokugawa in the 1600's.

大泉水と蓬莱島
Daisensui Pond and Hōrai-jima Island

151

富士山を写景的に縮景、阿蘇山の伏流水を生かした立体絵画的大名庭園

阿蘇山の伏流水が湧き出した川と池に、僧、玄宅（げんたく）により建立されたのが水前寺。改易された加藤清正の後、寛永9年（1632）ここに入封したのが熊本3代藩主細川忠利。忠利は、水前寺の寺を移して自らの別邸とすべく寛永14～15年頃から作庭を開始、5代綱利のとき「成趣園」と名付け、8代重賢（しげかた）のとき完成した。作庭の指揮は、細川家茶頭ほか数名の家臣によるが、園内各所に茶亭を配した池泉周遊式で、面積は20,000余坪。元来名門の細川家は、和歌や茶道に秀でて八条宮智仁親王に古今伝授をした幽斎以来、文化芸術に力を入れた家風であり、成趣園の中央に位置する藩主愛用の粋月亭址には、大正元年細川家に下賜された「古今伝授の間」が移築されている。

庭園の主役は、毎秒2～3トンもの湧水による水深20～50cmの清らかで浅く広がる豊かな水面と主景の富士峯である。

日本庭園の典型的手法である「縮景」の代表的モチーフは何んといっても天下の富士山だが、成趣園の富士峯は実に優美で秀麗である。

近景に広がる水景、中景のやわらかく連なる山々が、まるで富士をより雄大に見せるように長くやさしく裾野を引く。そして遠景にそそり立つ富士峯をフォーカスする。主景の富士山の高さは、

12. Jōju-en Garden of Suizen-ji Temple

(Kumamoto City, Kumamoto Prefecture, 1637)

The Suizen-ji Temple was founded by the priest Gentaku in a place where an underground stream from Mt. Aso surfaced and created a natural pond. Hosokawa Tadatoshi, the regional *daimyō* (lord) of the Kumamoto domain from 1632, relocated the temple and began to create his own villa and garden at this location around 1637-1638. The garden, named Jōjuen by the fifth-generation *daimyō* Tsunatoshi, was completed by the eighth *daimyō*, Shigekata. The tea master and retainers of the Hosokawa clan directed the construction of the garden in a *chisen kaiyū* (pond circuitous strolling) style with a number of tea pavilions over the 6.6 hectare site.

The Hosokawa family was distinguished in traditional arts and excelled particularly in waka poetry and tea ceremony. In 1912, the "Kokindenju no ma," a celebrated structure for poetry teaching, had been given to the Hosokawa family. This thatched-roof building was moved to the former site of the Suigetsu-tei pavilion that had been a favorite teahouse of the *daimyō* for its stunning view of the *shukkei* (miniaturized) Mt. Fuji across the pond. The

水面から20数メートルの独立峰で、特に頂部はより高く見えるように凸型に築造され、安息角を超える尖りを保持するために芝生で蔽い、前からは見えない背後に鉄条網をめぐらして立入禁止にしているほどである。

実際の富士山と比較して、頂はより鋭角に、裾野はより長く引くことで本物以上に富士山らしく見せている。強調・省略法である。全山を芝草で統一して広がりとやわらかさを明るく演出している点も注目したい。なお明治以後は細川家の祖先を祀る出水（いずみ）神社の境内となっている。

reduced Mt. Fuji scenery is a popular attraction in Japanese gardens built in the 17-18th centuries and the one in Jōju-en is particularly elegant and graceful.

The central and dominant feature of the garden is the large, crystal clear pond, 20-50cm deep, fed by spring water that is abundant in this region.

The waterscape serves as foreground scenery and the gentle range of "foothills" in the middle ground is arranged to make Mt. Fuji in the background appear even more grand. The shukkei "Mt. Fuji" is freestanding and rises over 20m from the water surface with the flanks of the mountain feature exaggeratedly steep to make it appear much higher than it actually is.

The peak of this hill is at more of an acute angle and its base is proportionally much broader than the actual Mt. Fuji. Paradoxically, this exaggerated form allows it to appear even more like Mt. Fuji than the real one.

13, 旧芝離宮恩賜庭園 （1686年大久保家楽寿園を造園：東京都港区）

中国杭州西湖堤を汐入の庭中央に写し、知仁の楽寿を得るべく作庭

1678年江戸幕府の老中となった小田原藩主大久保忠朝（おおくぼただとも）(1632-1712)が、芝金杉築地103,78坪を下賜され、杭州の西湖堤を写した汐入りの庭「楽寿園」を造園した。1696年にも海手の1900坪を埋めて拡張し海と富士への眺望を改善した。楽寿園としての歴史は140年間つづき、徳川家の御三卿、御三家の別邸を経て、明治の初めに有栖川宮家の邸地、そして皇室財産芝離宮となる。1923年の震災で荒廃、翌年東京市に下賜「旧芝離宮恩賜庭園」として公開。1975年国指定名勝となる。開園面積は43,407平方メートル。

現代都市東京都心の庭園、高層ビル地域の中の別天地

A contrast between worlds, a beautiful garden with the background of modern skyscrapers in downtown Tokyo

江戸期の大名庭園には、中国の景勝地杭州の西湖十景をテーマとした造園が少なくない。西湖堤（せいこづつみ）と呼ばれる石造の直線堤の中央には石橋が架けられる。本物では洪橋（アーチ橋）だが本園では単純化している。また、蘇堤以外は現存しないが当初は"断橋の残雪""花港の観魚"、"三譚印月（さんたんのいんげつ）（水中の石灯籠）"など「西湖十景」を園景のモチーフとしていた。江戸期大名の文化的素養の高さがわかる。

園名を「楽寿園」としたのも儒家が好んだ人生観「智者楽水、仁者楽山」の生き方を庭園に託したもの。智力のある人は流れるように行動し、愛に満たされる仁者は愛に生きるというのである。

なお、「大久保加賀守芝金杉上屋敷之図」（1776〜82年）に描かれた彩色絵がある。絵では、右手前に州浜があり、その上に西湖堤、堤は中島につながる。中島には丸く刈り込まれた遠山風植栽を背景に枝振りの良い松が幾本も見える。刈込みの間には石塔が見える。島の奥の入江は深く正面に富士型の築山がある。その左方には外部をかくすように大刈込みの遠山や大木が描かれる。激しいビジネス都心に存在する「楽寿園」の時代的意義を思うと、これら史料を参考に名園の復元整備が強く求められる。

13. Shiba Detached Palace Garden Rakuju-en

(Minato District, Tokyo, 1686)

This garden has its origin in 1678, when 3.435 hectares of land in the Shiba-Kanesugi Tsukiji area of Tokyo was bestowed on Ōkubo Tadamoto, the lord of the Odawara domain and a high official of the shogunate. On this site, he created Rakuju-en, modeled after West Lake, a place of scenic beauty in Hangzhou, China. The garden was built around a large seawater pond with unparalleled views of the ocean and Mt. Fuji, partially on reclaimed land recreated by a landfill project extending into Edo Bay in 1696. The garden was donated to Tokyo City in 1924 by the Imperial Household and opened to the public after additional improvements were made.

Though the garden has lost much of its original splendor, magnificent colored perspective drawings and a blueprint of the original Rakuju-en Garden from its golden era have survived and exist today. On the drawing, a sandy beach is shown in the foreground to the right, and above it is a West Lake Embankment emulation and bridge which connects Naka-jima (central island) with the rocky shoreline. On the island, plants that have been pruned into rounded forms to suggest distant mountains, provide a backdrop for a number of pines with graceful branches. Uki-jima (floating island) was carefully made at the right elevation to appear like it was floating at high tide.

The inlet at the far end of the island is deep, and in front of it is a man-made mound shaped like Mt. Fuji. In the middle of the greenery are cascades of water that appear to feed the pond.

The scale, complexity and magnificence of this garden, especially in its original form, are of a scale unimaginable for present day garden construction.

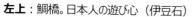

右上：楽寿園型雪見灯籠
右下：中国の道教世界、蓬莱島
(山)の象徴

Upper right: Rakujuen-style *yukimi-dōrō* (snow-viewing lantern)

Bottom right: A Hōrai-jima emulation representative of the world of Chinese Taoism

左上：鯛橋。日本人の遊び心（伊豆石）
左中：湖中の浮灯籠

Upper left: The Sea Bream Bridge made from volcanic Izu rock (the rock slab is shaped like a sea bream). An example of playful spirit in Japanese Garden design.

Bottom left: *Uki-dōrō* (floating lantern)

西湖堤（中国の名所、杭州西湖の蘇堤の写し）
Emulation of the famous West Lake Causeways in Hangzhou, China

14，養浩館庭園（福井藩松平家御泉水屋敷）

（1699年周遊式林泉庭園完成、1993年焼失した茶屋の復原整備公開：福井県福井市）

大胆な意匠と地場石材を活用した越前松平家 茅屋泉水一如の舒服世界

徳川家康の次男結城秀康（ゆうきひでやす）を藩祖に福井藩68万石が成立。2代忠直以後は徳川御家門松平家として幕府に重きをなし16代慶永（よしなが）（春嶽〔しゅんがく〕と号す）は幕末維新で活躍、橋本左内や由利公正など人物を輩出した。3代忠昌（ただまさ）のころ、藩の別邸「御泉水屋敷」は既に存在。「養浩館」の名は明治17年（1884）春嶽が孟子の「浩然の気を養う」の意でつけたもの。五重の環郭式平城であった福井城本丸から北東400mの至近に立地。敷地は外堀の土居に接し、藩主一族の居住や休養、迎賓、宴遊、接待の場として機能した。現在は福井市によって、戦災で消失した御茶屋が1989年（平成元年）から3ヵ年をかけて復元工事、池底の浚渫、景石据直等整備し、1993年（平成5年）に一般公開。復元は文政6年（1823）の『御泉水指図』（136×160cm）を踏まえたもので庭園維持管理の成果もあって、現在、江戸の大名別邸の舒服感覚（シューフー、ゆったりし、おおらかな感覚）が味わえる。

14. Yōkō-kan Mansion Garden

(Osensui Residence of the Matsudaira Clan, Fukui Domain)
(Hōei, Fukui City, Fukui Prefecture, 1699)

The Fukui Clan was founded by Yūki Hideyasu, the second son of Tokugawa Ieyasu, the founding father of Tokugawa Shogunate. Beginning with his son, Tadanao, the Fukui clan assumed the name Matsudaira and served the shogunate. The 16th *daimyō*, Matsudaira Yoshinaga took an active role at the end of the shogunate, supporting the return of imperial rule, otherwise known as the Meiji Restoration in 1868. The Osensui Villa Residence was already in existence by the time of the third shogun Tadamasa, and in 1884 Yoshinaga gave it the new name, the Yōkō-kan Mansion, a reference to the words of the Chinese Confucian philosopher Mencius which meant "to cultivate an open, relaxed spirit".

Yōkō-kan was located northwest of the main enclosure of Fukui Castle, a plain castle with five layers of moats. The building functioned as a place for rest, as a guest house and an entertainment venue. In 1989, Fukui City began a three-year project to restore the mansion that had been lost in a fire during World War II, dredge the pond, and reconstruct rock arrangements. The garden

『指図』では南北45間（82メートル）×東西85間（155メートル）となっており、面積は約4,000坪（12,710平方メートル）で、本園は大名庭園として決して広くないが、ゆったりとした水景と数奇屋造の御茶屋の美事な「庭屋一如」の庭園景観を醸成している。全国に名高い東尋坊の柱状節理の石、また北前船で金沢から北海道にまで運ばれた笏谷石、三国湊の安島石（あんとうせき）など福井の地場材を多用した造園でもある。昭和57年（1982）国指定名勝である。

has been restored to its original state as depicted in the *Osensui sashizu*, a historical drawing from 1823 of the buildings and grounds in the Edo period.

　According to the drawing, the main garden measured 82 meters north to south and 155 meters east to west and was approximately 1.32 hectares in area. The garden is not as large as a *daimyō* garden but its large body of water and the restored *sukiya*-style teahouse were beautifully integrated. In addition, the garden is quite unique with an abundance of rocks indigenous to Fukui prefecture, such as columnar rocks, porous volcanic rocks and rhyolite. In 1982, the garden was designated a Place of Scenic Beauty by the Japanese government.

園池の水源は芝原用水（北東8km先の芝原郷で九頭竜川から引入れた城下の飲用水）で、滝口、遣水（やりみず）、砂利浜護岸とせせらぎ等細部は、道路拡幅のため『指図』とは大きくアレンジしているが美しく納まっている。又、復原された「御茶屋」や「小亭・清廉」、すぐ近くの大泉水、露地、築山など変化に富んだ中景。そして植栽を見切りとし往時福井城天守や隅櫓への遠望を、借景したであろうことも偲ばれる。これら近景・中景・遠景の景観効果は、小面積の弱点を補ってあまりある。

特に付記したいのは、御茶屋復原に当った文化庁の見識によって、建築と園池の関係性が守られた点。発掘された遺跡の保存を留意するあまり、盛土した上で復元するため視点高が元の見え方と一変してしまうこともよくあるが、養浩館では元の基盤の上に直接再建したので、座敷からの眺めが昔ながらの水上に居るような親水感が保持されている。

復原整備された「養浩館」（**左頁写真と上左**）と小亭の「清廉」（**上右**）。清廉の左側には、狭い空間でありながらも、沢山の自然石立石で造られた厳しい峡谷、谷川のせせらぎ、石橋など、深山峡谷の山水画の世界が表現されている。

Previous page and upper left: The restored Yōkō-kan Mansion
Upper right: The restored Seiren Gazebo with landscaping on the viewer's left designed to be reminiscent of Chinese *Shan Shui* ink painting landscapes, featuring austere, vertical canyon wall-like vertical rocks, a stream and rock bridge, creating a separate world in a small space.

The pond is fed by water originally intended as potable water drawn from the Kuzuryū River nearly 8 kilometers away. The waterfall, *yarimizu* (narrow winding stream), gravel beach revetment, and stream have been slightly altered over the last century but are beautifully composed to form a uniquely regional garden. The foreground and the pond can be viewed from the restored teahouse; the diverse elements in the middle ground include the tea garden, man-made hill, dry creek and the distant view of the Fukui castle.

The Cultural Agency, in charge of restoring the teahouse, decided to preserve the original relationship between the architecture and the pond. Yōkō-kan mansion was rebuilt directly on the original foundation, preserving the close relationship with the water and looking from its guest room, one feels like the building is practically in the middle of the pond.

159

15，駒込の六義園 （1695年、7年かけて完成：東京都文京区）

りくぎえん

和歌の名所(などころ)88カ所を石柱で表示した、雅(みや)びな文芸趣味の柳沢吉保の大名庭園

徳川3代将軍家光の四男が5代将軍綱吉（つなよし）である。綱吉は学問好きで、幕府の運営方針を武力から文化力に転換しようとした。綱吉に仕えた学問好きの家臣、柳沢吉保（やなぎさわよしやす）（1658-1714)は大名にとり立てられ、遂に幕府の重役、大老格にまで出世する。

吉保は1695年、もとは加賀藩の下屋敷であった駒込の敷地46,000坪（現在の面積は約8.8ヘクタール）を拝領し7年余をかけ、1702年に六義園を完成、将軍のお成りの栄に浴している。

吉保の構想と指図で作庭した園名が「六義園」（りくぎえん：むくさのその）

である。「六義」は、詩道の基本となる六つの「体（てい）」をいう。吉保自身、和歌を嗜み、京都から公家（貴族）出身の夫人を迎え和歌を楽しむほどであった。

小石川後楽園が儒教や漢詩の世界であるなら、吉保は歌枕や名所の風景を88か所選び和歌の世界をめざした。

これが「六義園88境」。池の汀線（水辺）には、吹上（ふきあげ）の浜、出汐の湊（でしおのみなと）。中島には妹山（いものやま）、背山（せのやま）の石組。橋は土橋（どばし）の山陰（やまかげ）の橋、石橋（いしばし）の渡月橋（と

15. Rikugi-en Garden

(Bunkyō-ku Ward, Tokyo, 1695-1702)

Yanagisawa Yoshiyasu who, served under the fifth Tokugawa shogun, received 15.18 hectares of land (the present area of the garden is approximately 8.8 hectares) in 1695 that had previously been the estate of the Kaga clan. After seven years, he completed this representative *kaiyū*-style or pond-strolling garden in Edo (now Tokyo).

The garden was named Rikugi-en. *Rikugi* refers to the six styles that were considered basic to *waka* poetry. Yoshiyasu, who was a devoted scholar of Japanese arts, sought to reference sites famous in *waka* and make the garden into a world of poetry, thus the name Rikugi-en. Specifically, he selected 88 places or views that various poets had written about in *waka*, using a rhetorical device called *uta makura* (poem pillow - a device that allows for greater allusions and intertextuality across Japanese poems), where the name of a place is associated with beauty or a mood. He then arranged scenes that symbolized them in various places within the garden and linked them with a strolling path. The result was the 88 Sites of Rikugi-en. A stela with a poetic inscription was erected at

げつきょう）など。それぞれに書家の細井広沢に書かせた碑石柱を立てた。いわば文字でその場所をイメージさせる造園手法で、現在もいくつかの石柱が残っている。

1878年、三菱財閥の岩崎弥太郎（やたろう）が買収して別邸として整備、子の岩崎久弥（ひさや）が 1938年、これを東京市に寄付。今日では都民共有の財産、国指定の特別名勝になっている。

each place and the words inscribed on the stela themselves were intended to evoke famous sceneries. A number of the stelae still stand in the garden.

Yatarō Iwasaki, the founder of the Mitsubishi corporation, bought the garden in 1878 and made it his villa. In 1938, his son, Hisaya, eventually donated the garden to the City of Tokyo to add to their public park system. It is interesting to compare Rikugi-en, which is very Japanese and feminine in style with gentle lines and soft colors, with Kōraku-en (also within the Tokyo Park system), which is more Chinese Confucian and formal in style with sharp masculine lines and bold features.

六義園では、日本の詩歌で詠まれている名所88か所の名前を石に刻み、庭園内各所を景勝地に見立てる手法を使っている。上は、出汐湊(でしおのみなと)（上）とその石柱（右）。出汐とは、舟が湊(港)に入るために満潮を待っていることで、紀州の和歌浦の場所をイメージさせる石柱。

Rikugi-en's design is based on 88 famous select sites referred to in *waka* poetry. Each of the scenic viewpoints had a stone stela marker with a poetic inscription. One of the views was an emulation of a scenic harbor in which ships waited for high tide to enter into port (Deshio-no-Minato) in Wakayama (**top**) the name of which is inscribed in Chinese calligraphic kanji characters on a stela (**right**).

下は、和歌浦と吉野山をつなぐ川である紀乃川の場所性の表現（左下）と、その石碑（右下）。石柱は書の大家の細井広沢(ほそいこうたく)の筆。

An emulation of a famous view of the Kinokawa River between Nara and Wakayama prefectures (**bottom left**). The *kanji* inscribed stela in the renowned calligraphy of Confucian scholar Koutaku Hosoi (**bottom right**).

162

16, 岡山後楽園　（1700年：岡山県岡山市）

地元花崗岩を多用、芝生地に流水、封建制基調の「農」景観をデザイン

　備前岡山藩主池田光政・綱政に仕えた津田永忠(つだながただ)(1640-1707)は、百間川開削(かいさく)、閑谷(しずたに)学校建設、元禄13(1700)年概成の後楽園作庭を指揮した。

　対岸の岡山城防備の機能も兼ねて構成された旭川の中州約40,000坪の敷地に、中央部に大芝生地に、そのなかをひと筆書きで曲折する流れ、処々に池を湛え、茶畑、梅林など田園風景を基調に、東海道五十三次を縮景している。日本三大名園のひとつ。

　広大な芝生園地は、当初「菜園場(さいえんば)」とも呼ばれた農地ゾーン。封建時代の農地開発法を象徴する9枚の水田（井田法：せいでんほうと呼ぶ）を中央に、園の周辺には茶畑、竹林を配し、紅葉、桜、梅 が季節を彩る。

　芝生は、苔と違ってこの庭園に明るくモダンなイメージを与えている。大芝生地の緑の広がりの中をマサ土独特の白っぽいまっすぐな園路が伸び、緑と白のコントラストともに現代的である。園内をゆったり曲折する流れの花崗岩製間知石積(けんちいしづみ)の護岸は、京都など古典庭園とは異(ちが)う、さわやかな気分を出している。

　水系と水景デザインには、津田永忠

16. Okayama Kōraku-en Garden

(Okayama City, Okayama Prefecture, 1700)

The Kōraku-en Garden in Okayama was completed in 1700 by Ikeda Tsunamasa, the second lord of the Okayama domain. Approximately 13.3 hectares in area, it is built on a sandbank of the nearby Asahi River. The Okayama Castle is on the opposite shore and the garden served a defensive function as well. An embankment three meters tall is built on the periphery and densely planted with bamboos to offer protection from river flooding events.

　The garden is a peaceful space with an extensive lawn, a large pond and nine rice paddy fields in the middle, a gently curving stream flowing through it and tea fields and bamboo groves arranged on the outer edges. Groves of Japanese maple, Japanese plum and cherry add color to the landscape in different seasons. Unlike moss-covered ground, the expanse of grass gives the garden a contemporary character. The straight path that crosses the lawn and the contrast between the white decomposed granite paving and the green grass also appears distinctively contemporary. The gently meandering stream with stone-clad edges is well-suited to the spacious lawn and the bold pattern of the garden path. The simplicity of

の非凡な土木技術がつかわれた。敷地は旭川の中州で、隣を流れる河川を引き入れることは無理。そこで上流で取水、開削した後楽園用水で北側対岸まで引き、そこからサイホンの原理による埋設木管で園に導水。これが「沢の池」、「花葉の池」、「花交の池」、「曲水」など水景の豊かさを見せている。

庭園の外周は3メートルの高さに築堤、矢竹やモウソウ竹を密生させ、外敵や洪水への備えとしている。また、園内には12か所も、男女の性器を象徴し子孫繁栄を願う「陰陽石（いんようせき）」が配石されている。当初は「菜園場」、次に「後園（こうえん）」、明治4年（1871）以降は「後楽園（こうらくえん）」と呼ぶようになった。

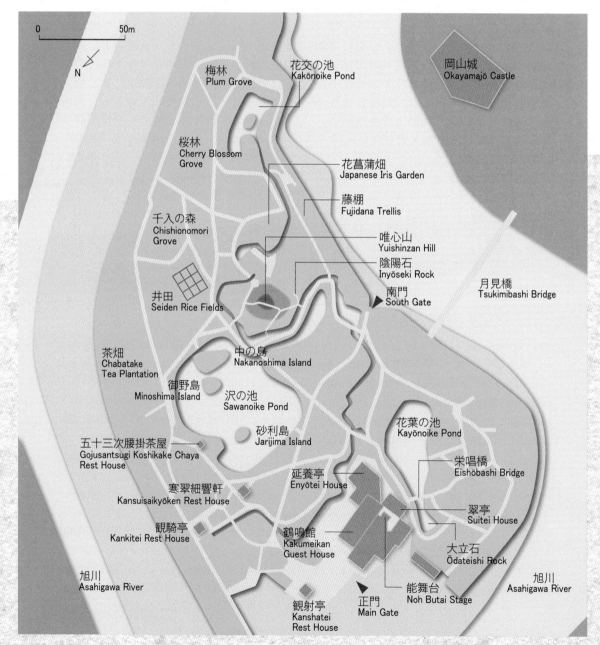

0　　　　50m

N

梅林
Plum Grove

花交の池
Kakōnoike Pond

岡山城
Okayamajō Castle

桜林
Cherry Blossom
Grove

花菖蒲畑
Japanese Iris Garden

藤棚
Fujidana Trellis

千入の森
Chishionomori
Grove

唯心山
Yuishinzan Hill

陰陽石
Inyōseki Rock

月見橋
Tsukimibashi Bridge

南門
South Gate

井田
Seiden Rice Fields

茶畑
Chabatake
Tea Plantation

中の島
Nakanoshima Island

御野島
Minoshima Island

沢の池
Sawanoike Pond

砂利島
Jarijima Island

花葉の池
Kayōnoike Pond

五十三次腰掛茶屋
Gojusantsugi Koshikake Chaya
Rest House

栄唱橋
Eishōbashi Bridge

延養亭
Enyōtei House

寒翠細響軒
Kansuisaikyōken Rest House

翠亭
Suitei House

観騎亭
Kankitei Rest House

鶴鳴館
Kakumeikan
Guest House

大立石
Ōdateishi Rock

旭川
Asahigawa River

能舞台
Noh Butai Stage

旭川
Asahigawa River

観射亭
Kanshatei
Rest House

正門
Main Gate

左：大芝生地と唯心山　右：芝生地をゆったり流れる水路脇の点景となる灯籠と冬の野焼きの芝生

Left: Yuishin-zan hill that affords an expansive view in spite of its mere 6 meter elevation and the flat and spacious park lawn. **Right**: A stone lantern acts as a landscape focal point, placed amidst the scenery of the canal meandering through the lawn garden, which is managed by seasonal controlled burning.

左：延養亭の全景　右：延養亭からの眺め（藩主の御座所）

Left: Enyou-tei House　**Right**: View from the feudal lord's office in the Enyou-tei House

these arrangements creates a pleasant and cheerful atmosphere that is quite different from the ambiance of the classical gardens of Kyoto.

The waterways and waterscapes of the garden reveal remarkable technical skills. A siphon was used because water could not be introduced directly from the nearby Asahi River into the garden. Water was drawn at a point four kilometers upstream, carried by a canal excavated for this, and is then further lifted another 50 cm in elevation to the garden via a 160 meter long buried wooden pipe siphon. This water feeds all three of the garden ponds (Sawa Kayō and Kakō Ponds) the sum total area of which is 5,000 m².

Unique features found in the garden are the Yin and Yang Rocks, a rock grouping symbolizing the male and female sexual organs, that represent hope for the prosperity and flourishing of descendants to come.

165

園内の唯心山（ゆいしんざん）と園外、操山（みさおやま）中腹の多宝塔の借景
View from within the park with Yuishin-zan hill in the midground and Mt. Misao and the Tahoto Pagoda on its flank in the background outside the park, serving as *shakkei*.

左：花葉の池にある、大立石。実は巨大な花崗岩を100個ほどに割り、再び組み上げたもの
Left: Kayou-no-ike pond (Lotus Pond) and Odate-ishi rock. This spectacular granite rock, due to its size, was broken down into nearly 100 pieces and moved then reassembled in the garden.

左：武士が刀を研ぐための砥石からできた石橋、常在戦場の気持ちを表現　**右**：陰陽石とは男根を陽石、女陰の形に似る石を陰石と呼び、子孫繁栄の象徴とされる石組
Lower left: A bridge, made from sharpening stones used by samurai for their swords, lends a mood of vigilance to the garden.　**Right**: This Yin and Yang rock grouping mimics the male and female sexual organs, expressing hope for the prosperity and flourishing of descendants to come.

166

上：岡山城をランドマークとして、強調　中：9つに分けられた田圃は、中国から伝わった、井田法（せいでんほう）の象徴。「井」字形のうち、周囲の八区画は八戸の家がそれぞれ「私田」として耕し、中心の一区画は「公田」として共同で耕して、収穫物はみんなのため公共的に活用する。その奥は庭園景観としての茶畑。　下左：梅林、下中：紅葉林、下右：茶畑

Above: The dramatic landmark of Okayama Castle in the background **Middle**: The nine rice paddies included in the park design, giving it an agrarian scenery component, arranged in the pattern of the Chinese character 井 (well) based on a traditional Chinese land distribution system wherein the outer squares were allocated to citizens for personal food growing but the middle square's communal harvest was given as tribute or for famine distribution. **Bottom**: Further agrarian design components - a plum tree grove containing around 100 trees of different varieties with staggered blooming and varied colors (**left**); Japanese maples planted for their rich fall colors is metaphorically named Chishio-no-mori ("Dyeing Grove") in reference to the term *chishio*, which means "to dye a cloth multiple times", just as the maple leaves dye themselves when they change colors (**middle**); the harmonious curves of the tea garden from which high quality tea was harvested for the feudal lords and can still be sampled at the annual Tea Picking Festival (**right**)

上左：賓客の接待、藩主の休憩所などに使われたた2階建ての数寄屋造りの流店（りゅうてん）。

上右：一階部分の中央に水路を流し、色彩に富んだ奇石六個を配し曲水の宴に使った。

The Ryūten Rest House used by feudal lords as a resting place and hosting space with simple but exquisite proportions in a two story sukiya-style (**left**) with a stream passing through the middle of the first floor with six unique stones placed in it (**right**) used for *kyokusui-no-en* drinking and poetry writing parties where cups of *sake* were floated down the stream and if the next participant in line could not improvise a poem, they had to drink the sake.

中：東海道五十三次の絵馬を並べた腰掛茶屋

Middle: Teahouse wall decorated with wooden prayer plaques on which the 53 stations of the Tokaido Road are colorfully illustrated

下：石山寺や八ツ橋、釣り亭、蘇鉄、菊花展など日本各地の点景が池沿いに配された回遊式庭園

Bottom: Five different features from the circuitous strolling garden including the Ishiyama-dera Temple, Yatsu-hashi zig-zag bridge, Tsuri-tei fishing gazebo, a grouping of cycad trees and a chrysanthemum display, all representative samples from famous views and scenery around Japan.

17, 浜離宮恩賜庭園

（浜御殿1707年、鴨場建設1778年・1791年：東京都中央区）

徳川将軍家の宴遊、社交、武芸、軍事など多面的機能を充足した政治色が濃い苑地

　江戸東京を通した代表的名園。敷地は、江戸初期（1650年代）に江戸湾の海辺を埋め立てて造成されたもので、やがては将軍家の「浜御殿」、「浜の苑」として、江戸造園の特色である鴨場、汐入の庭、黒朴（くろぼく）石積が見られる名園である。造園がもっとも充実したのは11代将軍家斉（いえなり）（1773-1841）の時代で家斉は248回も浜を訪れている。1870年からは明治政府宮内省所管の「浜離宮」、1945年からは「東京都立浜離宮恩賜庭園」として今日にいたる。面積75,000余坪（25ヘクタール）。江戸期を代表する回遊式大名庭園で、国指定の特別名勝・特別史跡である。

　浜の御庭は、観賞・接待機能、将軍ファミリー時どきの住居機能のみならず、将軍家が要請する多面的機能を発揮してきた。

　その立地から江戸湾、品川の海、富士への第一級の眺望を得るのみならず汐入の池の周囲には、いずれも戦後順次復元されたものだが、中の島の御茶屋、松の御茶屋、燕の御茶屋、鷹の御茶屋など園の点景、又もてなしの場としての御茶屋が配される等、大面積に多様な風景を展開し最上の遊観所となっている。

17. Hama Detached Palace Garden

(Hama Garden of the Tokugawa Shogun)

(Chuo-ku Ward, Tokyo, 1778)

This site was reclaimed from Edo (Tokyo) Bay in the early Edo period around the 1650s. In 1870, it became the Hama Detached Palace of the Tokugawa shogunate and eventually its ownership was transferred to the Ministry of the Imperial Household during the Meiji Restoration in 1868. From 1945, the Tokyo Metropolitan government was entrusted with the ownership of the garden and it was incorporated into the Tokyo public park system. Twenty-five hectares in total area, it is a representative *kaiyū*-style *daimyō* garden of the Edo period.

　The Hama Detached Palace Garden has proved to be highly flexible and has been adapted to serve various functions. It is not simply a garden but closer to the broader, contemporary concept of a park. Its exceptional views of Edo Bay, the Sea of Shinagawa beyond and Mt. Fuji in the distance were valued by both the shogunate and present day visitors. In addition, the palace grounds were equipped with two duck-hunting facilities that still survive to today.

上：汐入の庭　大泉水中島の御茶屋とお伝い橋（**左**）と、その夜景（**右**）**下**：復元された、燕の御茶屋と鷹の御茶屋（写真提供：菊池正芳）

Top: The Naka-jima Teahouse, built on stilts within the Daisensui Pond which draws seawater from the Tokyo Bay, connected by the Otsutai-bashi Bridge (**left**); night view of the teahouse (**right**)
Bottom: The restored Tsubame Teahouse and Taka Teahouse

Photo credit: Masayoshi Kikuchi

徳川期には京都の公家や僧侶らの接待場としての社交機能も大きかったし、明治期には国賓級ゲストの接待所、西洋風石造の延遼館も設けられ外交機能を果たす離宮であった。武芸の鍛錬に不可欠な馬場、弓場、鴨場などが配されたのはもとより、何よりも正面入口が大手門と桝形（ますがた）の構えとされ、四周が濠と石垣で堅固な城郭的構造となっている。なお、将軍が江戸城から脱出するには築地川を下り、浜の御庭のお船入から御殿で休み、江戸湾の軍艦から外洋に出るようになっていた。大名庭園の政治性が如実に表われた庭園である。

The garden changed from a place of recreation and social gatherings to a place for research into raising agricultural and industrial productivity at the end of the shogunate, and then to a military base. The status of the shogun was most evident in the castle style of the main entrance to the garden; there was a main gate with a square, enclosed court. The garden itself was surrounded on four sides by the solid fortification, of a moat and a stone wall. The state garden was originally used for the samurai class as a training place for martial arts such as horse-riding and archery. Later, during the Meiji Period, the garden was a place for both social and diplomatic functions. With several teahouses within the garden and a diverse landscape, the garden was a special place to entertain distinguished guests.

170

18, 金沢の兼六園

（始まりは1676年、兼六園の命名は1822年：石川県金沢市）

園林文化重要視の名門加賀藩前田家代々が育んだ普遍的「名園」

　前田家は、加賀百万石の大大名。江戸の藩邸、現在の東京大学構内には「育徳園」、江戸郊外の板橋区には217,000坪の広大な下屋敷（現在、区立加賀公園）、駒場や鎌倉にも西洋館庭園などを。一方、国元の金沢市には、金沢城惣構え、兼六園、近年復元された玉泉院丸庭園など園林文化の守護・推進者であり続けた。小堀遠州一門を家来に抱えたり、『作庭記』など造庭書を多数所蔵したり庭園文化のよき理解者であった。

　兼六園の園名は松平定信が中国の『洛陽名園記』から引用したもので、当初から"兼六"をテーマとした作庭ではない。「洛陽名園記」にある「園圃の勝の六」は名園の条件を示すもので「宏大・幽邃、人力・蒼古、水泉・眺望」の3対6語。

　これは造園設計に一般化できる規範でもあり、兼六園の実体ともいえる。たとえば「水があるのは低地や谷地で、どうしても眺望は難しい」。だから「水泉と眺望」の両方があるのはめずらしい。ところが兼六園では、台地上のゾーンは卯辰山（うだつやま）への眺望に恵まれているし、唐崎（からさき）の松や徽軫（ことじ）灯籠で有名な霞ヶ池とか、辰巳用水の取水口山崎山からの眺望、西北部は雁行橋の流れの水景に秀れている。

　霞ヶ池一帯には、12代藩主がつくった建坪4,000坪という広大な「竹沢（たけざわ）御殿」と京都の庭師に作庭させた前庭があったが、13代藩主斉泰（なりやす）(1811-1884)は浪費の象徴といわれた竹沢御殿を撤去して霞ヶ池を拡張し蠑螺山（さざえやま）を築き一体的に整備した。

18. Kenroku-en Garden

(Kanazawa City, Ishikawa Prefecture, 1822)

The Maeda family governed the Kaga Domain, a major domain of Tokugawa Shogunate, in present day Kanazawa in Ishikawa Prefecture. The Maeda family had their main residence in Edo (now the site of the University of Tokyo). In addition to the main residence, the family owned a large villa in Itabashi Ward on the outskirts of Edo, (today's Tokyo) and more properties in and around Tokyo. At their Kanazawa estate, they built the Kenroku-en Garden facing the Kanazawa Castle. The Maeda clan was a well-known advocate of *sadō* or *chadō*, the Way of Tea, and Japanese gardens. Their library had an extensive collection of classic garden treatises including Sakuteiki.

Kenroku-en (Garden of Six Attributes), is the name given to the garden by lord Matsudaira Sadanobu which he took from the Chinese garden book, *Chronicles of the Famous Luoyang Gardens*, which described three pairs of opposing attributes that are present in the ideal garden: spaciousness vs. seclusion; creation via human effort and technique vs. the beauty of aging and nature; lush, treed waterviews vs. expansive panoramic views. He felt that this garden was an example of balance of these three fundamental opposing element pairs.

The garden was built on a plateau that affords a borrowed view of Mt. Udatsu to the northeast. Its northwest zone has many points of interest that unfold along the flow of the waterway: the Kikkō (Tortoiseshell) Bridge (also known as the Flying Geese Bridge); the Kasumigaike Pond; the Karasaki pine trees; the

手前に石橋、左に唐崎の松、右に琴柱灯籠、先に霞ヶ池が広がる秋の兼六園（写真提供：共同通信社）
Stone bridge in foreground, Karasaki pine trees on the left, Kotoji Lantern on the right, and Kasumigaike Pond Photo: Kyodo News

　台地上の造園では、竹沢御殿跡地の利用と「兼六園」のコンセプトを生かしながら霞ヶ池を拡張、蓬莱（ほうらい）島を築き、近江八景の唐崎松から松の実生（みしょう）を取り寄せ、内橋亭（うちはしてい）を移築するなど作庭感覚を大いに発揮している。さらに台地の斜面と、その下の金沢城と百間堀をはさんだ低地部（谷部）に「蓮池亭（れんちてい）

（庭）」を設けることで一体化している。

　マスタープランにもとづいて施工されたわけではないが、代々の藩主が部分々々を少しずつ造り込み、やがてそれらがつなぎ合わされて一大庭園へと成長してゆく。兼六園は、幾代もかけてつくり育てられ完成度を高めていく日本庭園変遷史の典型だといえる。

Rainbow Bridge and the Kotoji Lantern. Kenroku-en in winter is famous for its *yukitsuri* ropework where ropes are tied atop a wooden pole lashed vertically to the tree trunk and the ropes splayed at even intervals down to the ground in a tent-like shape. Horizontally spread branches are then tied to the ropes and suspended thereby protected from breakage from the weight of snow accumulation on the branches. It is craftsmanship that combines function and beauty.

　The twelfth lord of the Kaga domain Maeda Narinaga (1782-1824) built Takezawa Palace as a retirement estate. Maeda Nariyasu (1811-1884) the thirteenth lord, declared the Palace too extravagant and had it dismantled and

made Kasumigaike Pond in the same spot and the pond excavation dirt was used to create a mound known as Sazae-yama and a Hourai-jima island in the pond. Karasaki Pine seedlings were ordered from the Ōmi region close to Kyoto, and the teahouse, Uchihashi-tei was moved from another site and located in the garden.

　The garden began with an overall concept; then individual components were carefully created and eventually joined together over time into one great garden. The history of the evolution of Kenroku-en illustrates the way gardens evolve through a process of creation, cultivation, and care by successive generations. It is considered one of the three great gardens of Japan.

172

19, 偕楽園　（1842年開園：茨城県水戸市）

千波湖を借景・城外の台地上に民衆と楽しむ広大な梅林、ツツジや萩の芝庭

「日本三名園」の一つ偕楽園は、細部構成には頼らない造園に特徴がある。おおらかな郊外の全域梅林という園地である。敷地外の千波湖への眺望を含め全体景観がゆったりした休養緑地的デザインに、大名庭園にはめずらしい偕楽園のオリジナリティがある。

構想者は、水戸藩9代藩主徳川斉昭（なりあき）（1800-1860）である。江戸幕府最後の将軍慶喜（よしのぶ）の実父である。

コンセプトは園名どおり、家臣や領民と「偕（とも）に楽しむ」という儒教的思想である。斉昭は、「自然の万物は陰陽の理」に順うべきだとして、藩校弘道館で学問を勧め偕楽園で休養すべきとした。天保12(1841)年には水戸城内に藩校、天保13(1842)年には郊外の眺望絶好の台地12,000坪に梅樹数千株を植えた大園地を設けた。なお現在の梅林は、100種3,000本。国指定史跡名勝（指定名称は常盤公園）。

唯一の建物で、学問を意味する好文亭が偕楽園のランドマークとなっている。最上階を「楽寿楼」と呼ぶ。楽寿楼に上るには、暗く急な階段を曲折して登る。三階に上るとにわかに明るくなり、視野が広がる。園外の東には千波湖の水景、西には筑波山が遠望できた。もとも

19. Kairaku-en Garden

(Mito City, Ibaraki Prefecture, 1842)

Kairaku-en, considered one of the three most famous gardens of Japan, is characterized by its grandeur of scale, and a design which consists almost entirely of groves of Japanese plum trees. Kairaku-en is unique in its refreshing expansive views that extend outside the garden to Senba Lake, making it much different than other *daimyō* gardens.

The garden was conceived by Tokugawa Nariaki (1800-1860), the ninth *daimyō* of the Mito Domain and the father of Yoshinobu, the last Tokugawa shogun.

As the word *kairaku* ("to enjoy with others") suggests, the concept of the garden is Confucian in spirit, i.e. the garden was to be shared with the retainers and the common residents of the domain alike.

Small shrines and other objects that originally occupied the site were moved elsewhere, several thousand Japanese plum trees and shrubs were planted, and a large expanse of lawn was established. Its only landmark building is the three-story Kōbun-tei (Plum Pavilion). The plum blossoms remain increasingly popular to the present day. The groves include 3000 Japanese plum trees of 100 different varieties, generating an atmosphere that attracts large numbers of visitors eager to view the early harbingers of spring.

とは水戸城から千波湖の柳堤を経て、丘の下の大理石製の吐玉泉（とぎょくせん）、そして斜面の杉木立の真暗な坂を登り、台地上の好文亭を上って、その最上階の楽寿楼に到りはじめて明るいパノラマを眺めるというのが、水戸偕楽園ならではのダイナミックなシークエンスと千波湖水景の借景体験である。

園名の由来や庭園利用における利用者のマナーなどを斉昭直筆で記された『偕楽園記碑（高さ2.5mの自然石）』がある。当時の Open Garden の思想を知れておもしろい。

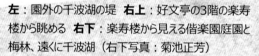

左：園外の千波湖の堤　右上：好文亭の3階の楽寿楼から眺める　右下：楽寿楼から見える偕楽園庭園と梅林、遠くに千波湖（右下写真：菊池正芳）

Left: Willows on the levee of Senba Lake outside the garden creates a *shakkei* background scenery for the garden
Upper right: The 3rd floor of Kōbun-tei, known as Rakujurō, offers panoramic views.
Lower right: The spectacular plum groves and Senba Lake in the distance as seen from the 3rd floor of Rakujurō. Lower right photo credit: Masayoshi Kikuchi

The reconstructed Kōbun-tei is a three-story wooden structure. The third floor, called Rakujurō, is accessed by a steep, dark and winding stairway. At the top, one suddenly finds themselves in a brightly lit space that affords a panoramic view, creating a dramatic sense of contrast. The view from this building extends beyond the garden to Senba Lake to the near east and formerly Mt. Tsukuba was also visible in the distant west.

Originally one would journey to Kairaku-en from Mito Castle, by way of the levee on Senba Lake, to the Togyoku-sen well, where springwater flows from a marble block, then ascend a dark slope in a cedar forest to the top of the plateau occupied by Kairaku-en and then climb to the third floor Rakujurō to enjoy its panoramic views. This dynamic sequential experience of contrast and *shakkei* is unique to Kairaku-en.

（３）近現代日米の庭園

III. Modern Era Japanese Gardens of the Japan and the US

20, 向島百花園（1809年新梅屋敷と『群芳暦（植物目録）』で出発：東京都墨田区）

隅田河畔で田園を愉しむ江戸庶民の行楽拠点・民営園地の魁け

庭門正面上の額は「花屋敷」。左右の柱には「春夏秋冬花不断」、「東西南北客争来」の聯（れん）が架かる。

開園面積3,300坪（1ヘクタール）の小さな園地である。江戸の町人文化が花盛りの文化文政期（1804-30）に、骨董屋の佐原鞠塢（さはらきくう）（1762-1831）が、知己の文人らの支援と協力によってつくった庶民のための民営園地「新梅屋敷」が出発点である。いわゆる川向（かわむこう）、江戸郊外、墨東（ぼくとう）地域の田園の名所であるが、立地も規模もつくりも、大名庭園の対極にある。

国指定の名勝・史跡だが、向島（むこうじま）の場所性と非日常性を発揮した気楽で格式ばらない"草の庭（そうのにわ）"で、庶民に愛され殊に自由を求める文化人によって、30余りの歌碑、句碑が立てられ文芸趣味が表出している。ひょうたん池に藤棚や萩のトンネルがあるだけで、灯籠、景石ひとつない。なお草庭が完成した文化6、7（1810）年ごろ『群芳暦（ぐんぼうれき）』と名づけた植物目録を刊行しており、江戸庶民に当時愛された

20. Mukōjima Hyakka-en Garden

(Sumida-ku Ward, Tokyo, 1809)

In the Edo period Mukōjima had a magnificent waterfront, where shogun planted cherry trees on the inviting shores, making it a popular sightseeing attraction. Hyakka-en written in *kanji* (Chinese characters) means "a garden of a hundred flowers," referring to the plum blossom garden and referencing the fact that Japanese plum trees bloom before "a hundred [other] flowers." It was a venue for events throughout the year including plum blossoms in early spring, cherry blossoms to follow, the moon viewing in the fall and snow in winter.

Although small in scale, this garden is a well-known site in the *shitamachi* "old town" district near Sumida River in Tokyo. The district has a traditional atmosphere with the culture of commoners. It was developed and operated by an antique dealer, Sahara Kikū, in conjunction with a group of accomplished writers and artists in the area. The garden is only one hectare in size and has its origins in a privately owned Shin Ume-yashiki, ("Japanese Plum Garden") created in the

植物名を知ることができる。

　もちろん向島は、将軍による墨堤（ぼくてい）への植桜、雄大なウォーターフロントを立地とする江戸市民の行楽地へと発展した地域でもある。

　百花園の意味は百花に先駆けて咲く梅林

の意味だが、佐原鞠塢の凄さは早春の梅見に始まり、春秋の七草や野菜、春の花見、虫聞きの会、月見の会、晩秋の枯野見、冬の雪見、晩春の白魚漁の他、園内に祀られる「福禄寿」を含めた「隅田川七福神めぐり」を組み立てるなど、各種出版物の刊行やイベントと合わせたメディアミックスのソフトウェアに秀でたランドスケープ・マネージメントの先駆けといえる人物だった点にある。

左：「春夏秋冬花不断」と「東西南北客争来」の対聯（ついれん）　**中**：水仙　**右**：七草籠は、身近な薬草を7種まとめて春を感じさせる

Left: Poem excerpts from the famous poet and calligrapher Okubo Shibutsu inscribed on wooden plaques at the garden gate **Middle**: Narcissus in bloom **Right**: The seven medicinal herbs of spring planted in a basket which creates an ambiance of spring.

Bunka Bunsei era (1804-1830), a period in which the culture of the common townspeople (*chōnin*) in Edo flourished.

　Consisting only of a pond (fiddle-shaped in outline), and a few trees and flowering plants, this garden has no stone lanterns or picturesque rocks. It is the polar opposite, in both location and size, of a *daimyō* garden and it is typical of private gardens created during the Edo period. Designated a Place of Scenic Beauty and a Historic Site by the Japanese government, it has become a well-known and popular botanical garden in the district east of the Sumida River. The framed calligraphy over the gate reads "Flower Garden," and the pair of plates on the pillars read "Flowers are in bloom throughout the year" and "Visitors come from everywhere."

　As a private garden that reflected the *shitamachi* district's down-to-earth character, it was a relaxed place where social status and ceremony were not important, and was a garden open to and for the enjoyment of the general public unlike other gardens. It expressed the distinct character of the Mukōjima district and the area around Sumida River in general. It was notably described in many forms of poetry, song and literature of the era and was the inspiration for Sawara's botanical plate catalog publications.

　As the founder of Mukōjima Hyakka-en, Kikuu Sahara is also recognized as one of the great pioneers of effective and creative use of public park space for events and public amenity, which helped to knit together other scenic components of the district as well as becoming a focal point for the local waterfront culture of the commoner side of the river, in contrast with the aristocratic culture on the opposite side of the river.

21, 東京深川の清澄庭園 (1891年・近代日本の林泉庭園：東京都江東区)

三菱財閥創始者　岩崎弥太郎が構想した企業園地で日本各地の庭石の博物館

1896年、三菱財閥の創始者岩崎弥太郎（やたろう）（1835-1885）が隅田川近くの土地約30,000坪を購入し、自らの構想で作庭。1898年に完成して「深川親睦園（ふかがわしんぼくえん）」と命名した。弥太郎没後は、弟の弥之助（やのすけ）がその志を継ぎ、施工半ばの園を充実拡大、名園へと発展させ、弥太郎の息子の久弥を経て、東京市に寄付された。

岩崎弥太郎は、明治維新後の日本の政商、海運王として活躍した。弥太郎の庭園観はおよそ「常に心を泉石丘に思いを寄せる。憂悶（ゆうもん）を感じる時は名園を見た

い。人為の工は少なく、天然の妙趣があるものがいい。巨巌と老樹の豪宕（ごうとう）な深山の風致をつくりたい。」というもの。

隅田川畔の立地、江戸の名残りのある敷地に汐入りの庭と全国から名石、庭石を運びこみ、イギリス人ジョサイア・コンドルJosiah Conder（1852-1920）の設計による西洋館（赤レンガ造2階建てバルコニー付、現存せず）も建てた。

1923年の関東大震災で被害を受けたが、久弥は比較的園景が残った東半分（14,000坪）を東京市に寄付、1932年から市民に公開された。

21. Tokyo Fukagawa Kiyosumi Garden

(Kōtō-ku Ward, Tokyo, 1891)

In 1878, Iwasaki Yatarō, the Meiji period industrialist and founder of Mitsubishi Corporation, purchased approximately 9.9 hectares of land in this location and began to design and create his own garden. In 1880, when the garden was nearly complete, he named it the "Fukagawa Friendship Garden." After his death, his younger brother Yanosuke completed the garden, and then finally his son Hisaya donated the garden to the City of Tokyo in 1924.

Yatarō, a fan of Japanese gardens and dabbler in creating them had once expressed how he was drawn to natural landscapes and that when his mind or heart was not at ease, he would go to view a beautifully made garden, preferring something that is not too artificial.

Furthermore he expressed, that if he was to ever to make a garden of his own, it should instead have the subtle charm of nature with the splendid presence of large rocks and old trees.

Yatarō's dream, combined with the favorable conditions of the garden site along the Sumida River, made water transportation of large boulders convenient and led to the successful creation of this garden. A Western-style building and a Japanese-style building were also constructed. The former, designed by Josiah Conder, was a Tudor-style, two-story red brick building, equipped with balconies and set on a lawn. The 1923 Great Kanto Earthquake and the resulting fires burned both buildings to the ground.

上：涼亭　**Top**: Ryo-tei - *Sukiya*-style building originally used to entertain foreign dignitaries

清澄庭園の特色は、全国の庭石をふんだんに使っている点にある。相州や伊豆の石はもちろん全国各地から船便で集めたもので、「海運王・三菱」ならではといえる。庭石は、変成岩、花崗岩、粘板岩など地域色豊かな自然石で、ふつう地名で呼ばれる。重い庭石を全国から集めるのは容易で

ないが、ここでは紀州や伊予の青石、佐渡の赤玉石など各地の銘石が全園に配石されていて、趣味人によろこばれる「庭石博物館」ともなっている。

沢飛石が数ヶ所に打たれた大きな心字池の正面には、富士山や水上に浮ぶ涼亭（茶室専門の保岡勝也設計）を望む池泉周遊式庭園。

Today, the Kiyosumi Garden is only half its original size. What is notable about this garden is the extravagant use of splendid garden rocks. Rocks were transported by boat from all over Japan. The garden demonstrates Mitsubishi's capability in water transportation. Well known rocks, such as green schist from the Kishū area of remote south-central Honshu and Iyo area in western Honshu, and jasper from Sado Island are sprinkled throughout the garden, making it a veritable museum of garden rocks.

右上：仙台石の自然の石橋
右下：自然石による沢飛石
Upper right: *Sendai-ishi* slate natural stone slab bridge **Lower right**: Unmilled natural stone used to create a *sawa-tobiishi* style stepping stone path across the pond.

22, 新宿御苑 (1906年・西洋式庭園としての新宿御苑：東京都新宿区、渋谷区)

ヴェルサイユ園芸学校マルチネ設計の整形式、風景式、日本式もある庭園

高遠藩（たかとおはん）内藤家は江戸半ば100,000坪の下屋敷に玉川上水を引いて「玉川園」（現在の玉藻池）を作庭。

明治新政府の時代になると、農業重視の政策が始まり、政府は内藤家の邸宅を購入し、敷地を約175,000坪に拡張。農業の近代化拠点として1872年内藤新宿試験場（農事試験場）を開設した。西洋式の牧畜、野菜、果樹、花、養蚕、製紙、製茶、樹藝、害虫の試験を開始。外国人教師を招いて農事修学場（後、農学校、駒場農学校、東大農学部の前身）を付設し、人材育成も始めた。

1879年になると、所管は宮内省に移管され「新宿植物御苑」と改称、皇室行事に供用するブドウ、メロン、缶詰などの試作、サボテン、カトレア、プリムラ、フリージア、イチゴの栽培を行った。その後は西洋式の皇室庭園（パレスガーデン）として整備、1906年「新宿御苑」と改称した。植物御苑の時代には、現在日本庭園となっているところを中心に鴨池、養魚池、動物園（大正15年上野動物園に下賜）が造られるなど、皇室の御料地・農園として運営がなされた。

なお、新宿御苑の西洋式造園計画は、宮内省植物御苑係長・式部官に任命（1898）された当時の日本を代表する造園家福羽逸人（ふくばはやと）（1856-1921）が、1900年のパリ万博に出張したおり、ヴェルサイユ造園学校教授アンリ・マルチネー（Henri Martinet, 1867-1936）に設計を依頼したところから始まる。

22. Shinjuku Gyoen National Garden

(Shinjuku-ku, Tokyo, 1906)

A Western-style garden, representative of modern Japan, Shinjuku Gyoen National Garden straddles Shinjuku and Shibuya wards. The former feudal lord Naitō's family mansion estate of 30 hectares was purchased by the Japanese government as part of the Meiji Restoration, and then later additional land from other holders, to establish the 58.3 hectare Naitō Shinjuku Experiment Station in 1872.

Over the years, a succession of different agencies had jurisdiction over this land including the Finance Ministry, the Interior Ministry, the Imperial Household Ministry, and after World War II, the Health and Welfare Ministry and the Ministry of the Environment.

At first, in 1872, the aim was to create a modern agricultural experiment station that would conduct research related to livestock farming, vegetables, fruit trees, sericulture, paper manufacturing, tea processing, arboriculture and pest control. In 1879, under the jurisdiction of the Imperial Household Ministry, it was renamed Shinjuku Imperial Botanical Garden. Experiments were carried out with the cultivation of grapes, melons, cacti, primrose, freesia, and strawberries as well as canning processes.

元、東京市の公園課長で、東京の公園行政の基礎を築いた井下清氏によると、新宿御苑のスズカケノキやユリノキは、東京市の街路樹の母樹として使われた。
写真提供：環境省新宿御苑管理事務所

Large numbers of Old World London Plane and Tulip trees used in the green boulevards of Tokyo city were from mother trees in Shinjuku Gyoen National Garden.
Photo: ©Shinjuku Gyoen Management Office

福羽は、マルチネの設計図どおり正門部分はフランス整形式庭園、園内の中央にはイギリス風景式庭園の皇室庭園・宴遊の場を目指した。鴨池跡は、日本式林泉へと改装整備された。

明治天皇を迎え開苑式も行われ、宮中行事としての観桜会も1917年から、観菊会は1929年から開かれ、近年まで首相主催のイベントなどとして継承されていた。

敗戦後、1949年（昭和24年）からは「国民公園・新宿御苑」として広く国民に公開。現在は環境省所管で生物多様性の普及活動を実施する。

マルチネ案の広場では、大正、昭和天皇の大喪の礼（たいそうのれい）が挙行された。大喪の礼の会場にあてられたのは、同案で並木のビスタ正面には宮殿が予定されていたほどに高い格調を感じさせる空間構成のゆえだからと考えられる。

新宿御苑は、広大な芝生園地と自然樹形のプラタナス、ユリノキ、タイサンボク、メタセコイアなど、樹高20mを超える自然形大木をゆったりと点綴（てんてい）し、都心中の都心に、おおらかさを与えている。

Hayato Fukuba (1856-1921), a horticultural expert with the Imperial Household Ministry (who became the director of the Shinjuku Imperical Botanical Garden in 1898) visited Paris to inspect horticultural exhibits for the Paris Exposition of 1900. During his visit, Fukuba met Henri Martinet (1867-1936), then a professor of the Versailles Horticultural School and asked him to re-design the Shinjuku Botanical Garden. The garden was then remodeled based on Martinet's design. The area around the main gate is French formal in style, but the garden overall is an English *fūkei* (natural scenery) garden design style and also includes a Japanese-style garden on the former site of the duck pond. It was subsequently renamed the Shinjuku Gyoen (Imperial Garden) in 1906.

As the garden was designed with the intention of being used for formal occasions, the design employed symmetry to create a grandiose atmosphere. Consequently, the garden served as an official location for government and imperial court events including formal cherry-blossom and chrysanthemum viewing parties starting in 1917 and 1929 respectively, and for the funeral ceremonies of both Emperor Taishō and Emperor Shōwa.

The gentle curves, expansive lawns and Tulip trees, London planes (Platanus), Southern Magnolias and Dawn Redwoods of over 20 meters in height in the English *fūkei*-style garden, provide a refreshing contrast with the neighboring skyscrapers and dense urban environment of neighboring Shinjuku.

23, 旧古河庭園 （1919年：東京都北区）

ジョサイア・コンドルのバラ園と西洋館、小川治兵衛の日本庭園併存財閥邸園

主役のジョサイア・コンドル設計の西洋館（1917年竣工）が台地上に建つ。西洋館の南斜面にはバラが主体の西洋式テラスガーデンが、一方、東斜面と南低地には庭師の植治こと小川治兵衛(1860-1933)作庭の池泉庭園（1919年竣工）がある。

この土地はもと明治の元勲陸奥宗光（むつむねみつ）邸であったが、宗光次男の潤吉が古河市兵衛の養子になったので古河家のものになり、古河財閥3代当主で男爵を賜った虎之助（市兵衛の実子、1887-1940）により、1917年に完成した。

洋館の全景は東側と南側から眺められる。洋館の東は芝生の平坦園で、建築の全貌が眺めやすいように建物高の3〜4倍の引きがある。

南斜面、3段のテラスガーデン、上から1段目はサワラ、ハクチョウゲの刈込みとバラ花壇、2段目はツツジの植込み。3段目からはシイノキの大木もあり、自然に下の日本庭園に馴じむよう配置している。

その先の低地は植治流の池泉庭園となっており、池には大小の島、荒磯（ありそ）、洲浜（すはま）、石橋がある。池畔の磯浜の雪見灯籠（ゆきみどうろう）は、財閥臭を感じるほど大きく高さ八尺(2.5m)もあり、他にも財閥好みの大ぶりの石造美術品が10余基もある。一方には、枯滝、見晴台がある。

なお、コンドル設計の西洋館はレンガ造二階建だが、外壁は伊豆の真鶴産の新小

23. Furukawa Garden

(Kita-ku Ward, Tokyo, 1919)

This land originally belonged to an elder statesman in the Meiji period, Mutsu Munemitsu. When the founder of the Furukawa *zaibatsu* (a powerful business conglomerate) Furkawa Ichibei adopted his second son Junkichi after the death of Munemitsu's wife, the land was given to the Furukawa family. Construction of the residence and garden began in 1914 under the direction of the third head of the Furukawa *zaibatsu*, Toranosuke, and it was completed in 1917.

Ogawa Jihei (also known professionally as Ueji) designed the Furukawa Garden around a Western-style residence designed by Josiah Conder in 1917 (the author of the classic Japanese garden book, "Landscape Gardening in Japan"). The residence overlooks a terraced rose garden on the south hillside below and a Japanese-style pond garden on the east hillside and the lowland to the south.

To the east of the residence is a flat lawn, the length of which is three to four times the height of the building, allowing for a full view of the building. The lowest part of the site is a natural-style garden in the style for which Ueji was known for. On the hillside just below the lawn is a large waterfall, a ravine, and a large pond. In the pond are

松石（安山岩）で覆い、屋根は天然スレート葺きである。外観と1階は完全に西洋式であるが、2階内部は和室の居間、客間、仏間になっている。

　2006年国指定名勝、面積約30,800平方メートル。西洋館の管理は、現在大谷美術館による。

傾斜地を生かしたJ.コンドル設計の西洋建築（**上**）、その前庭のバラ園（**中**）、小川治兵衛の和風庭園（**下**）

Western-style residence designed by British architect Josiah Conder (**top**); rose garden in front of the Western-style residence (**middle**); Japanese-style garden designed by Ogawa Jihei (Ueji) (**bottom**)

as a result the garden is its own little world. The large pond in the middle creates an impression of spaciousness and depth. A tea garden on a level area halfway down the hillside adds another dimension to the garden.

The Furukawa Garden, unlike other western influenced gardens of the era, which often had incongruent and forced mixtures of western and eastern architecture and landscape architecture, has a tactful, fluent and integrated design. This can likely be largely attributed to Josiah Conder's in-depth understanding and sense for Japanese landscape architecture. Conder lived in Japan for over 40 years (1877-1920) and took a keen interest in Japanese culture, especially Japanese gardens. This gave him the uncommon and highly skilled capacity to successfully combine Eastern and Western design styles.

islands, large and small, a rocky coast, sandy beach, stone bridge, dry waterfall, and elevated viewpoint. Surrounded by topographical features and a clay wall, the garden does not permit long, uninterrupted views; more than 200 chinquapin pine trees were planted, and

24，川合玉堂美術館の庭園 （1961年開館作庭：東京都青梅市）

近代数寄屋建築家吉田五十八の美術館と造園家中島健の現代的枯山水

青梅線の御嶽（みたけ）駅を出ると御嶽山が仰瞰され、駅前の橋を渡って渓谷におりると、日本画家の川合玉堂（かわいぎょくどう）（1873-1957）の美術館に到る。敷地面積1,500㎡の美術館は、現代数寄屋建築の巨匠吉田五十八（よしだいそや）（1894-1974）の設計。多摩川の清流を望み水音も聴こえる立地に、モダニズムを感じさせる数寄屋風の建築と造園家中島健（なかじまけん）（1914-2000）の設計したシンプルな枯山水が見事に一体化している。

漆喰（しっくい）塗の低い築地塀は、庭と外を截然（せつぜん）と区切りつつも庭前の渓谷の水音や気配を十分に感じさせてくれる。庭園は、現地多摩川御岳渓谷から採取した大小の自然石をやさしく配石した実に簡素な枯山水である。深い庇（ひさし）、禅院のような磚（せん）の舗装テラスと砂敷の砂紋の広がりが連続し、静寂な露地風の境地を醸成する。

川合玉堂が愛した御岳渓谷の場所性に加え、地場材の多摩川石が数石、効果的に

24. Kare Sansui Garden of the Gyokudō Art Museum

(Ōme City, Tokyo, 1961)

Crossing the bridge in front of the Mitake Station on the Ōme Line in eastern Tokyo and descending to the bottom of the gorge, one arrives at a compound surrounded by a clay wall: an art museum dedicated to Gyokudō Kawai (1873-1957). Kawai was a master of modern *Nihonga* (Japanese-style painting). Here at the Gyokudō Art Museum, one finds a simple *kare sansui* garden, where natural rocks harvested from the Mitake Gorge of the nearby Tamagawa River are arranged.

Standing between the hillside and the river, the museum is a contemporary masterpiece that skillfully integrates a refined *sukiya* style (teahouse inspired) building designed by the architect Isoya Yoshida and a *kare sansui* garden by the landscape architect Ken Nakajima.

The garden is sublimely simple. Nakajima distilled and expressed the character of the gorge into a simple *kare sansui* style garden. A continuous space of deep eaves, a terrace paved with bricks (*sen*) and a raked sand expanse, suggestive of a Zen temple, produce an irresistible sense of stillness. The low clay wall with white plaster clearly separates the garden from the outside world, however, one can still sense the presence of the gorge beyond the wall.

The large trees outside the garden, the hillside opposite the shore, the surrounding topography, and the distant view of the gorge all beautifully envelop the garden and give it a sense of tranquility and stability.

配石。やさしい砂敷空間に直線形のアクセント効果をねらった延段は、多摩川産小石を天端(てんぱ)を平らに敷きつめている。

　庭園から眺められる近景の大樹、背後の杉林、中景の民家や対岸の斜面林、遠景に紅葉が、美しい渓谷美へと連ながり一幅の日本画のようである。谷地形に囲まれ安らぎと安定感を感じさせる現代東京の名園である。妹家（いもうとや）というレストランもいい。

上：玉堂美術館前の多摩川の渓谷風景美

Top: The beautiful scenery of the Tamagawa River where it flows past the Gyokudo Art Museum.

下：多摩川の風景をモチーフとしたシンプルかつモダンな枯山水。場所性を生かし、地場材(多摩川現地産の景石)を活用している。

Bottom: A modern and simplified, *kare sansui* emulation of the scenery of the Tamagawa River in the museum garden. The use of locally sourced rock gives the garden a uniquely regional flavor.

25, 足立美術館　（1970年・美術館開館：島根県安来市）

アメリカ人観光客に大好評の借景効果抜群の現代日本の枯山水庭園

　貧農に生まれた足立全康（あだちぜんこう）（本名・義元、1899-1990）は、大阪に出て30余の仕事を経て金儲けに励み実業家として成功。69歳のとき故郷安来市（やすぎし）の生家跡に15,000坪（後、50,000坪に拡張）の日本庭園の造園と美術館建設に着手。庭園設計図は大阪芸大中根金作（なかねきんさく）教授による築山林泉と枯山水だが、1970年の開館以来美術館本館建築など次々と拡張。その度に足立全康の思いで整備改修されほとんど原設計の面影は残らないほど「足立ワールド」が現出している。

　足立全康は「自分の人生は、庭と女性と日本画ーすべて美しいもの」と語る。子供のころ近くの禅寺雲樹寺の手入れの行き届いた枯山水に感動し、美しい女の子に憧れ、ひと目見た横山大観の日本画を忘れられず、必死に働き日本画のコレクターとなる。美術館のコレクションには近代日本画家らの作品、他に近代陶芸家の作品などがある。

　オーナー個人の熱い思いは、亡くなる92歳まで20余年に及ぶ。『庭園日本ー足立美術館をつくった男』（日本経済新聞出版社、2007）には、故郷の勝山、京羅木山、月山への眺望を借景し、今までにないスケールの日本庭園を構想するまでの情熱的なチャレンジが綴られる。

25. Garden of Adachi Museum of Art

(Yasugi City, Shimane Prefecture, 1970)

Zenkō Adachi (Yoshimoto Adachi, 1899-1990), was born to a poor farming family, made his way to Osaka, and eventually became a successful entrepreneur. At 69, he began building a Japanese garden and art museum occupying 4.95 hectares of land (which later expanded to 16.5 ha) in his hometown of Yasugi City in Shimane Prefecture.

　The garden was originally designed by Professor Kinsaku Nakane of Osaka University of Art as an amalgamation of a *kaiyū*-style (strolling) garden and a *kare sansui* garden. However, the museum grew in stages after opening in 1970, and the garden was enhanced each time in accordance with the owner's ideas and preferences. Today, little of its original design remains with it instead reflecting Adachi's own taste.

　Adachi described his life as one spent in preoccupation with beauty: the beauty of gardens, the beauty of women, and the beauty of Nihonga (Japanese-style paintings). As a youth, he was moved by the *kare sansui* garden of the nearby Unju-ji Temple. He was also deeply impressed by the Nihonga paintings of Yokoyama Taikan, so much so that, according to him, he set out to amass wealth in order to collect the artist's work. Today the museum's collections include works of prominent modern *Nihonga* painters such as Taikan, as well as works of celebrated modern ceramic artists.

旅行中の車窓からみた赤松800本を石川県の能登で入手するエピソード。新見石、佐治石を見つけたこと。大観作「那智の滝」の絵画から高さ15mの亀鶴の滝を思いついたり、大観作「白砂青松」を庭に再現したこと。庭師小島佐一（こじまさいち）の苔庭への思い入れ等、自らの絵心と大観の描いた日本画世界を、足立全康は「日本庭園こそ一幅の絵画」と考え見事にパノラマ園景に表現したのである。

借景による遠景・中景・近景の奥行と、左右前面に展開する日本画世界のインパクトは、景観効果抜群。手入れも完璧。米国の日本庭園専門誌の来日観光客によるランキングでは数十年トップが続くのも納得できる。

Adachi remained passionate about his garden for over two decades, until his death at 92. In his autobiography, "The Man Who Created the Garden of the Adachi Museum of Art, the Finest Garden in Japan" (2007), he described the challenge of creating a Japanese garden of unprecedented scale, one in which distant views of the local mountains of Mt. Katsuyama, Mt. Kyōragisan, and Mt. Gassan are incorporated as borrowed scenery.

In his book, he recounts numerous episodes, such as the acquisition of 800 Japanese red pines in the Noto Peninsula in Ishikawa Prefecture that he happened to see from the window of a train while also discovering specimens of Niimi and Saji stones. He was so inspired by the painting, "Nachi-no-taki" by Taikan that he created an actual waterfall 15 meters high. He also recreated another Taikan masterpiece, "Hakushya Seishō" ("White Sands and Green Pines") as part of the art ensemble he created in his garden. Adachi's garden design philosophy was born out of his deep passion for *Nihonga* paintings and his belief that a Japanese garden composition should be like the expansive and panoramic scenes in those paintings.

The garden, with the distinct establishment of foreground, middle ground and background, creates a clear sense of spatial depth and it is indeed a successful interpretation of Adachi's world of *Nihonga*, complete with quintessential borrowed scenery. Accordingly, the garden has been recognized as the top Japanese garden in Japan by the *Sukiya Living Magazine: The Journal of Japanese Gardening* for twenty consecutive years running.

26, 新宿京王プラザホテル外空間 （1971年ホテル開業：東京都新宿区）

東京の原風景である武蔵野の雑木林を東京都心ホテルの「外空間」に再現

新宿の淀橋浄水場跡地に東京の新都心を建設することになり最初に建てられた超高層ホテルが、京王（けいおう）プラザホテルである。このホテルの外構、いわばオープン・ガーデンのテーマを異色の造園家深谷光軌（ふかやこうき）（1926-1997）は、江戸東京の原風景の再生を構想した。

京王プラザホテルは、1971年6月オープンした。ホテル北側2階のグラウンドレベルに「レストラン・樹林」があり、建物の壁面から幅15メートル、長さ90メートル、面積1,400平方メートルの「外空間（がいくうかん）」が続く。都庁舎に向かう歩道の左手、南側は斜面になっていて、ここに

も雑木（ぞうき）が植えられ、歩行者は緑の谷道を通っているように感じる。道路から建築線の空間は緩やかな斜面になっていて、雑木林に奥行き感を演出している。

雑木林のところどころには、まるで武蔵野の窪地にできた井戸のような水景を配し、しっとり感を演出している。半地下のレストランの壁は石積みになっているが、壁の途中何カ所かに吐水口（ハケ）があって滝のように水が落ちる。武蔵野台地の端部の崖緑地形の湧水を表現している。

歩行者はまるで武蔵野の雑木林のなかを歩いているように感じ、人工都市に生きる東京人を暖かく包んでくれる。武

26. Outdoor Space of Keio Plaza Hotel, Shinjuku

(Shinjuku-ku Ward, Tokyo, 1971)

Part of the new center of Tokyo, built on the former site of the Yodobashi Water Purification Plant in Shinjuku, the Keio Plaza Hotel was the first super high-rise hotel in Japan. The exterior landscape of the hotel, open to public viewing, designed by landscape architect Kōki Fukaya, emulates the native flora of the Musashino Plateau where present day Tokyo exists and evokes nostalgic imagery of classic Tokyo scenery.

The hotel opened in June 1971. The second floor, on the north side, is a restaurant situated at ground level. An outdoor space of 15 x 90 meters (1,400 m²) continues along the restaurant's glass wall. On the south side, to the left of the sidewalk, as one walks from the direction of Shinjuku Station toward Tokyo City Hall, the ground slopes and the trees are planted to create the impression for pedestrians, that they are passing through a green valley.

The space between the street and the building is a gentle slope, creating the illusion that it is a remnant of natural woodland. The stand of trees is dotted with pools of water and small channels,

蔵野の主役は、クヌギやコナラ、ときにはイヌシデ、アカシデ、アカマツが混じる雑木林である。歩道並木の主役となっているケヤキとともにひとまとまりの緑の懐かしい風景軸をつくっている。

なお栃木県那須地方から産出される芦野石（あしのいし）が、野面（のづら）加工されて全敷地の歩行面や石積として活用され Agingの美と深い味合いを醸し出している。歩行面に埋められた砕石が靴底を刺激し、足裏の感覚を呼び起こす効果をねらっている。

suggestive of the natural springs found in the hollows of a Musashino forest, produces a distinct sense of calmness and peace. The sub-basement level restaurant has a masonry wall from which water surges out, representing spring water falling from verdant bluffs on the edges of the Musashino Plateau. The recreated woodland consists primarily of Japanese *konara* oak, hornbeam and Japanese red pine, with Zelkovas lining the sidewalk, creating a green oasis gently embracing the busy people moving through this densely-populated urban center of Tokyo.

27, ガーデンアイランド下蒲刈島

（1988年計画「2015年度サントリー地域文化賞」受賞：広島県呉市）

朝鮮通信使、おもてなしの島を「新下蒲刈八景」で全島庭園化

世界にはひとつの島が美しく造園修景されて、正に"島そのものが名園"となっているものがある。北イタリア、マッジョーレ湖の「イソラ・ベラ(Isola Bella)」や南ドイツ、ボーデン湖の「花の島マイナウ島(Mainau)」など。

日本では古来「島（しま）」の呼称は「庭園」と同義で、ミクロコスモスとしてもリゾートとしても「島」はもっと生かされるべきである。

このように考えていた私に、広島県下蒲刈町の竹内町長から蘭島美術館周辺修景計画の依頼があった。竹内弘之は1976年から27年間を務めた名物町長だが、会ってす

ぐ庭園癖の人だと実感した。そこで竹内町長の行動力に造園家の構想力をプラスすれば「全島庭園化構想」も可能だろうと計画を策定（東京農大進士研究室、1988年）、概成した全体像を進士著『庭園の島／21世紀日本のまちづくりモデル・ガーデンアイランド・下蒲刈』（写真集、マルモ出版2003）としてまとめた。

下蒲刈島は江戸時代、朝鮮通信使が長期滞在し徳川将軍家に"安芸の蒲刈ご馳走一番"と奉答したと言われる"おもてなしの島"で、通信使は「下蒲刈八景」を詠んでおり、著者進士は町が候補にあげている島内開発拠点を「新八景」に位置づけ各景

27. Shimokamagari Garden Island

(Created in 1988, Kure City, Inland Sea, Hiroshima Prefecture)

There are islands around the world that are entirely landscaped into beautiful gardens. Among them is Isola Bella on Lake Maggiore in north Italy and the "flowering island" of Mainau on Lake Constance in south Germany. Since ancient times, *shima*, the Japanese word for "island," has also meant "garden." The author believes, more islands should employ this unique geographic capacity and be developed as a micro-cosmos in this way to draw more visitors.

Mayor Takeuchi of Shimokamagari Island in Hiroshima Prefecture, asked the author to design the landscape around the Rantōkaku Art Museum. Mayor Takeuchi, a long-time resident and leader of the island, served as the head of the island municipality for 27 years, beginning in 1976. Takeuchi loved gardens and believed it was possible to realize this visionary idea to transform the entire island into a garden if his passion could be combined with the skills and abilities of a landscape architect. The Shinji Research Lab prepared a master plan in 1988 (later documented and published as "An Island Garden: Shimokamagari, A Model of Community Development for the 21st Century" Marumo Publishing, 2003).

風光明媚な瀬戸内海の下蒲刈島は、いまや観光客で賑わいボランタリー活動も盛んで、2015年にはサントリー文化財団の「サントリー地域文化賞」を受賞している。著者の狙いは、熊本県アートポリスが建築家によるのに対し、造園家版ガーデン・アイランドを構想したのだが、文化賞の受賞で評価を得たと考える。

の造園を当代の代表的作庭家に依頼し、多様性に富み美しい『庭園の島』に仕上げた。

蒲刈大橋の三之瀬公園は伊藤邦衛、松濤園は野沢清、美術館前は井上剛宏、大地

写真：伊藤邦衛設計の防波堤。瀬戸内地方の花崗岩を多孔質な空積みとし、生物が共生できるようにする。さらに近くの島と相似形の石を堤体に組み込むことで遠景と近景を一体化させている。それが全島庭園化の心である。

Picture: Designed by Japanese landscape architect Kunie Ito, this seawall was made of local granite stones, dry-stacked, allowing for spaces between the rocks, creating habitat for a multitude of diverse organisms. He also incorporated a rock arrangement into the wall that emulates the islands across the bay, uniting both the near and distant views. This design embodies the spirit of this whole-island garden composition ambition.

Shimokamagari Island has long had a reputation for excellent hospitality. In the Edo period, a notable Korean diplomatic mission declared they experienced incredible generosity, and that their stay on Shimokamagari was their most joyful experience during their stay in Japan. The mission composed a poem remembering the so-called Eight Views of Shimokagari. These eight historical views provide a conceptual framework for this project. Five celebrated garden artists were selected and each given a commission to create a garden for each designated site, initiating the transformation of Shimokagari into a "garden island."

Kunie Itō designed Sannose Park where the Kamagari Bridge is located; Kiyoshi Nozawa designed the Shōtōen Garden; Takahiro Inoue designed the garden in front of the art museum; and Takurō Mayuzumi designed the artificial beach in Ōjizō. In addition, Toshio Watanabe collaborated with the mayor and local volunteers to organize garden design workshops and identify new scenic locations on the island, following the historical journey undertaken by the Korean diplomatic mission to Shimokamagari Island. Shimokamagari is now a popular tourist destination and is well known for community volunteer activism, receiving the Suntory Prize for Community Cultural Activities in 2015.

28, 杉本博司・江之浦測候所　（2017年：神奈川県小田原市）

現代美術作家からのメッセージ、「アーティストよ、人類意識の現場・天空のうちにある自身の場に立ち戻れ」

　世界的な現代美術作家、杉本博司（1948-）はニューヨーク近代美術館収蔵作品の写真家としてデビューし、伝統建築家、文筆家、歴史家、演劇家、能楽師等々、多彩な作品と活動でアートの本質を追求しつづけてきた作家であり思想家でもある。著者らは2017年11月、開館1ヶ月後の小田原文化財団・江之浦測候所を訪ね、杉本氏自身の解説で氏の作家活動の総まとめでもあり、その歴史的意味を構造化したという正に「杉本ワールド」を拝見。これこそ現代日本が世界に誇れる「日本庭園の思想的造景」と確信した。

　たとえば日本庭園の最重要事、立地・敷地選定だが、10,000平方メートルの海に岬状に突き出た元ミカン畑のこの土地は、少年期の杉本の原体験・原風景の地でもあり、相模湾から世界の海・太平洋が眼前に広がる。

　この江之浦に杉本は長い隧道を通す。冬至の朝、相模湾を上る「朝日」が隧道を通過する。1年に1度だけの光景だ。「アートは人間の意識の最先端を提示し続けてきた」と杉本は考える。しかし今それが失われつつある。今こそアーティストたちに人類意識の発生現場に立　ち戻る契機を与えたい。冬至や夏至の光を浴びて「天空のうちにある自身の場を再発見してほしい」という。

　だからここを「江之浦測候所」と命名

28. Enoura Observatory

(Odawara City, Kanagawa Prefecture, 2017, created by Hiroshi Sugimoto)

Hiroshi Sugimoto (1948 -) is an artist and philosopher, who made his debut as a photographer. His works are now in the collection of The Museum of Modern Art, New York and has continued to explore the essence of art through diverse works and activities including as a traditional architect, writer, historian, dramatist and Noh actor.

The Enoura Observatory of the Odawara Art Foundation, which opened in 2017, represents Sugimoto's view of the world, a recapitulation of Sugimoto's creative works and, in his word, the "structuralization" of their historical significance. This is indeed a work of landscape architecture based on the same philosophy behind the Japanese garden design tradition. The selection of the location and site is the most important in the design of a Japanese garden. This particular piece of land, a former tangerine grove measuring 10,000 ㎡, projecting into the sea, was the primary landscape of Sugimoto's childhood memories. It affords a view of Sagami Bay and to the Pacific Ocean beyond.

Here in Enoura, Sugimoto created a long buried passageway. On the winter solstice, light from the morning sun rising

する。園内には方位・地形に順って、氏の代表作のフォトギャラリーをはじめ石舞台、硝子舞台、茶室、竹林に回遊路が巡り、太陽と月と海の水平線の雄大なランドスケープと、日本建築と築地による結界内に法隆寺の若草伽藍の礎石など日本の歴史の、数々のマイルストーンが場所を得て据えられる等、景観軸と時間軸の原点を美事に実感させる。

世界中の人たちに杉本博司の思想「天空を観測することで、未来への道が開く」を、江之浦測候所で体感してほしいと願っている。

（写真と図の提供：江之浦測候所）

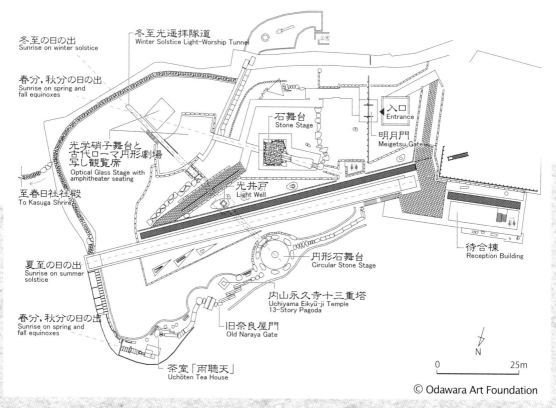

冬至の日の出
Sunrise on winter solstice

冬至光遥拝隧道
Winter Solstice Light-Worship Tunnel

春分，秋分の日の出
Sunrise on spring and fall equinoxes

石舞台
Stone Stage

入口
Entrance

明月門
Meigetsu Gate

光学硝子舞台と古代ローマ円形劇場写し観覧席
Optical Glass Stage with amphitheater seating

光井戸
Light Well

至春日社社殿
To Kasuga Shrine

夏至の日の出
Sunrise on summer solstice

円形石舞台
Circular Stone Stage

待合棟
Reception Building

春分，秋分の日の出
Sunrise on spring and fall equinoxes

内山永久寺十三重塔
Uchiyama Eikyū-ji Temple 13-Story Pagoda

旧奈良屋門
Old Naraya Gate

茶室「雨聴天」
Uchōten Tea House

N

0   25m

© Odawara Art Foundation

「雨聴天」茶室と石造の鳥居

写真提供：江之浦測候所

Uchoten (Listen-to-the-Rain) Tea House and stone *torii* gate

Photo Credit: Odawara Art Foundation

192

from Sagami Bay, passes through the tunnel. This is naturally an event that can be witnessed only once a year. Sugimoto believes that "art has long represented the leading-edge of human consciousness and the environment." However, he also believes art is now losing this character. He wants to provide an opportunity for artists to return to the birth of human consciousness and be immersed in the light of the winter and the summer solstice to rediscover "their own place under the firmament."

This is why he named this place the Enoura "Observatory." Within the grounds,

and well adapted to the orientation and topography of the land, a gallery, a stone stage, a glass stage, a teahouse, and a bamboo grove are arranged and linked by a path. It is a magnificent landscape of the sun, moon, and ocean horizon. A number of milestones from Japanese history are installed, including a foundation stone from what is reputed to be the original Hōryū-ji monastery. Enoura Observatory is a place where Japan's spatial and temporal axes are on display and examined, echoing Sugimoto's idea that "the path to the future opens up through the observation of the firmament."

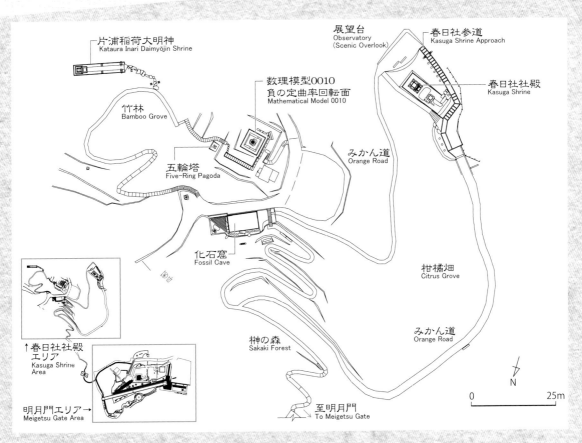

江之浦測候所、明月門エリア全景

Enlarged view of the Meigetsumon (Bright Moon) Gate area ©Odawara Art Foundation

上左：石舞台
上右：冬至光を遥拝する隧道
（写真提供：江之浦測候所）

Upper left: Stone stage
Upper right: Winter Solstice Light Worship Tunnel and lightwell

Photo credit: Odawara Art Foundation

中：海抜100メートル地点に立つ、夏至光を遥拝する杉本博司氏の写真代表作展示ギャラリー
下：夏至の朝、海から昇る太陽光が数分間、この空間に差し込む（写真提供：江之浦測候所）

Middle: Summer Solstice Light-Worship 100 Meter Gallery (built at 100m above sea level). The gallery features photos by observatory creator Hiroshi Sugimoto. (Photo Credit: Odawara Art Foundation)
Right: As the summer solstice sun rises from the ocean horizon, it shines through the front glass corridor of the 100 Meter Gallery, front to back, for just a few minutes every year.
Photo Credit: Odawara Art Foundation

29, 世田谷区二子玉川公園内の帰真園

（2013年開園：東京都世田谷区、旧清水邸書院と日本庭園）

高齢社会下ユニバーサルデザイン対応の初の公設日本庭園

二子玉川園（東急電鉄経営遊園地、1922-1985）跡の再開発により新設された世田谷区立の「二子玉川公園」（総面積6.3ヘクタール）の中央部に2013年4月開園した本格的日本庭園が「帰真園」（面積5800平方メートル）。本園は多摩川畔で二子玉川駅至近に位置。緑の国分寺崖線と水の多摩川の2つのエコシステムが交わる場所にあり、富士山や丹沢の山々への眺望と武蔵野と玉川八景気分を味わえる。

作庭意図は源流から海までの多摩川水系軸と武蔵野の松や雑木、伊豆の根府川石、武家庭園ならではの直線護岸ほか江戸東京地域の文化的自然表現にある。一方、高齢社会下のユニバーサルデザインを目指して車イスで園全体を周遊できるものにした。

ところで市民主権の現代社会では、公的資金で「日本庭園」を開設するには、多くの課題を解決しなければならない。世田谷区では、市民福祉・環境共生・文化教育・公民連携を柱に、以下①～⑦をクリアして事業を推めた。帰真園はその好例であろう。

①企画・監修：世田谷の熊本区長は東京農業大学長の進士五十八教授を委員長に造園事業全ての監修を依頼。

②発注方式：造園学会賞受賞者数名を指名、プロポーザル方式で作庭家と設計者を選定、公平性を担保。設計者に戸田芳樹、

29. Kishin-en Garden

(Public Japanese Garden/ Former Shoin of the Shimizu Residence in Futago-Tamagawa Park, Setagaya-ku, Tokyo, 2013)

Kishin-en (5,800 ㎡) is a full-scale Japanese garden that opened in April 2013 in the center of Futako-tamagawa Park (6.3 hectares) as part of the redevelopment of the former Tokyu Futakotamagawa Amusement Park. The park is located alongside of the Tamagawa River, close to Futagotamagawa Station. Located at the convergence of two ecosystems, the forests of the Kokubunji Escarpment and the waterway of the Tamagawa River, it offers views of Mt. Fuji and the Tanzawa Mountains and gives visitors a taste of the Musashino Plain and the so-called Eight Scenic Spots of Tamagawa.

The garden design is intended to represent the cultural and natural environment of the Edo/Tokyo region: the water system of the Tamagawa River from its source to the sea; the pines and the woodland of the Musashino plain; the display of andesite known as Nebukawa-ishi from Izu; and the straight shoreline unique to gardens of the samurai class during the Edo period. The entire garden is wheelchair-accessible in an effort to achieve a universal design for an aging society.

In today's citizen-sovereign society, many issues must be resolved before a publicly funded "Japanese garden" can be established. In the case of Setagaya Ward, the following seven conditions needed to be met in compliance with the basic tenets of civic welfare, environmental coexistence, cultural education and community coordination:

195

作庭家に高崎康隆を決定。

　③バリアフリー化：伝統的日本庭園では、高低差のある敷地、親水性のための沢飛石、反橋など各種バリアによる景観変化の演出が多用された。ところが高齢社会の居住空間にはユニバーサルデザインが不可欠。スロープ園路の帰真園は車イスで水と触れ花植えも楽しめ視点場を巡れるよう設計する。

　④予算：コスト低減が求められ「企業のCSR」による支援の可能性を模索。「庭屋一如」が日本庭園の基本だが公園予算では本格的日本建築は不可。そこで区の文化財部

門が保存してきた清水建設㈱の元副社長宅の柱材の活用を発意。大手ゼネコンの社会貢献事業として「旧清水邸書院（世田谷区登録有形文化財）」復原工事を要望、園の主景が完成。

　⑤次世代育成：グローバル社会を生きる世田谷の子供たちは、やがて世界を舞台に活躍する。そこで重要なのはアイデンティティ（＝日本文化）。しかし高層マンション育ちの現代っ子に日本建築・日本庭園・和室・床の間・縁側・茶華道文化の体験は皆無。世田谷区が「日本語教育特区」として小中学校生徒の日本文化教育を推進していることから帰真園をその体験場と位置づけた。

1. Design Leadership: General supervision commissioned to a singular professional in the field of landscape architecture. The author was commissioned to supervise the entire project as the chair of its planning committee.

2. Project Commission: The garden designers and architects were selected through a competitive proposal process so that impartiality was assured. Candidates were selected from former recipients of the annual Japanese Institute of Landscape Architecture award. From this process, Yoshiki Toda and Yasutaka Takasaki were selected as the architect and landscape architect.

3. Accommodating a barrier-free environment: In traditional Japanese gardens, unintended barriers such as differences in ground level, steppingstones over a stream or pond, and arched bridges are used to promote unique kinetic and visual experiences. Kishen-en was the first public Japanese garden to adhere to the principle of universal design for an aging society.

園内主要園路は車椅子で移動可能。休憩鑑賞可能のユニバーサルデザインの風景場面

All of the main paths in the garden were designed in accordance with universal design principles making them easily accessed by wheelchairs or guests with other disabilities and allowing them places to rest as well as prime viewpoints from which the garden can be appreciated and garden elements can even be touched from a wheelchair.

⑥公民連携：清水建設株式会社はじめ、区内の五島美術館寄贈の石灯籠などを再利用し、公民連携の見える化を図る。

⑦園名のネーミング：「帰真」の意味は、Return to Nature。自然回帰、本質に立ち帰ることの意義を標榜。著者が「帰真園」を選んだ理由は東洋庭園の園名には造園の思想が表出されるべきで、『江南園林史』の著者、楊鴻勛（YANG HONG XUN）先生が中国山東省濰坊市（ウェイファン）人民公園に設計した「帰真園（2006開園）」に共感したからである。

著者としては社会的要請のクリアと作庭理念を両立してこそ、公共的に日本庭園を開設することが可能となる現実を読者に伝えたいのである。

古くから日本の象徴である富士山を眺めるための、富士見台。富士山形の築山で、晴れていれば眼下に清流多摩川、遠くに富士が大きく眺められる

The Fujimi-dai emulation mound of the iconic Mt. Fuji from the top of which, on a clear day, you can see the real Mt. Fuji.

4. Budget: Consultants and contractors were sought to participate in "Corporate Social Responsibility (CSR)" in response to the demand for cost reduction. Traditionally, a garden and its architecture are integral parts of a qualitative whole, but given the project budget, designing and constructing a full-fledged Japanese building was difficult to achieve. The Cultural Asset Department of the city conceived the idea of utilizing the structural members preserved from the residence of the former vice president of the Shimizu Corporation. The city asked a general contracting firm to restore the former *shoin* of the Shimizu Residence (a registered tangible cultural asset of Setagaya Ward) to comply with their CSR mandate, and the garden was thus provided with its architectural focal point.

5. Training the next generation: Setagaya's children, living in a globalized society, will soon be active on the world stage and their identity is important (i.e., awareness of their Japanese culture). However, children growing up in high-rise condominiums of today have no experience with traditional Japanese architecture, Japanese gardens, Japanese-style rooms, *tokonoma* alcoves, verandas and the culture of tea ceremonies and flower arrangements. Setagaya, as a special Japanese-language education zone (designated by the Ministry of Education, Culture, Sports, Science and Technology) has been promoting education about Japanese culture among elementary and junior high school students, and decided to use Kishin-en as a site for this experience.

6. Public-private partnership: Stone lanterns and other items donated by the Shimizu Corporation and the Goto Art Museum were reused. This is a tangible example of public and private partnership.

7. Naming of the garden: *Kishin* means "return to nature." It is important to go back to what is essential. The name Kishinen was selected to express the philosophy behind the garden design, which was inspired by remembering a garden with the same Chinese characters in its name, designed by Yang Hong Xun in Weifang city in Shandong Province of China.

This garden demonstrates that a contemporary Japanese garden is only possible when it satisfies both the social needs and the philosophy of garden design.

197

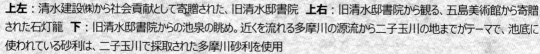

上左：清水建設㈱から社会貢献として寄贈された、旧清水邸書院　上右：旧清水邸書院から観る、五島美術館から寄贈された石灯籠　下：旧清水邸書院からの池泉の眺め。近くを流れる多摩川の源流から二子玉川の地までがテーマで、池底に使われている砂利は、二子玉川で採取された多摩川砂利を使用

Upper left: The rebuilt structure made from the structural components of the former *shoin* study of the Shimizu Residence, donated by Shimizu Corporation.　**Upper right**: A stone lantern, one of many items donated by the Gotoh Museum, as seen from the Shimizu-tei *shoin* study.　**Bottom**: In emulation of the nearby iconic Tamagawa River, the park has a waterway emulating the main stages of the river using gravel and large river stones and boulders from the Tamagawa River in the waterscape, evoking strong imagery and connection.

30, アメリカ ポートランド市のジャパニーズガーデン(オレゴン州)

（1967年・戸野琢磨設計）

森林公園の変化ある地形を生かし半世紀かけて育まれた日本式庭園
日本の伝統文化と美をアメリカ人に伝える本格的文化センター

日本とアメリカをつなぐ文化施設をつくりたいと考えた日米有志の手で、1967年に開園された。庭園設計は、アメリカ・コーネル大学でLandscape design（造園）を学び東京農業大学で教鞭をとった戸野琢磨(1891-1985)により、教え子の平欣也が初期工事(1964-1969)を担当した。

海外の日本庭園の多くは、メンテナンスとマネージメントに課題があるが、本園の場合は、施工後も日本からの庭園ディレクターたちが次々と常駐し、高質のメンテナンスと拡張整備を続けた。木や苔の成長成熟によって、庭園の質は年々高まり、北アメリカを代表するジャパニーズガーデンへと成長した。

近年は財団CEOスティーブ・ブルームの強力なリーダーシップで、また庭園主任学芸員内山貞文らスタッフによる国内外でのピースシンポジウム活動などにより、海外で開設されている代表的日本庭園として注目されている。財団CEOスティーブは「Inspiring Harmony and Peace（調和と平和をもたらす日本庭園）」をスローガンに、世界のジャパニーズ・ガーデン界のネットワークをリードしている。

ポートランドのジャパニーズガーデンは、市の森林公園の一画にあり、高低差に富んだ複雑な地形を生かして、基本設計者

30. Portland Japanese Garden

(Oregon, USA, 1967)

Dedicated in 1961, the Portland Japanese Garden was formally opened in 1967. The garden was created with hope for "forging a healing connection to Japan on the heels of World War II." It was designed by Takuma Tono (1891-1985), who studied landscape architecture at Cornell University and taught at the Tokyo University of Agriculture. The construction was initiated (1964-69) by Kinya Hira, one of Tono's former students.

The Portland Japanese Garden occupies part of a forested city park. The complex topography of the site, with many different levels, makes it possible to bring together, without any anomaly, several different gardens of diverse styles - a flat garden, a strolling pond garden, a tea garden, and a rock garden - and integrate them into one overall kaiyū-style (circuitous strolling) garden.

Many Japanese gardens outside of Japan face challenges of maintenance and management. However, the Portland Japanese garden, thanks to a succession of eight resident garden experts or "Garden Directors" from Japan from 1964 to 1990, has continued to enjoy high-quality maintenance as well as steady improvement and significant expansion.

の戸野の後、3-4年交代で滞米した8名の庭園ディレクターが各々平庭、池庭、茶庭、石庭をつくり、多彩な庭園様式を違和感なく共存させて、各型式をつなげた回遊式庭園を完結させている。本園のもうひとつの特色は、ソフトウェアの充実で、当初から日本文化の展示・講演ホールを、庭園と同等に重視してきたことである。

2017年竣工の文化交流館は、世界的建築家隈研吾(1954-)の設計で、質の高い展覧会を継続的に企画している。アメリカでは最もアクティブな日本文化センターと評価され、多彩な日本文化がアメリカ人に体験され吸収されている。来園者らは、時代を超えて受け継がれてきた日本の心と関係者の異文化交流への情熱に感動している。

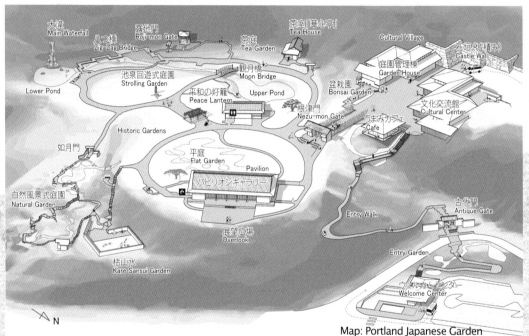

Map: Portland Japanese Garden

左：1970年代に小樽の商家から移築された正門　右：日本の代表的造園家で、本園の設計者 戸野琢磨の枯山水庭園（1967年設立）

Left: Antique gate with autumnal Japanese maple. (Photo: William Sutton) **Right**: Dappled light on *kare sansui* garden (Photo: Wayne Williams)

右：平庭とパビリオン（百畳敷の書院）
下：園内の平庭と外部の森林の連続性の演出に注目
Right: The Garden and Pavilion Gallery (Photo: Jonathan Ley) **Below**: The Garden: subtle but skillful delineation of the garden with the forest behind (Photo: Tony Small)

右下：文化交流館(カルチュラル・ビレッジ)
隈研吾設計、2017年設立
Bottom right: Cultural Village campus and Learning Center building (Photo: Bruce Forster)

The growth and maturation of trees and moss have also helped to improve the quality of the garden year after year and as a result, the Portland Garden is the best-known Japanese garden in North America and regarded as the best outside of Japan.

In 2008, following the eight garden directors, Sadafumi Uchiyama became the first garden curator (2008-2013), which coupled with the strong leadership of CEO Steve Bloom and the efforts of their staff, have helped the Portland garden become well known for their work as advocates of cultural diplomacy using art, culture, and nature to create inter-cultural under-standing through peace-centric programming including organizing international peace symposiums and other such events.

One unique and notable feature of this garden is the existence of a facility called the "Cultural Village" added in 2017. The Cultural Village, designed by Kengo Kuma, organizes high quality exhibitions, lectures and other cultural activities. The garden is said to be the most active Japanese culture center in the United States and for over a half a century has introduced Americans to diverse aspects of Japanese culture. Visitors are most impressed by its authentic Japanese spirit which has been kept alive by the vision and enthusiasm of the community associated with this garden.

Raising Public Awareness of Japanese Garden Culture in North America

1. Facilitating world peace through communication between diverse cultures

The Portland Japanese Garden, a U. S. public benefit foundation, was established in 1963 as an extension of the voluntary work of the citizens of Portland to bridge the deep divide left by World War II between Japan and the United States. In the search for a way to overcome the destruction and tragedy of the war and to build a bridge between two different cultures, a common desire to "love nature" that transcended culture was crystallized in the form of the Japanese Garden. In 1955, the mayor of Yokohama gifted Portland a peace lantern inscribed with the words "Casting the Light of Everlasting Peace."

2022 Tokyo Peace Symposium
(Photo: Ken Katsurayama)

ピース・シンポジウム東京2022でピース・ランタンについて語る、ポートランド・ジャパニーズ・ガーデンCEO、スティーブ・ブルーム氏

アメリカにおける日本庭園文化の発信と普及

（1）異文化コミュニケーションで世界平和へ

ポートランド市民の自主的な活動の延長線の上に、第二次世界大戦が残した両国の深い溝を市民レベルで埋めるためのアメリカ合衆国公益財団法人「ポートランド日本庭園」は1963年に設立された。戦争による破壊や悲惨さを乗りこえ、二つの異なる文化を繋ぐ架け橋を 作る方法を模索した結果、文化を超えた「自然を愛する」という共通の思いが 日本庭園という形で結晶することとなった。本園にはその後1955年横浜市長平沼亮三氏から「Casting the Light of Everlasting Peace」という英文が刻まれたピース・ランタン（平和の灯篭）が寄贈されている。

Peace lantern donated by Kew Gardens in London in 2022
2022 年 ロンドン キュー植物園に寄贈されたピース・ランタン

2. Encouraging understanding of the complex Japanese culture through experiential events

The 12 acre (4.8 hectare) garden is located on a western hilltop in Washington Park overlooking the city of Portland and is enjoyed by nearly 500,000 visitors a year.

Completed in 2017, the Cultural Center commonly referred to as the "Cultural Village" was built through a shared vision with architect Kengo Kuma. It is a place to experience diverse aspects of Japanese culture through dialogue with the garden and nature, as well as through a wide range of Japanese arts and crafts that are showcased in the garden.

Performance by Youth Taiko Group at Children's Day event (Photo: Jonathan Ley)

子どもの日イベントにおけるユース太鼓グループによる演奏

（2）多彩な日本文化の体験と理解

庭園（12エーカー＝4.8ヘクタール）は、ポートランド市街を見下ろすワシントンパークの丘にあり、ポートランド市民はじめ年間約50万人に及ぶ来園者に親しまれ、日本の庭園文化を継承しつつ、次世代につなぐ新しい日本文化発信・交流プラットフォームとしての可能性を広げている。

2017年に完成した文化センター（通称「Cultural Village」）は、建築家・隈研吾氏との共通ビジョンによって実現され、日本の自然観・芸術・工芸を幅広く世界に発信し、また、庭や自然との対話を通じて多様な日本文化体験場になっている。

Lion Dance performance at the New Year's Day event (Photo: Jonathan Ley)

正月イベントにおける獅子舞パフォーマンス

Ikebana Demonstration accompanied by Shamisen (Photo: Jonathan Ley)
三味線演奏をバックにした生け花のデモンストレーション

Tea Ceremony Presentation (Photo: Jonathan Ley)
茶道のプレゼンテーション

3. Japanese garden design and maintenance techniques training

In 2020, the garden expanded its international activities and partnerships by launching a new organization, the Japan Institute, to share the Garden's vision and unique activities with the world. The Institute offers innovative international programs such as the Peace Symposium series which will be held on six continents, as well as the promotion of global collaboration. The Institute consists of the following three components:

Photo: Portland Japanese Garden

(1) Center for Culture and Art
(2) International Exchange Forum
(3) International Japanese Garden Training Center

The most notable of these three components is the Japanese Garden Training Center, which was launched in 2015, prior to the Institute's establishment. Major renovation and expansion of the Training Center's operations occurred in 2017, and in 2022 with a new 5 acre (2 hectare) campus site purchased to accommodate all of the Training Center's programs and activities.

（3）日本庭園の作庭・管理技術のトレーニング

2020年には、庭園のビジョンとユニークな活動を世界へ発信・共有するための新組織「ジャパン・インスティテュート」を立ち上げ、国際的な活動とパートナーシップを拡大する。6大陸での開催を目指す「ピースシンポジウム」など、斬新な国際プログラムやグローバルコラボレーションの促進や体験教育を特徴とするインスティテュートは、次の3つから成る。

1) Center for Culture and Art（文化芸術センター）
2) International Exchange Forum（国際フォーラム）
3) International Japanese Garden Training Center（日本庭園トレーニングセンター）

Photo: Portland Japanese Garden

その中でも注目されるのが、インスティテュート設立に先立って（2015年）始動していた日本庭園トレーニングセンターである。2017年の大規模改修に伴い、トレーニングセンターの事業も拡充。2022年には、新たに2ヘクタールにおよぶキャンパス用地を活動拠点とした。

The North American Japanese Garden Association was established in 2011 to answer the need for an institution that offered training to improve the skills of Japanese garden professionals in North America. Though initially intended for North American Japanese garden professionals, the center now welcomes participants from more than a dozen countries around the world. The center offers a comprehensive learning program about Japanese gardens in English, including practical design and construction skills. It is the only educational program that is dedicated to addressing the needs of Japanese garden professionals outside of Japan.

2011年には、北米日本庭園協会も設立されて関心は高いが、海外日本庭園専従者の技術向上を目的とした訓練教育機関の必要性は高い。当初、北米の日本庭園技術者を対象としていたが、現在は世界十数か国からの参加者を迎えている。センターは、実技を含む日本庭園の英語での総合学習プログラムを提供している。海外日本庭園関係者のニーズに対応した唯一の教育プログラムである。

Photo: Portland Japanese Garden

4. NORTH AMERICAN JAPANESE GARDEN ASSOCIATION (NAJGA)

NAJGA traces its roots back to the 2009 International Conference on Japanese Gardens Outside Japan held at California State University, Long Beach, where leaders in the field of Japanese gardens residing in North America met. The conference reaffirmed the need to establish an organization to maintain and enhance Japanese gardens in North America. In 2011, NAJGA was formally established as a "501 C (3)" non-profit organization by Japanese garden practitioners, administrators, landscape architects, researchers and other Japanese garden enthusiasts.

NAJGA's vision was to create a healthy and peaceful world through Japanese gardens and to educate and support the art, craft, and spirit of Japanese gardens in North America. NAJGA works to share knowledge, improve techniques, and promote research in order to maintain and pass on the sustainability, lasting value, and social impact of Japanese gardens in North America and beyond.

NAJGA's main activities include the publication of a newsletter, journal, and workshops focusing on practical exercises in garden design, construction, and maintenance. NAJGA also holds biennial conferences, during which a broad network is developed through lectures, round-table discussions, and workshops.

NAJGA currently has more than 300 members in the U.S., Canada, Japan and Europe, and is governed by a volunteer Board of Directors and Executive Committee. Partnerships have also been established with the Japanese Garden Society, Academic Society of Japanese Gardens, both in Japan, the Japanese Garden Society in UK and European Japanese Garden Association.

(Text by Sadafumi Uchiyama, Curator Emeritus, Portland Japanese Garden)

（4）北米日本庭園協会について

NAJGAのルーツは、2009年にカリフォルニア州立大学ロングビーチ校（CSULB）で開催された北米在住の日本庭園分野のリーダー達による「日本国外における日本庭園に関する国際会議」に遡る。会議では、北米の日本庭園を維持・向上させるための組織を設立する必要性が再認識された。2011年、NAJGAは、造園家、研究者、管理者、実務家を含む200人により「501 C(3)」非営利団体として正式に設立された。

NAJGAのビジョンは、日本庭園を通じて、健康的で平和な世界を創造し、北米における日本庭園の芸術、技術、心を啓蒙・サポートするとされた。北米における日本庭園の持続可能性、永続的な価値、社会的インパクトを維持・継承するため、知識の共有、技術向上、研究促進などを目的とした活動をおこなっている。

NAJGAの主な活動には、ニュースレターの発行、年刊誌の発行、庭園設計・施工・管理など、実技演習に焦点を当てたワークショップなどがある。また、隔年ごとにはカンファレンスも開催し、そのなかでは講演、座談会、ワークショップなどを通して幅広いネットワークが構築されている。

現在NAJGAは、アメリカ、カナダ、日本・欧州に300名以上の会員を擁し、ボランティアで構成される理事会と実行委員会によって運営されている。日本庭園協会、日本庭園学会、英国日本庭園協会やヨーロッパ日本庭園協会などとのパートナーシップも確立している。

（文責 内山貞文、ポートランド日本庭園 名誉キュレーター）

Translators' Musings

This journey started in early 2020 when the author (our father/father-in-law) asked us to look at a draft proposal for a Japanese and English bilingual book on Japanese garden design. The publisher had already had that version translated into English and we were asked to check the English for readability for native speakers. After review and contemplation, we concluded the book needed to have a fundamental shift in its writing and translation style to make it more compatible for comprehension of English speakers. With that, in close collaboration with the author, the editing and redrafting process began.

This was an especially challenging process; trying to fix the writing style, reform the content and not only correct the issues in the original English translation but reconcile it with the new Japanese version that was forming. In many ways it was harder than starting a project from zero. Like reversing the momentum of a freight train already in motion. We also faced the inherent and common challenge that all Japanese English translators know all to well, reconciling the differences of order in Japanese logic and expression with that of English, as well as the many ways that cultural differences affect language (the extent of which is always a surprise and the occasional cause of bicultural marital arguments). We also had to fill in knowledge gaps of common Japanese history and context for English speakers, who are without the benefit of twelve years or more of Japanese schooling. At the same time, we questioned if some of the details provided in the Japanese version had relevance in the English version and felt that with other topics, more explanation was needed in the English. It was akin to untangling a ball of yarn with many knots in it. In addition to all this, a significant amount of content and photographs, along with detailed captions, were added and translated, to make the book more complete and comprehensible for English readers that lack familiarity with famous sites, their cultural context and that of the historical figures who created them.

As if this was not enough, multi-talented Mariko took on the colossal task of creating a more interesting, unique and appropriate book design, layout and cover design.

Knowing the author very well, and over the years having had the privilege of countless, in-depth conversations about his impressive life's work in Japanese garden landscape architecture, its cultural implications and its application in municipal amenity design and environmental conservation and sustainability, above all, we wanted the true essence of his message, to come through clearly in English to be shared with the larger world. We believe the real value of this book is in the scattered nuggets of original insight and conclusions throughout the chapters, gleaned from the author's expansive and prolific career. The author wanted this to be more than a typical book on Japanese gardens. He wanted it to provide readers with a more in-depth perspective on gardens, their design philosophy and techniques so they could appreciate them at a deeper level.

It will be apparent to bilingual readers that this book is not a direct translation. The author gave explicit direction to us to take liberty to add, omit and rephrase in the English version. While having experience in the field of translation, we have much less training in the field of English book editing, but with this book being created by a skeleton staff with no access to a professional English editor, we, along with other English speaking team members, endeavored to edit it to the best of our ability. We apologize for any deficiencies.

This project was more time-consuming and expansive than anyone expected, consuming much of our free time as a married couple, on top of running a full-time eco-building company. We apologize to and thank our three children, Noah (14), Aman (12) and Aleythia (10) for needing them to pick up the slack, taking over many domestic duties and for being deprived of time spent together. We also want to thank the author and his wife Mihoko Shinji for their support and guidance on so many levels throughout this endeavor. Special admiration and respect for Mihoko Shinji for her art contribution for the jacket cover, with an amazing interpretation of Japanese garden design in the medium of oil painting, with a very original twist.

Beyond the interesting and enlightening content of this book itself, through this process of translating and redrafting, we gained even deeper insight into the cultural and language differences between Japanese and English on which our marriage and family have as part of its foundation. We hope this book aids in furthering sharing, understanding and relationship-building between these two cultures and beyond.

Mark and Mariko Benson

Mark Benson and Mariko Shinji met in 1998 at an international environmental conservation conference in the Shiretoko National Park in eastern Hokkaido, Japan, where Mark was working as a conference translator and Mariko as a conference organizer. They were hired post-conference to write a bilingual summary report of the conference on behalf of the organizer, the Association of National Trusts in Japan.

Mark at the time was a scholarship-recipient graduate student in his master's program at the Tokyo University of Agriculture at the Okhotsk campus in the faculty of Bio-Industry in Abashiri, Hokkaido where he was researching organic agriculture methods, while Mariko was working as a researcher with the Association of National Trusts in Tokyo after graduating from the Tokyo University of Agriculture with a degree in Landscape Architecture. From this first translation project together their relationship bloomed. They now live in Canada, on beautiful Pender Island, a small island in the Salish Sea between Vancouver and Vancouver Island, with their three children, chickens, garden and orchard and enjoy sea kayaking, hiking and cold water snorkeling as a family.

Mark, with the help of Mariko, runs an eco-building company on Pender and Mariko, besides being a mother of three, enjoys writing, art, gardening and teaches classes on sourdough bread making and natural fermentation occasionally, when not working on a team translation project with Mark.

ちょうど四年前。

万里子の父から、日本庭園の本を日英二か国語で出版する話があり、英語がすでに作業を進めている出版社があり、英語のネイティブスピーカーの最終確認が必要なので、監訳をしてくれないかという依頼があった。気軽に引き受けたものの、いただいた英語ドラフトを読んでいるうちに、もっと違う角度でまとめるべきではないか、という疑問をまとめてきた。

というのは、カナダ在住の私たちを、日本にいたときよりも客観的に見られるようになった。時折、それは言語に関しても同様だったが、日本文化の価値の重みを日本にいる人々より感じつつも、英語以上に感じられるようにもなっていた。その論理性の違いにそれは言語に圧倒されるようになりつつ、この美しさに圧倒される日本語に関しての論理性の違い、日本語の美しさにも同様、私たちがお世話になりつつある海外の人々に、日本庭園の絶好の機会を世に出すことだけは、どうしても避けたかった。

そこから私たちの戦いが始まった。日本語だとさらっと書けるが、〜的などの表現を使ってみると、なぜかしっくりこない。英訳し、文法は正しくても論理性がなく聞こえてしまうところや、ネイティブスピーカーでないと気づかないような、ひとつひとつ直していくしかなかった小さな隠れたミスを見つけては、驚くことも多々あった。だからっけに発信する思いというのは言葉の裏にあるというところだけは、伝わってこない英訳も多い。父の「言葉に込めた思い」は完全に伝えることだけは避けたかった。

私たちの個人的な意見だが、この違いの多くは、日本語が漢字という漢字熟語や、〜的などの表現を使っている。そこから私たちの戦いが始まった。

けれども、私たちはそれを手に取る人にそれを外から客観的に見ていた。

イディオグラム（表意文字）を含んでいるからではないか。英語は、国際的な言語だからこそ、言葉に対する縛りがあり、定義がはっきりしていることに加え、語彙が多いことにより、誤解を招かないようよく知られず、日本漢字では、背景や雰囲気も知らず、熟語などの意味も完全にわかってもらえず、なんとなくいざ直接的に再現しようとしても、細かいニュアンスに手を伝えている、同じ意味の英単語をいくつもつなげて流し読みできてしまう。また、日本語のように物事をまた、日本語で論みに伝えようとするのは困難でもあり、それが言語の完璧に抵抗がある文化があり、私たちはこれを理論している（笑）。私たちは、これを西洋のように論理的に示すことに物事を影響している文化があり、これが言語の島国の水田文化と大陸の狩猟文化に差別化している（笑）。

さらには、日本の長い歴史と日本人の歴史への親近感は、日本語ノン・ネイティブスピーカーの理解を妨げ、特に日本庭園は歴史そのものであり、歴史上の人物名などは、ノン・ネイティブスピーカーにとってあまり意味をなさないことが多く、主旨を組み込みつつ、細かすぎないようにするためにどう圧倒されないのか、考えあぐねた。そこで私たちは、父と数えきれないほどのオンラインミーティングを重ね、父との強いコラボレーション、そしてスタッフの助けもあり、チームワークで日本語・英語ともの編集と再編を完成した。

しかし、このプロセスはある意味、ゼロから始めるよりも複雑で、幾重にも絡まった糸を解きほぐしながら、お互いの文化が異なる国際結婚の夫婦に、多少の夫婦喧嘩になったことは、今では笑い話だ。父からの強い要望で、英語は直訳することではなく、できるだけ意訳すること。

イディオグラムに決めた。時には、あえて日本語にはなくても、普遍的に伝えたい本質に焦点をしぼる内容にした。また、特にノン・ネイティブスピーカーの理解に必要なビジュアル（写真や図）を増やし、キャプションの翻訳にも力を入れ、万里子自らが読者の目で効果的なレイアウトにまとめた。

不十分な日英対訳をやめに決めた。

この本が目指したのは、日本庭園の総論で、それがわかりやすいコンセプトは、日本庭園に関する基礎知識を網羅したから深い。かたや日本庭園の著者はそれを既存の海外の本のように庭園哲学や庭園行政や持続可能な生物多様性を、幅広く活躍する著者だからこそ、散りばめられた技術、造園界のみならず、造園行政や技術などを、環境適応可能な生物多様性も、世界のひとりでも多くの人々に知ってもらうことが私たちの願いである。

本書の範疇を超えた既存の海外の日本庭園の本の著者はそれを、本書の理解できる基礎知識を網羅し、日本庭園のコミュニティを目指す環境行政や技術行政などに、配慮した深い識を込め、ユニティを目指す環境行政や、オリジナリティに満ちた庭園界にメッセージを、世界のひとりでも多くの人々に知ってもらうことが、私たちの願いである。

最後に、私事ではあるが、コロナ禍もあって予想以上に長丁場となってしまった本作りのためにも、幼いながらもサポートしてくれた息子のノア、エイボとント自作のアドベンチャーを全面的に借りてくれたアレイシアにも、心より感謝したい。また、私たちの父、進士五十八の造園人生を、しみじみ深い愛で包み込んでくれた母、私たち姉妹を深く愛情で描いてくれた母の絵、表紙絵では、私たち家族をよくご存じの、伝統色を新しい風を吹かせたいと願い、素敵な花を添えてもらえた、どうにかにかに。

（ベンソン万里子・マーク）

ベンソン万里子／ベンソン マーク

ベンソン万里子（旧姓 進士）は、進士五十八・美保子の長女として神奈川県に生まれる。幼少の頃から、父の影響で環境問題に深い関心をもって育つ。東京農業大学造園学科卒業後、自然保護や環境教育関連の仕事に従事。

ベンソンマークは、カナダ生まれ。若い時から海外にあこがれていたマークは、全学費・生活費支給のスカラーシップで、北海道へ6年間の留学を実現。時代に先駆け、オーガニック農業に関する論文をまとめた。東京農業大学生物産業学部（北海道オホーツクキャンパス）の大学院時代には、オーガニック農業研究会を設立したり、食糧問題は環境問題であることについて、実践から解決策を提案した。

マークと万里子の出会いは、1998年の北海道知床国立公園での自然保護国際会議。万里子は主催者（社）日本ナショナル・トラスト協会の担当として、マークは通訳として会議に参加。国際交流基金の助成で、会議後にまとめた日英2か国語の報告書が、二人はじめての翻訳／通訳の仕事に。

マークのカナダ帰国後、万里子は何度かカナダを訪れ、2006年に結婚。現在、ブリティッシュ・コロンビア州のセイリッシュ海が美しい、ガルフ諸島ペンダー島へ移住。ニワトリや果樹園のある庭で、森と自然に囲まれて暮らす。

翻訳をしていないときの二人は、マークがエコ建築建設の自営、万里子は、マークのビジネスサポートと忙しい3人の子育てに加え、ガーデニングはもちろんのこと、執筆、アート、天然酵母パン作り教室などを楽しむ。家族でのカヤック、ハイキング、寒中水泳などが趣味。

著者プロフィール

進士 五十八 （1944年京都市生まれ。東京農業大学卒業、農学博士。福井、東京、神奈川在住）

　造園家。東京農業大学名誉教授・元学長、福井県立大学名誉教授・元学長。政府の日本学術会議第20期21期会員（環境学委員長）、自然再生専門家会議委員長。東京都文化財庭園専門委員長、福井県里山里海湖研究所長、福井県政策参与など歴任。

　「日本庭園の特質に関する研究」で日本造園学会賞、日本農学賞、読売農学賞など受賞、紫綬褒章を受章。「日本庭園と農の融合による『みどりのまちづくり』の計画・政策・実践」に関する功績で内閣総理大臣から、みどりの学術賞を受賞。その他井下賞、田村賞、北村賞、今和次郎賞、上原敬二賞等受賞。土木学会景観デザイン賞、GOLDEN FORTUNE 表彰。ウクライナ国農業大学、ペルー国ラ・モリーナ大学の名誉博士。

　本書関連の著書に、日本庭園の特質　様式・空間・景観（東京農大出版会1987）、アメニティ・デザイン（学芸出版社1992）、日本の庭園（中公新書2005）、日比谷公園（鹿島出版会2011）、グリーン・エコライフー「農」とつながる緑地生活（小学館2010）、地球社会の環境ビジョン（日学新書2013）、進士五十八と22人のランドスケープアーキテクト（マルモ出版2016）、進士五十八の風景美学（マルモ出版2019）他多数。

About the Author

Isoya SHINJI

Born in Kyoto in 1944. Resides in Fukui Prefecture, Tokyo and Kanagawa Prefecture.

Landscape architect. Undergraduate degree and PhD from Tokyo University of Agriculture in Landscape Architecture. Former president and professor emeritus of the Tokyo University of Agriculture, former president and professor emeritus of Fukui Prefectural University. He is also recipient of honorary doctorates from the Ukrainian National University of Life and Environmental Sciences (formerly known as the National Ukrainian Agricultural University) and from La Molina National Agrarian University in Peru. He has served as or currently sits in a number of prestigious positions including the chair of the Environmental Science Committee for the prime minister's cabinet's Science Council of Japan, chairperson for the Japanese Minister of the Environment's Committee for Ecological Restoration, chief advisor for Greater Tokyo's Japanese gardens cultural asset management, Chief Policy Advisor of Fukui Prefectural Government and director of Fukui Prefectural Satoyama-Satoumi Research Institute among other positions.

Recipient of the Japanese Institute of Landscape Architecture Prize for his doctoral thesis "Characteristics of Japanese Gardens", the Association of Japanese Agricultural Scientific Studies Award, the Yomiuri Newspaper Agricultural Science Prize and the prestigious Japanese Emperor's Purple Ribbon Medal in recognition of his life's work. He also received the Japanese Prime Minister's Midori Academic Prize for his work on green municipal development.

Additionally he received the Inoshita Award, Tamura Award, The Keikan Design Prize for civil engineering, The Golden Fortune Award, The Kitamura Award, The Wajirou Kon Award, The Keiji Uehara Award among many other significant recognitions of achievement.

Author of Nihon Teien no Tokushitsu · Yoshiki, Kuukan, Keikan ("Characteristics of Japanese Gardens: Styles, Spaces, Vistas") (Tokyo Nodai Shuppankai, 1987), Nihon no Teien – Zokei no Waza to Kokoro ("Gardens of Japan - The Technique and Soul of Scenery Building") (Chuo Koron Shinsha, 2005), Amenity Design (Gakugei Shuppansha, 1992), Green Eco-life (Shogakukan, 2010), Hibiya Koen ("Hibiya Park") (Kajima Institute Publishing, 2011), Chikyu Shakai no Kankyo Vision ("Environmental Vision for Global Society") (Nichigaku Shinsho, 2013), Shinji Isoya to 22 Nin no Landscape Architects ("Isoya Shinji Interviews 22 Landscape Architects") (Marumo Publishing, 2016), Shinji Isoya no Fukei Bigaku ("Shinji Isoya's Philosophy of Scenic Aesthetics") (Marumo Publishing, 2019), as well as many other books and countless articles.

日本庭園　技心一如で自然に順う（日英2か国語版）

著者：進士 五十八

英訳：ベンソン マーク & 万里子

素訳：渡辺 洋

英語編集：ベンソン マーク

表紙デザイン、本文レイアウト、日本語編集：ベンソン 万里子

表紙絵（油絵）：進士 美保子

ポートランド日本庭園コラム寄稿、英語編集協力：内山 貞文

著者サポート：金村 奈津美、坪田 佳恵

出版：澤崎 明治、吉田 重行、大村 和哉

Copyright © 2024 進士五十八

ISBN 978-4-86797-061-4

Theory of Japanese Gardens (Japanese & English Version)

The Spirit and Techniques of Design in Accordance with Nature

Author: Isoya SHINJI, PhD

Translators: Mark & Mariko Benson

Initial rough draft translation: Hiroshi Watanabe

Project manager: Mariko Benson

English editing: Mark Benson

Book layout, design and Japanese editing: Mariko Benson

Jacket design: Mariko Benson

Front jacket art: Mihoko Shinji

Portland content and English editing contributor: Sadafumi Uchiyama

Author support staff: Natsumi Kanemura, Yoshie Tsubota

Publication: Meiji Sawazaki, Shigeyuki Yoshida, Kazuya Omura

Copyright © 2024 Isoya Shinji

ISBN 978-4-86797-061-4

進士五十八の日本庭園　技心一如で自然に順う　（日英2か国語版）
著者　進士　五十八

2024年3月13日　初版印刷
2024年3月28日　初版発行
発行者　澤崎　明治
印刷　新日本印刷
製本　ブロケード

発行所　株式会社　市ヶ谷出版社
東京都千代田区五番町5（〒102-0076）
電話　03-3265-3711（代）
FAX　03-3265-4008
www.ichigayashuppan.co.jp

Theory of Japanese Gardens (Japanese & English Version)
The Spirit and Techniques of Design in Accordance with Nature
Author: Isoya SHINJI

Publisher: Ichigaya Publishing Co. Ltd, Japan
Address: 5, 5 ban-cho, Chiyoda-ku, Tokyo, 102-0076
Phone: +81-(0)3-3265-3711
http://www.ichigayashuppan.co.jp
desk@ichigayashuppan.co.jp